Propaganda and Persuasion 2nd Edition

To Ada and May, who lived through two World Wars and who, in another time and place, took me to the movies.

Garth S. Jowett

My portion of this book is dedicated to Helen A. O'Donnell in memory of a special woman who loved life, people, pets, movies, and me.

Victoria O'Donnell

Propaganda and Persuasion 2nd Edition

Garth S. Jowett
Victoria O'Donnell

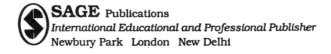

SAGE Publications
International Educational and Professional Publisher
Newbury Park   London   New Delhi

For information address:

SAGE Publications, Inc.
2455 Teller Road
Newbury Park, California 91320
E-mail: order@sagepub.com

SAGE Publications Ltd.
6 Bonhill Street
London EC2A 4PU
United Kingdom

SAGE Publications India Pvt. Ltd.
M-32 Market
Greater Kailash I
New Delhi 110 048 India

Printed in the United States of America

Library of Congress Cataloguing-in-Publication Data

Jowett, Garth.
    Propaganda and persuasion / Garth S. Jowett, Victoria O'Donnell.—
2nd ed.
        p.   cm.
    Includes bibliographical references and index.
    ISBN 0-8039-4677-5 (cl).—ISBN 0-8039-4678-3 (pb)
    1. Propaganda. 2. Persuasion (Psychology) I. O'Donnell,
Victoria. II. Title.
HN263.J69 1992
303.3'75—dc20   92-15929
                                                                          CIP

96 97 98 99 00 10 9 8 7 6 5

Sage Production Editor: Astrid Virding

Contents

Preface to the First Edition   vii

Preface to the Second Edition   xi

Acknowledgments   xv

1. What Is Propaganda and How Does It Differ From Persuasion?   1

2. Propaganda Through the Ages   36

3. Propaganda Institutionalized   79

4. Propaganda and Persuasion Examined   122

5. Propaganda and Psychological Warfare   155

6. How to Analyze Propaganda   212

7. Propaganda in Action: Three Case Studies   229

8. How Propaganda Works in Modern Society   263

References   272

Index   283

About the Authors   293

Preface to the First Edition

This book grew out of the discovery that both the authors were interested in the study of propaganda; however, we come to this interest from the perspectives of different academic disciplines: Professor Jowett from that of communication history and Professor O'Donnell from persuasion and rhetoric. To any discerning reader, this will make the primary authorship of the individual chapters obvious, but to keep the record straight Professor Jowett wrote Chapters 2, 3, and 5; Professor O'Donnell was responsible for Chapters 1, 4, and 6. Chapters 7 and 8 are the result of the joint exchange of ideas.

We were both intrigued with how poorly propaganda had fared in recent years as part of general communication studies, and further informal investigations revealed that few students were being given the opportunity or encouragement to examine this subject in a systematic manner. When we questioned our colleagues, we were assured that propaganda as a topic within the communications curriculum still held great interest, but because the subject was so vast in scope, it was difficult to cover it in anything but the most cursory way. This problem was compounded by the lack of suitable classroom materials designed to allow a systematic treatment, without forcing the student to consult a wide array of disparate sources. This book was written with a view to solving some of these problems by presenting an overview of the history of propaganda as well as a review of the social scientific research on its effects and an examination of its applications. We have tried to restrict the narrative so that it will serve as a guide to further reading on specific issues rather than be encyclopedic in scope.

In the past seventy years there have been many hundreds of books dealing with various aspects of propaganda. There have also been almost an equal number of books and journal articles dealing with persuasion, and very often these two subjects have come to be regarded as synonymous. With the growth in the study of persuasion in the last two decades, propaganda has received scant attention as a subject in its own right within the spectrum of communication studies. With the advent of a whole range of new communication technologies, and the immininent promise of a myriad of channels for disseminating information, the opportunities for increased propaganda activities are obvious. For this reason we believe that the time has come to revive the study of propaganda as a separate topic, and of great significance at this particular point in time.

This book is offered as a modest treatment of a very old subject, and we trust that the reader will be sympathetic to the fact that we could not include a detailed history of propaganda nor a lengthy review of all of the research ever done to evaluate its effectiveness in specific campaigns. Our aim was to provide the reader with a challenge to become involved in the fascinating world of propaganda in the hope that it would stimulate further research and discussion. We both owe an intellectual debt to T. H. Qualter (1962), whose excellent slim volume *Propaganda and Psychological Warfare* was all that was available for a long time, and whose recent detailed monograph *Opinion Control in Democracies* (1985) is a landmark study, but that unfortunately was only received after this volume had been sent to the printer. Other than Qualter and the important work by David L. Altheide and John M. Johnson (1980) *Bureacratic Propaganda*, the three-volume compilation of important articles by Harold D. Laswell, Daneil Lerner, and Hans Speir, *Propaganda and Communication in World History* (1979), and Richard A. Nelson's (1986) forthcoming detailed bibliography on the subject, there have been very few systematic examinations of propaganda in recent years, and it is our intention that this book fill some of the gaps in the current literature.

What may appear to the readers to be a relatively short book is, in fact, the result of several years of reviewing a vast literature, which is unfortunately reflected only in a minor way in the bibliography. We chose to present in this book both a digest of important and classic ideas on the subject and our original ideas. It has been our goal to produce a work that, we hope, will enable students of modern-day propaganda to recognize, analyze, and evaluate propaganda in their midst while giving them an appreciation of its history and development. Although respectful of the work of Jacques Ellul, we could not incorporate many of his ideas within the text of this book. We aimed to clarify and distinguish propaganda as a form of communication, but found that we could not do so with Ellul's view of the pervasiveness of propaganda. Also, advertising, although presented as the most prevalent form of propaganda in the United States, does not receive extensive treatment. We felt that advertising as propaganda is such a complex and extensive subject that it required an entire series of studies in itself and that such a treatment was beyond the scope of this book.

Writing a book should always be a learning experience, and this book taught us that we all have a great deal to learn about the role and practice of propaganda in our everyday society. We have also learned that in order not to fear propaganda, we must first understand it.

GARTH S. JOWETT
Houston, Texas

VICTORIA O'DONNELL
Denton, Texas

Preface to the Second Edition

In the six years since the first edition of this book appeared, we have been gratified by the increased interest in the field of propaganda studies. Though it would be premature to declare that the study of propaganda is now an accepted part of all communication studies or political science programs, there are, nevertheless, indications that more and more such courses are appearing. As time separates the study of propaganda from the political ideologies that hovered over academe in the Cold War period, there is a clear revival of interest in the important role of propaganda in many aspects of modern life, not necessarily related to international intrigue or military campaigns.

The publication of the first edition of this book proved to be an important development in both of our academic careers. We presented joint workshops on teaching propaganda studies as part of the communication curriculum for the Speech Communication Association, which were well attended by enthusiastic participants and from whom we learned as much as we taught. Several things were made very clear in these workshops as well as from correspondence with others: First, it is very difficult to get anyone to agree on an exact definition of propaganda, although the definition offered in this book is now (thankfully) widely cited; second, it is a formidable task to get instructors and students to view propaganda as a "neutral" technique, which only in its specific application becomes either "positive" or "negative"; and third, that this is a subject that is guaranteed to raise emotions in the classroom, no matter how it is taught. Also, we have discovered that in the classroom it is only with a determined effort that discussions of propaganda can be removed from an association with war (and even more specifically, Nazi propaganda activities). This is a testament to the specifically negative connotation that the term *propaganda* has acquired in our society, and also to the persistent and somewhat troublesome strength of Nazi mythology and imagery. (This last fact is a topic that requires its own full-length treatment.) It is one of our stated intentions that the approach outlined in this book, which provides a wider and more systematic examination of propaganda throughout history and in the modern world, will help to enlarge the dimension of the propaganda discourse beyond these limiting subjects.

In the last six years, though the number of books dealing with propaganda in a systematic manner has not been as large as we would have liked to have seen, several publications deserve special mention. Ted Smith, III edited a splendid collection of original essays, *Propaganda: A Pluralistic Perspective* (1989), that contributes to opening up the discussion of what encompasses the discourse of propagandistic activities. A recent book by Anthony Pratkanis and Elliot Aronson, *Age of Propaganda: The Use and Abuse of Persuasion* (1991) is admirable in its sociopsychological examination of many aspects of propaganda in contemporary society. Also, the work of Michael Sproule in a series of articles on the history of propaganda analysis in the United States has significantly reshaped our understanding of this topic. Several books that have contributed to the reevaluation of propaganda are Roland Marchand, *Advertising the American Dream: Making Way for Modernity, 1920-1940* (1985); Maureen Honey, *Creating Rosie the Riveter: Class, Gender, and Propaganda during World War II (1984)*; Richard W. Steele, *Propaganda in an Open Society: The Roosevelt Administration and the Media, 1933-1941 (1985)*; Benjamin Ginsberg, *The Captive Public: How Mass Opinion Promotes State Power* (1986); Shearon Lowery and Melvin DeFleur, *Milestones in Mass Communication Research*, 2d ed. (1988); Philip G. Zimbardo and Michael Leippe, *The Psychology of Attitude Change and Social Influence* (1991), and Holly Cowan Shulman's, *The Voice of America: Propaganda and Democracy, 1941-1945* (1990). These and other specialized studies are collectively helping to give shape to the role and dimensions of propaganda in American society.

We have welcomed the opportunity to write a second edition of this book, as much for the chance to enlarge on certain topics as to try and keep up with current events. The few short years since the first edition have been witness to several important historical events that have contributed to the appreciation of propaganda in modern society. Perhaps the decade will be best remembered for the sudden demise of Communism in Eastern Europe. The first edition was written during a period when the USSR was still "the Evil Empire" described by Ronald Reagan. It was a strange experience in this edition to have to rewrite all of the descriptions of Soviet propaganda activities in the past tense. Even as this book is going to press we still do not know what types of propaganda may emerge from this region. (Today's newspapers, January 3, 1992, are full of stories about the dismantling and replacement of previous Soviet propaganda symbols, such as the giant statues of Lenin and Marx). The fact is we just have no clear idea what type of propaganda will now dominate the international scene. We can only be sure that there will be a continued battle for the "hearts and minds" of the world's population, and the decade of the nineties might see the emergence of an international polarization more along economic than political lines. The differences between the "have" and the "have not" nations will become more obvious, and this will generate its own type of propaganda battle.

This book has been greatly enlarged in certain areas. There is much additional historical material, including a case study of the Crusades, the demagoguery of Huey Long and Father Charles Coughlin, and the specific propaganda activities of the Korean and Vietnam conflicts. The Gulf War, while somewhat anticlimactic in the end, was a textbook example of both the positive and negative uses of propaganda, as well as providing a useful new case study for this edition. The section in Chapter 1 that defines propaganda has been greatly expanded based upon our classroom experience with the first edition and has two new models that conceptualize disinformation. The sections on the theoretical aspects of propaganda have been updated to include the latest research that pertains to persuasion and mass media effects and cultural studies. Only one of the original case studies, that involving the tobacco industry, has been retained, but an historical study about the U.S. government and women's work in World War II has been added, and there have been revisions and expansions in every chapter. (Victoria O'Donnell is making a documentary film about the Vanport City, Oregon, case study. It will be available for education uses.)

In the Preface to the first edition we noted that writing this book had been a learning experience for us. This learning experience has not stopped, for the more that we attempt to understand the subject of propaganda the more we discover what remains yet to be learned. In particular the past six years have witnessed the increasing use of professional "manipulators" of public opinion, especially in the political arena. Unchecked, this trend threatens, at worst, to subvert the very foundations of our democratic society, and, at best, to make the public even more suspicious about politics and the mass media. We need to be continuously vigilant about giving over our democratic rights to these highly skilled operators. It has been our experience that students who have studied propaganda are extremely adept at spotting, and even hostile to, such professional manipulation of public opinion. It is our fervent wish that all who use this book will acquire such skills because the future of democracy and the free expression of ideas depend upon it.

GARTH JOWETT   VICTORIA O'DONNELL
University of Houston   *Montana State University*

Acknowledgments

When we wrote the first edition of *Propaganda and Persuasion*, we were separated by 400 miles, but we were able to work together at intervals. For this edition, almost 2000 miles lay between our respective universities in Texas and Montana, thus we did everything by telephone, mail, computers, and the fax machine. The new technologies that impact the nature of propaganda also affected the writing of the second edition. We were fortunate to also temporarily reside in New York and London and respectively gathered valuable materials in those cities. To the film archivist at the Imperial War Museum who not only showed films in a private screening but who also made tea as well, a special thanks.

We wish to thank our publishers, especially our editor Ann West, for their infinite patience and enormous support of this new, enlarged edition. Also, the many reviewers of the first edition who reminded us of what we omitted and who lifted our spirits by liking what we included. A special thanks goes to Robert W. Smith of Alma College who made so many helpful suggestions. Our many students who took our propaganda courses and some who wrote theses on the subject gave us treasured insights and special information. As always, we probably learned more from them than they did from us.

1 What Is Propaganda and How Does It Differ From Persuasion?

Propaganda is a form of communication that is different from persuasion because it attempts to achieve a response that furthers the desired intent of the propagandist. Persuasion is transactive and attempts to satisfy the needs of both persuader and persuadee. A model of propaganda depicts how elements of informative and persuasive communication may be incorporated in propagandistic communication. References are made to past theories of rhetoric that indicate that propaganda has had few systematic theoretical treatments prior to the twentieth century. Public opinion and behavior change can be affected by propaganda.

Propaganda has been studied as history, political science, sociology, and psychology as well as from an interdisciplinary perspective. To study propaganda as history is to examine the practices of propagandists as events and the subsequent events as possible effects of propaganda. To examine propaganda in light of political science is to analyze the ideologies of the practitioners and the dissemination and impact of public opinion. To approach propaganda as sociology is to look at social movements and the counterpropaganda that emerges in opposition. To investigate propaganda as psychology is to determine its effects on individuals. Propaganda is also viewed by some scholars as inherent thought and practice in mass culture. A recent trend that draws on most of these allied fields is the study of propaganda as a purveyor of ideology and, to this end, is largely a study of how dominant ideological meanings are constructed within the mass media (Burnett, 1989). Ethnographic research is one way to determine whether the people on the receiving end accept or resist dominant ideological meanings.

1

This book approaches the study of propaganda as communication. Persuasion, another category of communication, is also examined. The two terms *propaganda* and *persuasion* have been used interchangeably in the literature on propaganda as well as in common usage. There is a certain amount of overlap, but the two terms can be differentiated. A communication approach to the study of propaganda enables us to isolate its communicative variables, to determine the relationship of message to context, to examine intentionality, to examine the responses and responsibilities of the audience, and to trace the development of propagandistic communication as a process.

We believe that there is a need to evaluate propaganda in a contemporary context free from value-laden definitions. Our objectives are to (a) provide a concise examination of propaganda and persuasion, (b) examine the role of propaganda as an aspect of communication studies, and (c) analyze propaganda as part of social, religious, and political systems throughout history and contemporary times.

Propaganda Defined

Propaganda, in the most neutral sense, means to disseminate or promote particular ideas. In Latin, it meant "to propagate" or "to sow." In 1622, the Vatican established the *Sacra Congregatio de Propaganda Fide*, meaning "the sacred congregation for propagating the faith of the Roman Catholic church." Because the propaganda of the Roman Catholic church had as its intent spreading the faith to the New World as well as opposing Protestantism, the word *propaganda* lost its neutrality, and subsequent usage has rendered the term pejorative. To identify a message as propaganda is to suggest something negative and dishonest. Words frequently used as synonyms for propaganda are *lies, distortion, deceit, manipulation, psychological warfare*, and *brainwashing*. Many of these synonyms are suggestive of techniques of message production rather than purpose or process.

When usage emphasizes purpose, propaganda is associated with control and is regarded as a deliberate attempt to alter or maintain a balance of power that is advantageous to the propagandist. Deliberate attempt is linked with a clear institutional ideology and objective. In fact, the purpose of propaganda is to send out an ideology to an audience with a related objective. Whether it is a government agency attempting to instill a massive wave of patriotism in a national audience to support a war effort, a military leader attempting to frighten the enemy by exaggerating his or her strength, or a corporation attempting to promote its image in order to maintain its legitimacy among its clientele, there is a careful and predetermined plan of prefabricated symbol manipulation to communicate to an audience in order to fulfill an objective. The objective that is sought requires the audience to reinforce or modify attitudes and/or behavior.

Many scholars have grappled with a definition of the word *propaganda*. Jacques Ellul (1965) focused on the technique of propaganda, notably psychological manipulation, which, in technological societies, "has certain identical results" whether it is used by Communists or Nazis or Western democratic organizations. Ellul contended that nearly all biased messages in society were propagandistic, even when the biases were unconscious. He also emphasized the potency and pervasiveness of propaganda. Because propaganda is instantaneous, he contended, it destroys one's sense of history and disallows critical reflection. Leonard W. Doob, who defined propaganda in 1948 as "the attempt to affect the personalities and to control the behavior of individuals towards ends considered unscientific or of doubtful value in a society at a particular time" (p. 390), said in a recent essay (1989) that "a clear-cut definition of propaganda is neither possible nor desirable" (p. 375). Doob rejects a contemporary definition of propaganda because of the complexity of the issues related to behavior in society and differences in times and cultures.

Both Ellul and Doob have contributed seminal ideas to the study of propaganda, but Ellul's magnitude and Doob's resistance to definitions are troublesome, for in order to analyze propaganda one needs to be able to recognize it. A definition sets forth propaganda's characteristics and aids our recognition of it. Furthermore, we want to place propaganda within communication studies in order to examine the qualities of context, sender, intent, message, channel, audience, and response. Finally, we want to clarify, as much as possible, the distinction between propaganda and persuasion by examining propaganda as a subcategory of persuasion as well as information.

Psychologists Anthony Pratkanis and Elliot Aronson have written a book about propaganda for the purpose of informing Americans about propaganda devices and psychological dynamics so that people will know "how to counteract their effectiveness" (1991, p. xii). Although their preface states that they understand the difference between persuasion and propaganda, they do not further expound, but state that not all persuasion is propaganda. They do, however, regard propaganda as the abuse of persuasion and recognize that propaganda is more than clever deception. In a series of case studies, they illustrate propaganda tactics such as withholding vital information, invoking heuristic devices, using meaningless association, and other strategies of questionable ethics. They define propaganda as "mass 'suggestion' or influence through the manipulation of symbols and the psychology of the individual," (p. 9) thus emphasizing verbal and nonverbal communication and audience appeals.

Two propaganda scholars have emphasized the communicative qualities of propaganda. Leo Bogart (1976, pp. 195-196) in his study of the U.S. Information Agency, focused on the propagandist as a sender of messages: "Propaganda is an art requiring special talent. It is not mechanical, scientific work. Influencing attitudes requires experience, area knowledge, and instinctive 'judgement of what is the best argument for the audience.' No manual can guide the propagandist. He must have 'a good mind, genius, sensitivity, and knowledge of how that audience thinks and reacts.'" (Within this quote is material from the original five-volume study of the USIA that Bogart's work condenses.)

Terence H. Qualter (1962) emphasized the necessity of audience adaptation: "Propaganda, to be effective, must be seen, remembered, understood, and acted upon . . . adapted to particular needs of the situation and the audience to which it is aimed" (p. xii). Influencing attitudes, anticipating audience reaction, adaptation to the situation and audience, and being seen, remembered, understood, and acted upon are important elements of the communicative process.

Our definition of propaganda focuses on the communication process and most specifically on the purpose of the process: *Propaganda is the deliberate and systematic attempt to shape perceptions, manipulate cognitions, and direct behavior to achieve a response that furthers the desired intent of the propagandist.*

Let us examine the words of the definition to see what is precisely meant. First of all, *deliberate* is a strong word meaning willful, intentional, and premeditated. It carries with it a sense of careful consideration of all possibilities. We use it because propaganda is carefully thought out ahead of time in order to select what will be the most effective strategy to promote an ideology and maintain an advantageous position. *Systematic* complements deliberate because it means precise and methodical, carrying out something with organized regularity. Governments establish departments or agencies to specifically create systematic propaganda. Although the general public is more aware of propaganda agencies during wartime, such agencies exist all of the time, for they are essential. Another form of systematic propaganda is an advertising campaign. The goal of propaganda is to "attempt" or try to create a certain state or states in a certain audience, thus propaganda is an attempt at directive communication with an objective that has been established a priori. The desired state may be perceptual, cognitive, or behavioral, or all three. Each one of these is described with examples as follows.

Shaping perceptions. The shaping of perceptions is usually attempted through language and images, which is why slogans, posters, symbols, and even architecture are developed during wartime. *Operation Desert Shield* was changed to *Operation Desert Storm* when U.S. forces invaded Iraq in January 1991. *Shield* to *Storm* was meant to change people's perception from "protective" to a "raging" forces. Saddam Hussein called President George Bush "Devil Bush" while Bush consistently mispronounced Saddam with the accent on the first syllable—SADdam. In the United States, yellow ribbons were put on trees, fences, buildings, and jewelry as momentum gathered to "Support the Troops." Throughout Iraq, ubiquitous murals of Saddam Hussein made him appear larger than life. Americans perceived Hussein as an atavistic villain; whereas, in Iraq the intention was to get Iraqis as well as other Arab nations to perceive Hussein as a heroic leader.

As perceptions are shaped, *cognitions may be manipulated.* One way that beliefs are formed is through a person's trust in one's own senses (Bem, 1970). Certainly, an attitude is a cognitive or affective reaction to an idea or object based on one's perceptions. Of course, once a belief or an attitude is formed, a person's perceptions are influenced by it. This does not happen in a vacuum. The formation of cognitions and attitudes is a complex process related to cultural and personal values. A study done at the University of Massachusetts during the Persian Gulf War found that the more people watched the news of the war on television, the stronger were their attitudes that the United States should be involved in the war (NPR radio, June 26, 1991). While it is tempting to say that the television images and patriotic messages created positive attitudes toward the war, it is possible that viewers who leaned toward support of the war watched more television. Without assigning particular causality to the media coverage or anything else, one can conclude that President Bush had his nation's support. Polls taken during the war indicated very strong support of the war and of President Bush. In mid-February 1991, pollsters found 80% approval of Bush's handling of the Gulf crisis (Can the pro-war consensus survive? 1991, p. 32) and 86% approval of a ground war in Iraq (Duffey & Walsh, 1991, p. 27). Contrasted to the Vietnam War, the government's efforts to elicit national support for Operation Desert Storm were successful. Even people who participated in antiwar demonstrations said they supported American troops in the Persian Gulf.

Often the *direction of a specific behavior* is the intent of a propaganda effort. During war, one desired behavior is defection of enemy troops. In the Persian Gulf War, the U.S. Fourth Psychological Operations Group dropped 29 million leaflets on Iraqi forces to attract defectors. A U.S. radio program, "Voice of the Gulf" featured testimonials from happy Iraqi prisoners of war along with prayers from the Koran and the location of the bomb targets for the next day. Seventy-five percent of Iraqi defectors said they were influenced by the leaflets and the radio broadcasts (A Psy-Ops Bonanza, 1991, p. 24).

These examples from the 1991 Persian Gulf War were part of deliberate and systematic plans on both sides to fulfill a purpose on behalf of an institution. Saddam Hussein's propaganda resembled that of Hitler and other dictators and was thus more recognizable. American propaganda in the Gulf War included a multitude of techniques, and analysis is required to fully understand it. (See Chapter 7 for a case study on the propaganda of the Gulf War.)

To continue with the definition, propaganda seeks to "achieve a response," a specific reaction or action from an audience "that furthers the desired intent of the propagandist." These last words are the key to the definition of propaganda, for the one who benefits from the audience's response, if the response is the desired one, is the propagandist and not necessarily the members of the audience. People in the audience may think the propagandist has their interest at heart, but in fact, the propagandist's motives are selfish ones. Selfish motives are not necessarily negative, and judgment depends upon which ideology one supports. For example, people who listened to the Voice of America broadcasts behind the Iron Curtain found satisfaction for their hunger for information, and thus it appeared that the VOA had altruistic motives. The information they received from the VOA, however, was ideologically injected to shape positive perceptions about America and her allies and to manipulate attitudes toward democracy, capitalism, and freedom. Most Americans would not regard these practices as negative, but the communist government officials did. (Later in the chapter in the section on Subpropaganda, there are examples of seemingly altruistic communication which was deliberately designed to facilitate acceptance of an ideology.)

When conflict exists, and security is essential, it is not unusual for propagandists to try to contain information and responses to it in a specific area. Recipients of propaganda messages are discouraged from asking about anything outside the contained area. During wartime, members of the press complain about restrictions placed on them in reporting the events of the war. Newspaper reporters covering the Civil War between the States complained in the 1860s as journalists did during the Persian Gulf War in 1991. Tom Wicker of the *New York Times* wrote that "The Bush administration and the military were so successful in controlling information about the war that they were able to tell the public just about what they wanted the public to know. Perhaps worse, press and public largely acquiesced in this disclosure of only selected information" (Oh, What a Censored War! 1991, p. 69). There is nothing unusual about journalists' complaints about information control during wartime. There is a saying that "the first casualty during war is truth."

Yet, contemporary technology is capable of instantaneous transmission of messages around the world, and because there has been a tremendous expansion of exposure to all of the mass media throughout the world, it is, as Bogart (1976) has pointed out, "increasingly difficult to maintain a country in isolation from ideas and information that are common in the rest of the world" (p. xviii).

Certainly, as communist governments toppled in Poland, Czechoslovakia, Hungary, East Germany, and Romania in 1989, the world saw dramatic evidence that propaganda cannot be contained for long where television exists. People living under the austere regime of East Germany received television from West Germany and saw consumer goods that were easily had and a life-style that was abundant rather than austere. Also, the technology of the portable video camera enabled amateurs to capture and display footage of the Czech police on the rampage, the massacre of Georgian demonstrators in Tiblisi, and the bloodbath in Tiananmen Square. When the Communist government controlled Czechoslovakia, rebellious protestors produced the "Video Journal" on home video cameras and sent it into Czech homes via rented satellite dishes. In Poland, Lech Walesa said that the underground Solidarity movement could not have succeeded without video. In Rumania, it was said that while the crowds protested against Nicholae Ceausescu, the television showed fear and doubt in his eyes and encouraged people to continue to fight against his regime despite his army's violence. Ironically, the center of the intense fighting between the army and Ceausescu's loyalists was the Bucharest television station. For a time, the new government was in residence there, making the television station the epicenter of the revolution and the seat of the provisional government. In this age of instantaneous television transmission, containment of information is no longer easy. Yet propaganda itself, as a form of communication, is influenced by the technological devices for sending messages that are available in a given time. As technology advances, propagandists have more sophisticated tools at their service. ABC's *Nightline* reported in December 1991 the first recorded use of the Fax machine for propaganda purposes in Riyadh. Leaflets describing how to prepare for a chemical warfare assault, presumably sent by the Hussein propagandists, came through thousands of Kuwaiti Fax machines.

The study of contemporary propaganda in both oppressed and free societies is a complex endeavor. We acknowledge that one's perception of a form of communication determines what is self-evident and what is controversial. One person's propaganda may be another person's education. In our definition, the elements of deliberate intent and manipulation along with a systematic plan to achieve a purpose that is advantageous to the propagandist, however, distinguish propaganda from a free and open exchange of ideas.

Forms of Propaganda

Although propaganda takes many forms, it is almost always in some form of activated ideology. Sometimes propaganda is *agitative*, attempting to arouse an audience to certain ends, usually resulting in significant change; sometimes it is *integrative*, attempting to render an audience passive, accepting, and nonchallenging (Szanto, 1978). Propaganda is also described as white, gray, or black in relationship to an acknowledgment of its source and its accuracy of information.

White propaganda comes from a source that is identified correctly, and the information in the message tends to be accurate. This is what one hears on Radio Moscow and the Voice of America during peacetime. Although what listeners hear is reasonably close to the truth, it is presented in a manner that attempts to convince the audience that the sender is the "good guy" with the best ideas and political ideology. White propaganda attempts to build credibility with the audience, for this could have usefulness at some point in the future.

National celebrations with their overt patriotism and regional chauvinism can usually be classified as white propaganda. On July 4, 1991 President Bush went to Marshfield, Missouri to watch one of the nation's oldest annual Independence Day celebrations. Wearing an American flag in his pocket, he praised the American troops who fought in the Persian Gulf and said that "the war had made everyone in the country proud to say 'I am an American and I love my country.'" (Dowd, 1991, p. C7)

International sports competitions also inspire white propaganda from journalists. During the 1984 Olympics, there were many complaints of "biased" coverage by the American reporters, particularly from the British Broadcasting Corporation. The absence of the Soviet Union athletes in Los Angeles provoked a less than enthusiastic reaction to the multiple victories of Americans from non-American news sources. Although the former gold medalists of past games lauded American performances, the home countries of the other athletes accused the American commentators of being "unfair." Daley Thompson, the decathlon winner from Great Britain, appeared on television wearing a t-shirt that read, "But what about the coverage?" The American Broadcasting Company's coverage was accurate reporting of the events and white propaganda. They appeared to stir up American patriotism deliberately while being genuinely excited about the American athletes' achievements. Doubtlessly, this was also intended to convey a message to the Soviet government that said, "We do not need you at the Games."

Black propaganda is credited to a false source, and it spreads lies, fabrications, and deceptions. Black propaganda is the "big lie," including all types of creative deceit. During World War II, prior to Hitler's planned invasion of Britain, a radio station known as "The New English Broadcasting Station," supposedly run by discontented British subjects, ran half-hour length programs throughout the day, opening with "Loch Lomond" and closing with "God Save the King." The station's programming consisted of war news. This was actually a German undercover operation determined to reduce the morale of the British people throughout the Battle of Britain. The same technique was used on French soldiers serving in the Maginot Line from the autumn of 1939 until the spring of 1940. Radio broadcasts, originating from Stuttgart, were hosted by Paul Ferdonnet, a turncoat Frenchman who pretended to be a patriot, warned the French soldiers to save France before the Nazis took it over. French soldiers heard Ferdonnet sympathize with their discomfort due to crowded and damp conditions in barrack tunnels, and they enjoyed the latest gossip about Paris. He then went on to tell them that French officers had dined at a famous restaurant in Paris where they ate delicious six-course lunches (Roetter, 1974). He also described British soldiers in French towns. Because they earned higher pay than their French counterparts, he said, they spent a lot of money and made love to French women. He also said the French soldiers were dupes to fight England's war and urged them to support a "new" government for France. The French soldiers were already miserable due to the conditions on the Maginot Line, and they resented the differences in pay between themselves and the British soldiers. Ferdonnet's broadcasts, although designed to weaken the French soldiers' morale, provided entertainment but not thoughts of defection. Perhaps the French soldiers were not deceived because they also received obvious Nazi propaganda in the form of pornographic cartoons showing British soldiers fondling naked French women. Huge billboards were set up within their view that said, "**Soldiers of the Northern Provinces, Licentious British Soldiery Are Sleeping With Your Wives and Raping Your Daughters.**" The French soldiers put up their own sign that said, "**We Don't Give a Bugger, We're From the South!**" (Costello, 1985, pp. 242-43). The French soldiers listened to Ferdonnet because they knew he would be more entertaining than their own official radio broadcasts (O'Donnell & Jowett, 1989).

Radio Free Hungary made its appearance ten years later with very successful black propaganda broadcasts. This station attracted world attention and sympathy in 1956 when the Russians sent their tanks into Budapest to squelch the popular revolution that tried to overthrow the Communist regime. Radio Free Hungary's fervent pleas for help from the United States aroused sympathy from the free world. The atrocities of the Russians were described in hideous detail, and the Russians were cursed and denounced in every transmission. The station was actually a totally brilliant fake operated by the KGB with the intention of embarrassing the United States. There was little chance that the United States would send troops to Hungary, even though Radio Free Europe had suggested that Americans would support a popular uprising in Hungary. The Soviet Union used Radio Free Hungary to demonstrate that the United States could not be relied upon to help a country in revolt. Radio Free Hungary was so effective that the U.S. Central Intelligence Agency did not know that it was a Russian propaganda device until after it ceased broadcasting (Kneitel, 1982).

Black propaganda includes all types of creative deceit, and it is this type of propaganda that gets the most attention when it is revealed. An exhibit, "Fake? The Art of Deception" was featured in the British Museum in 1990, and it included among the art forgeries several examples of propaganda. One type of forgery was the postage stamp. (See Figures 1.1 and 1.2.) Both British and German versions were displayed, and the exhibition catalogue reports that 160 different stamps were produced by both sides during the two world wars (Jones, 1990).

The success or failure of black propaganda depends upon the receiver's willingness to accept the credibility of the source and the contents of the message. Care has to be taken to place the sources and messages within a social, cultural, and political framework of the target audience. If the sender misunderstands the audience and

Figure 1.1. A German "black" propaganda parody of a British stamp, c. 1944. Note how the traditional crown has been replaced with a Star of David at the very top of the stamp. There is a hammer and sickle in place of the "p" in the ½p circle.

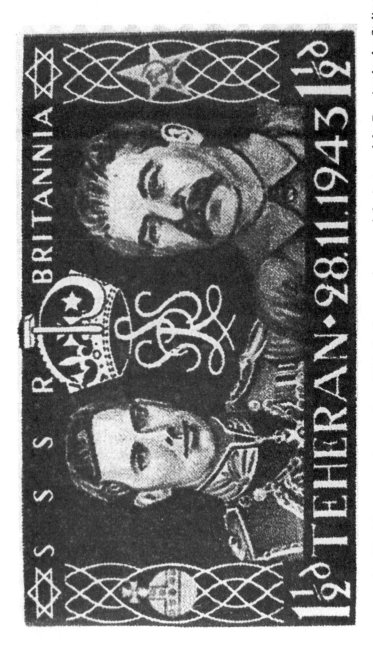

Figure 1.2. In this "black" propaganda parody, c. 1944, the Germans have used the image of the Russian leader Stalin in place of the traditional image of Queen Elizabeth. Other political symbols visible on this stamp include the Star of David and the Hammer and Sickle. The function of such parody stamps was more to create a symbolic awareness of the political association between the USSR and Britain than to undermine the economy of the postal system.

therefore designs a message that does not fit, black propaganda may appear suspicious and tends to fail.

Gray propaganda is somewhere between white and black propaganda. The source may or may not be correctly identified, and the accuracy of information is uncertain. In 1961, when the Bay of Pigs invasion took place in Cuba, the Voice of America moved over into the gray area when it denied any American involvement in the CIA-backed activities. When the Soviet Union invaded Afghanistan, Radio Moscow utilized gray propaganda when it attempted to justify the action. A documentary, "Afghanistan: The Revolution Cannot Be Killed," appeared on Soviet television on December 25, 1985. The program left the impression that the conflict had been instigated by outsiders, and maps with routes leading from Pakistan and Iran into Afghanistan were shown. Film clips suggested that the guerrillas were mercenaries. A captured man, identified as a Turkish national, said he had been sent to Afghanistan by the CIA. The film ended with music about the Afghan homeland and pro-Soviet troops being cheered by crowds (Ebon, 1987). In each of these cases, the source of the message was correctly identified, but the information was inaccurate.

Gray propaganda is also used to embarrass an enemy or competitor. Radio Moscow took advantage of the assassinations of Martin Luther King and John F. Kennedy to derogate the United States. The Voice of America did not miss the opportunity to offer similar commentaries about the invasion of Afghanistan or the arrests of Jewish dissidents.

Companies that distort statistics on annual reports, advertising that suggests a product will achieve results that it cannot, films that are made solely for product placement, and television evangelists who keep the money they solicit for religious causes all tend to fall in the gray propaganda category.

Another term used to describe propaganda is *disinformation*. It is usually considered black propaganda because it is covert and uses false information. In fact, the word *disinformation* is a cognate for the Russian *dezinformatsia*, taken from the name of a division of the KGB devoted to black propaganda.

Disinformation means "false, incomplete, or misleading information that is passed, fed, or confirmed to a targeted individual, group, or country" (Shultz & Godson, 1986, p. 41). It is not misinformation that is merely misguided or erroneous information. Disinformation is made up of news stories deliberately designed to weaken adversaries and planted in newspapers by journalists who are actually secret agents of a foreign country. The stories are passed off as real and from credible sources. Ladislav Bittmann, former deputy chief of the Disinformation Department of the Czechoslovak Intelligence Service, in testimony before the U.S. House Committee on Intelligence of the U.S. Congress in February 1980, said, "If somebody had at this moment the magic key that would open the Soviet bloc intelligence safes and looked into the files of secret agents operating in Western countries, he would be surprised. A relatively high percentage of secret agents are journalists. . . . There are newspapers around the world penetrated by the Communist Intelligence services" (Brownfield, 1984). Allan C. Brownfield (1984), a reporter for the *Washington Inquirer*, wrote that

> the documentation of the manner in which Moscow has placed false stories in the non-Communist press is massive. In one instance, Alezander Kasnechev, the senior KGB officer in Rangoon, Burma, who defected to the United States in 1959, described the Soviet effort to plant such stories. His department was responsible for receiving drafts of articles from Moscow, translating them into Burmese, and then seeing that they were placed in local publications to appear as if they had been written by Burmese authors. The final step was to send copies back to Moscow. From there they were quoted in Soviet broadcasts of publications as evidence of 'Burmese opinion' that favored the Communist line. (p. 6)

Among the more sensational Soviet disinformation campaigns was one that charged the United States with developing the virus responsible for AIDS, acquired immune deficiency syndrome, for biological warfare. The story first appeared in the October 1985 issue of the Soviet weekly *Literaturnaya Gazeta*, and it quoted the *Patriot*, a pro-Soviet newspaper in India. Although it was a Soviet tactic to place a story in a foreign newspaper in order to give it credibility, this time no such story had appeared in India. Despite U.S. State Department denials, the story appeared in the news media of more than sixty countries, including Zimbabwe while the nonaligned countries were having a conference there and in the October 26, 1986 issue of London's *Sunday Express* after the *Express* reporters interviewed two people from East Berlin who repeated the story. Subtle variations continued to appear in the world press, including an East German broadcast of the story into Turkey that suggested it might be wise to get rid of U.S. bases because of servicemen infected with AIDS. On March 30, 1987, Dan Rather read the following news item on *CBS Evening News*:

> A Soviet military publication claims the virus that causes Aids leaked from a U.S. Army laboratory conducting experiments in biological warfare.

The article offers no hard evidence but claims to be reporting the conclusions of unnamed scientists in the United States, Britain, and East Germany. Last October, a Soviet newspaper alleged that the Aids virus may have been the result of Pentagon or CIA experiments. (CBS Spreads Disinformation on Aids, 1987, pp. xvi-8)

There is increasing evidence that disinformation is widely practiced by most of the major world powers, and this reflects the reality of international politics. For a long time the United States denied using disinformation, yet a U.S. disinformation effort charged the Sandinistas in El Salvador with cocaine-running. The Iran-Contra hearings in 1987 along with Admiral John Poindexter's papers revealed, however, that the CIA and the Contras were involved in a massive Central American drug smuggling connection. Other disinformation stories planted by the United States were about carcinogenic Soviet spy dust, Soviet sponsorship of international terrorism, and attempts to assassinate the Pope by Bulgarians (Alexandre, 1988, pp. 114-15).

As a communication process, disinformation is described according to two models that we have developed (See Figures 1.3 and 1.4). In Figure 1.3, the propagandist (P) creates a *deflective source* (P1) which becomes the apparent source of the message (M). The receiver (R) perceives the information as coming directly from P1 and does not associate it with the original propagandist (P). In Figure 1.4, the propagandist secretly places the original message (M1) in a *legitimizing source* (P2). This message (now M2), as interpreted by P2, is then picked up by the propagandist (P) and communicated to the receiver (R) in the form M3, as having come from P2. This legitimizes the message, and at the same time, disassociates the propagandist (P) from its origination. One can see in both models that the propagandist's intent is to obscure the identity of the message-originator, thus creating a high degree of credibility for both message and apparent source.

Propaganda thus runs the gamut from truth to deception. It is, at the same time, always value- and ideology-laden. The means may vary from a mild slanting of information to outright deception, but the ends are always predetermined to favor the propagandist.

Subpropaganda/Facilitative Communication

Another dimension of propaganda is what Doob (1948) called "subpropaganda." Here the propagandist's task is to spread an unfamiliar doctrine, for which a considerable period of time is needed

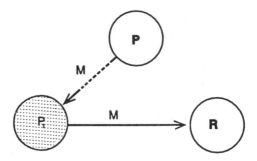

Figure 1.3. Deflective source model.

SOURCE: Reprinted by permission of Greenwood Publishing Group, Inc., Westport, CT, from *Propaganda: A Pluralistic Perspective* by T. J. Smith III. Copyright by T. J. Smith III and published in 1989 by Praeger Publishers.

to build a frame of mind in the audience toward acceptance of the doctrine. In order to gain the target audience's favor, various stimuli are used to arouse the attention of the audience and the related encoders and agents who mediate communication. L. John Martin (1971, p. 62), who was a research administrator in the U.S. Information Agency for nine years, called subpropaganda "facilitative communication," that is, an activity that is designed to keep lines open and to maintain contacts against the day when they will be needed for propaganda purposes.

Facilitative communication most frequently takes the form of radio newscasts, press releases, books, pamphlets, periodicals, cultural programs, exhibits, films, seminars, language classes, reference services, and personal social contacts. These are all arranged in an effort to create a friendly atmosphere toward those who may be needed later on. W. Phillips Davison (1971) gives examples of influencing

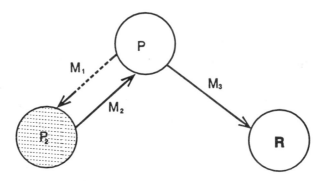

Figure 1.4. Legitimizing source model.

SOURCE: Reprinted by permission of Greenwood Publishing Group, Inc., Westport, CT, from *Propaganda: A Pluralistic Perspective* by T. J. Smith III. Copyright by T. J. Smith III and published in 1989 by Praeger Publishers.

journalists to give favorable press to the United States by offering rides and other services such as office space provided by the U.S. Committee on Public Information, parties, conducted tours of foreign cities, and news scoops.

Facilitative communication itself may not be propaganda, but it is communication that is designed to render a positive attitude toward a potential propagandist. In 1969, 450 active registrations of agencies distributing propaganda were on file with the U.S. government on behalf of foreign agencies. Davison points out that most were concerned with tourism, investment, or trade. This did not include embassies or consulates' activities, nor did it include mail and short-wave radio from abroad. Meanwhile, the U.S. Information Agency (USIA) employs a staff of 8,784 employees who work in 126 countries at a cost of $1,010.61 million per year "to give foreign peoples the best possible understanding of U.S. policies and intentions" (*U.S.I.A. Fact Sheet*, 1991). This agency alone publishes 14 magazines and commercial bulletins in 20 languages, produces more than 90 films a year, operates a radio-teletype network, and broadcasts more than 1,200 hours a week through the Voice of America in 45 languages to an estimated 130 million listeners. The Voice of America "Worldnet" is a satellite television network that was established in 1983. Television programs are set to 126 countries through a network of satellites.

Although the Cold War has ended, the use of propaganda is certainly not on the decline. Communication networks have expanded and changed, and information tends to be more accessible, but the institutions of modern society, government, business, and religion, still retain the need to deliberately manipulate responses.

A Model of Propaganda

The literature of propaganda often refers to "mass persuasion," suggesting that propaganda is persuasion on a one-to-many basis. Propaganda tends to be linked with a general societal process, whereas persuasion is regarded as an individual psychological process. Propaganda has not been successfully differentiated from persuasion by other writers. The model in Figure 1.5 is our attempt to differentiate between them and to demonstrate a separation according to purpose and process. The model also reveals the similarity between persuasion and propaganda with subtle differences of technique used according to purpose.

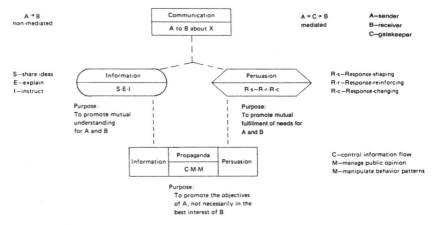

Figure 1.5. The Jowett-O'Donnell purpose model of propaganda.

Communication Defined

Communication is a process in which a sender transmits a message to a receiver through a channel. This process has been represented by both linear and transactional models. One of the earliest models of communication was developed by Aristotle (333 B.C.) who described a speaker, a speech, and an audience as the major components of the communication act. A linear model that influenced communication research was developed by Shannon and Weaver in 1949 for the study of electronic engineering. Its components were source, message, transmitter, signal, and receiver. Other linear communication models that followed were similar to Shannon and Weaver's because they emphasized source, message, channel, and response.

Communication involves attempts to share meaning through a process of symbolic interaction between and among human beings. A transactional model of communication represents it as a convergence process in which sender and receiver create and share information with one another in order to reach a mutual understanding (Rogers & Kincaid, 1981). Information exchange can reduce uncertainty after several cycles of exchange. In a convergence process, there is a tendency for the sender and receiver to move toward one point, or for one to move toward the other, or to unite in a common interest or focus.

A straightforward definition of the communication process is that which happens when A (sender) communicates to B (receiver) about X. A may be a person, a group, or a social system. B may be a person, a group, or a social system as well. Communication is often a human face-to-face transaction, but it is also often a mediated interaction whereby A communicates to B through C about X. Here C is a gatekeeper, an encoder of a message, or, quite possibly, an agent for B (Westley & MacLean, 1977).

It is important to examine both the message and the response to it in the study of communication. Responses may be in the realm of feedback, or they may be examined as effects on the audience. The elements of face-to-face and/or mediated communication must be examined in light of the context in which they occur, both in a specific and immediate sense and in the social-cultural framework of the times.

Propaganda and Information

Communication has been defined as a convergence process in which sender and receiver, either through mediated or nonmediated means, create and share information. When the information is used to accomplish a purpose of sharing, explaining, or instructing, this is considered to be informative communication. People seek information when they need to understand their world. Once gained, information tends to reduce uncertainty. Uncertainty reduction is normally acquired through the communication of messages; thus messages can be analyzed in terms of the amount of uncertainty they remove. Informative messages have an impact upon receivers by allowing them to acquire information, understand their world, and learn.

Generally speaking, informative communication is thought to be neutral because it is characterized by a very special and limited use of language. Informative discourse is communication about subject matter that has attained the privileged status of being beyond dispute. Whenever information is regarded as disputable by either the sender or receiver, it is difficult for the communication to proceed as information. An informative communicator differs from other kinds of communicators by having the purpose of creating mutual understanding of data that are considered to be accurate, of concepts that are considered to be indisputable, and of ideas that are based on facts.

Propaganda utilizes informative communication in a similar fashion. The difference is that the purpose exceeds the notion of mutual understanding. The purpose of propaganda is to promote a partisan or competitive cause in the best interest of the propagandist but not necessarily in the best interest of the recipient. The recipient, however, may believe that the communication is merely informative. As we pointed out in the example of the Voice of America, white propaganda is very similar to informative communication. Information is imparted from an identifiable source, and the information is accurate. The distinction between white propaganda and informative communication is that white propaganda informs solely to promote a specific ideology. Techniques of informative communication are also used in gray and black propaganda, but the information is not likely to be accurate or even based in reality.

Many writers grapple with the distinction between propaganda and informative communication in educational practices that include the communicative purpose of instructing for mutual understanding. Elliot Aronson (1980) questions whether educators are merely imparting knowledge or skill. One subject area that Aronson questions is arithmetic. He points out that most of the examples in elementary school arithmetic texts deal with buying, selling, renting, working for wages, and computing interest. He also cites Zimbardo, Ebbeson, and Maslach (1977) who feel that these examples do more than simply reflect the capitalistic system in which education occurs. The point is that arithmetic problems with a capitalistic ideological base endorse the system, legitimize it, and suggest that it is the natural and normal way. Aronson says that interpretation of an instructional practice depends largely on the values of the person who is interpreting it. William E. Griffith (1980), in his essay on Communist propaganda, refers to "propaganda" and "education" interchangeably. He says that educating the masses has been the same as propaganda (vol. 2, pp. 239-58).

By evaluating educational practices according to their ends rather than their means, however, one can observe the use of informative communication as a means of achieving a propagandistic end in practices such as the ones described in this chapter.

Propaganda and Persuasion

Persuasion Defined

Persuasion as a subset of communication is usually defined as a communicative process to influence others. A persuasive message has a point of view or a desired behavior for the recipient to adopt in a voluntary fashion. Victoria O'Donnell and June Kable (1982) define persuasion as "a complex, continuing, interactive process in which a sender and a receiver are linked by symbols, verbal and nonverbal, through which the persuader attempts to influence the persuadee to adopt a change in a given attitude or behavior because the persuadee has had perceptions enlarged or changed" (p. 9). Persuasion has the effect, when it is successful, of resulting in a reaction such as, "I never saw it that way before." What happens is that the recipient of the persuasive interaction relates or contrasts the message to his or her existing repertoire of information. The process of persuasion is an interactive or transactive one in which the recipient foresees the fulfillment of a personal or societal need or desire if the persuasive purpose is adopted. The persuader also has a need fulfilled if the persuadee accepts the persuasive purpose. Because both persuader and persuadee stand to have their needs fulfilled, persuasion is regarded as more mutually satisfying than propaganda.

Persuasion Is Transactional

People respond to persuasion that promises to help them in some way by satisfying their wants or needs. That is why the persuader must think in terms of the persuadee's needs as well as his or her own. Persuasion is a reciprocal process in which both parties are dependent upon one another. It is a situation of interactive or transactive dependency. Interactive suggests turn-taking; whereas, transactive suggests a more continuous and dynamic process of co-creating meaning. The persuader who understands that persuasion is interactive or a transaction in which both parties approach a message-event and use it to attempt to fulfill needs will never assume a passive audience. It is an active audience that seeks to have its needs fulfilled by the persuader, and it is an active persuader who knows that he or she must appeal to audience needs in order to ask the audience to fill his or her needs by adopting the message-purpose. A politician seeking votes must address the needs of the voters. If the voters are convinced that the politician will fulfill their needs, then they will fulfill the needs of the politician by casting positive votes at election time.

Responses to Persuasion

Persuasion attempts to evoke a specific change in the attitude or behavior of an audience. The change sought is a specific response from the audience. There are three different forms of response that are possible (Roloff & Miller, 1980).

First, there is response shaping. This is similar to learning, wherein the persuader is a teacher and the audience is a pupil. A persuader may attempt to shape the response of an audience by teaching it how to behave and offer positive reinforcement for learning. If audience responses favorable to the persuader's purpose are reinforced by rewards to the audience, positive attitudes are developed toward what is learned. The audience has a need for positive reinforcement filled, and the persuader has a need for a desired response from the audience filled.

Second, there is response reinforcing. If the people in the audience already have positive attitudes toward a subject, the persuader reminds them about the positive attitudes and stimulates them to feel even more strongly by demonstrating their attitudes through specified forms of behavior. Much persuasion in today's society is response reinforcing (blood drives, fund raising, pep rallies, helping others, etc.), but people have to be motivated to go out and do these things year after year. There is little controversy in these situations, but people's emotional needs have to be aroused to get them to get out and give blood or money or team support, and other activities requiring effort, time, and money.

Third, there is response changing. This is the most difficult kind of persuasion because it involves asking people to switch from one attitude to another ("Favor a tax increase"), to go from a neutral position to having a positive or negative attitude ("Support the community's waste recycling program"), to change behavior ("Practice safe sex"), or to adopt a new behavior ("Host an international student for the summer"). People are reluctant to change; thus, in order to convince them to do so, the persuader has to relate the change to something in which the persuadee already believes. This is called an "anchor" because it is already accepted by the persuadee and will be used to tie down new attitudes or behaviors. An anchor is a starting point for change because it represents something that is already widely accepted by the potential persuadees. Anchors can be beliefs, values, attitudes, behaviors, and group norms.

Beliefs

A belief is a perceived link between any two aspects of a person's world (Fishbein & Ajzen, 1975, p. 131). A belief expresses a relationship between two things ("I believe that a personal computer will help me get better grades") or a thing and a characteristic of that thing ("I believe that the world is round"). We have thousands of beliefs. In order for a persuader to change old beliefs or create new ones, he or she must build on beliefs that already exist in the minds of the audience. A persuader has to use anchors of belief to create new belief. The stronger the belief of a receiver, the more likely it is that it will influence the formation of a new belief.

Values

A value is a special kind of belief that endures and is not likely to change. A value is a belief that is prescriptive and is a guideline for a person's behavior. A value can be a standard for behavior (honesty, sensitivity) or a desired end (success, power). Values are concepts of right and wrong, good and bad, or desirable and undesirable.

Personal values are derived from cultural values that tend to be utopian, mythic, and pragmatic. For example, many people embrace a national vision that embraces the belief in popular participation of people in government, the right to say what you think without restriction, and good conquers evil. A West European research organization, Futuribles, through a grant from UNESCO, conducted a study of 1,125 experts throughout the world to predict their country's core values for the year 2000. The experts from North America, primarily the United States, predicted that the top-ranked values would include possession of material wealth, health, jobs and work, individual liberty, and social equality. In contrast, Latin American countries would place survival as the top priority, while Africans fear the loss of liberty.

When situations arise that pose a conflict between national and personal values, people often find it difficult to adapt. A nation's decision to go to war to protect economic assets creates conflict for the people whose children may die in battle. People regard their values as very personal and get quite upset when they are attacked; thus they make strong anchors.

Attitudes

An attitude is a readiness to respond to an idea, an object, or a course of action. It is an internal state of feeling toward or an evaluative response to an idea, person, or object. It is expressed in a statement that clarifies a position ("I like ballet" or "I disagree with political correctness codes"). An attitude is a relatively enduring predisposition to respond; therefore, it already resides in the minds of the audience and can be used as an anchor. As people form beliefs about an object, idea, or person, they automatically and simultaneously acquire an attitude toward it. Whereas each belief is an association of an attribute with an object, an attitude is essentially an attribute evaluation.

Attitude change is often the desired response in persuasion; thus attitudes may be used as anchors or they may be used as persuasive end-states. People have thousands of attitudes, some of which are important, others inconsequential. A persuader can use strongly held attitudes as anchors to promote related attitude change.

Behavior

Behavior can be used as an anchor not only because it is an overt expression of a way of being, but also because behavioral patterns are fair predictors of future behaviors. When a behavior is recurrent, a script for behavior develops to the point that a great deal of consciousness is not necessary to continue the same behavior. References to successful behavior can be motivational. By reminding persuadees that their behavior has meant need-fulfillment in the past, a persuader can urge them to use the same or similar behavior in the future. Conversely, if certain behavior has negative consequences, the persuader can urge the persuadee to avoid the consequences by discontinuing the behavior.

Another successful motivational strategy is to show persuadees models of behavior. Modeling influences new behavior in persuadees because it offers new information about how to behave (Bandura, 1986). Albert Bandura's Model of Observational Learning includes the necessity of symbolic representation in words and images for retention of a behavior and identification of the subject with the model. Powerful modeling can simultaneously change observers' behaviors, thought patterns, emotional reactions, and evaluations. Observational learning includes knowledge of the rules of thought as well as behavior itself.

Group Norms

Group norms are beliefs, values, attitudes, and behaviors that are derived from membership in groups. Group norms can be used as anchors because people have a tendency to conform to the norms of the groups to which they belong. Daryl Bem (1970) says that the major influence on people is people. Peer pressure influences how people dress, talk, and behave. When they are uncertain about what position to take or what to do, people often adopt the attitudes and behaviors of their peers. They also succumb to peer pressure because it is easier to conform than to depart from the norms of their groups.

Another form of group norm is derived from the norms of a reference group. Reference groups are groups that are admired or disliked by nonmembers who may be influenced in a positive or negative direction by those groups. People may admire the norms of a group such as Amnesty International or be repulsed by the norms of the Ku Klux Klan.

Resonance

A persuader who is well prepared knows the audience. Anchors can be discovered from knowledge of the audience's affiliation with groups as well as from insight into the audience's beliefs, values, attitudes, and behaviors. Because these categories constitute important attributes of the audience, they can be used to motivate the audience to accept the purpose of the persuader. Both persuasion and propaganda tend to produce messages of resonance; that is, the recipients do not perceive the themes of messages to be imposed upon them from an outside authority to which they are required or committed to defer. Rather the recipients perceive the anchors upon which the message is based as coming from within themselves. Paul Kecskemeti defines the propagandist's ideal role in relation to the recipient of the message as that of an alter ego, "Someone giving expression to the recipient's own concerns, tensions, aspirations, and hopes. . . . Thus, propaganda, . . . denies all distance between the source and the audience: the propaganda voices the propagandee's own feelings" (Pool et al., 1973, p. 264). Likewise, in persuasion, identification must take place between the persuader and persuadee. They share common sensations, concepts, images, and ideas that make them feel as one. A persuader analyzes an audience in order to be able to express its needs, desires, personal and social beliefs, attitudes, and values as well as its attitudes and concerns about the social outcome of the persuasive situation. The persuader is a voice from without speaking the language of the audiences' voices within. Yet persuasive communication may be dialectic in nature and preclude homogeneity. Conversely, the propaganda message is more often homogeneous because it is sent to a mass audience rather than to one person in an interpersonal setting. There are exceptions to this, of course, when the propagandist works one-on-one with various subjects.

Persuasion Seeks Voluntary Change

In general, practitioners of persuasion assume that the audience has access to information about the other side of a controversial issue as well as exposure to counterpersuasion. In other words, there is a recognition that any change that occurs within audience perceptions, cognitions, or behaviors will be voluntary change. Both parties, persuader and persuadee, will perceive the change due to persuasion as mutually beneficial.

Misleading and Manipulating An Audience

Of course, a persuader can mislead an audience regarding the true intention. Sometimes an audience is aware of this, which gives an aura of voluntary compliance; that is, the audience can decide to consent to change while knowing quite well that the persuader has a hidden agenda. Sometimes an audience will believe a persuader regarding the spoken intent, and, consequently, it will be manipulated and used without knowing what is happening. This we regard as propaganda. More commonly, however, the propagandist exploits an audience's beliefs or values or group norms in such a way as to fan the fires of prejudice or self-interest. When the audience goes along with such practices, mutual reciprocity occurs because both parties have needs fulfilled. The audience's needs—the reinforcement of prejudicial or self-serving attitudes—get fulfilled and spoken, but the persuader's needs—the attainment of a selfish end through the audience's compliance—get fulfilled but not spoken. No audience, no matter how perverse in its own needs, will put up with hearing that they are being manipulated and used to fulfill another's selfish needs. Thus the propagandist cannot reveal the true intent of the message.

Rhetorical Background and the Ethics of Persuasion

Since the beginnings of the study of rhetoric, which was synonymous with persuasion until the early twentieth century, theorists have been concerned with ethics. The form of government in ancient Greece encouraged public speaking. Citizens voiced their opinions openly and were encouraged to share in making political and judicial decisions. Because civic responsibility was presumed, there was strong encouragement to be honorable citizens and to acquire skill in public statement. The Athenian system disqualified any speaker who was "suspected of certain dishonorable acts . . . he could be prosecuted, not for the offense, but for continuing to speak in the assembly after committing the offense" (Bonner, 1933, p. 80). People studied the art of rhetoric almost as an entire system of higher education if not a way of life (Hunt, 1925).

Plato opposed the place of rhetoric in Athenian life as well as whatever part rhetoric had in influencing public opinion. As Hunt (1925) said, "He despised mere opinion almost as much as he did the public" (p. 3). He believed in a government ruled by philosopher-kings and not a government in which rhetoric was employed by those who did not possess true wisdom or knowledge. As a result, two of his writings, the *Gorgias* and the *Phaedrus*, attacked rhetoric as a system capable of making the worse appear the better reason. In the *Gorgias*, Plato criticized the study of rhetoric for misleading people into believing that by attempting through words to achieve what is good, that they can do good. Without insight and wisdom, a person who studied rhetoric was likely to become what we would call a propagandist. Plato, through his spokesman, Socrates, posed the questions:

> Do the rhetoricians appear to you always to speak with a view to what is best, aiming at this, that the citizens may be made as good as possible by their discourses? or do they, too, endeavor to gratify the citizens, and neglecting the public interest for the sake of their own private advantage, do they treat the people as children, trying only to gratify them, without being in the least concerned whether they shall become better or worse by these means? (Cary, 1854).

In the *Phaedrus*, Plato admonishes the rhetorician to have high moral purpose and knowledge of truth or else not attempt rhetoric at all.

Aristotle, the great philosopher and social interpreter of fourth-century Greece, produced many classical works about the nature of ideas and people. The work that is seminal in the field of persuasion is *Rhetoric* (Cooper, 1932). Although Aristotle studied under Plato and embraced many of the ideas that Plato expressed in the *Phaedrus*, *Rhetoric* tends to be detached from issues of morality. Rather, it is an amoral and scientific analysis of rhetoric, defined as "the faculty of discovering in the particular case what are the available means of persuasion" (p. 7). Yet, it is in *Rhetoric* that Aristotle establishes the concept of credibility (ethos) as a form of proof and a mode of persuasion. Ethos, an artistic proof established within the discourse itself, provides the audience with insight into the persuader's character, integrity, and good will. Other forms of proof are emotional appeal (pathos) and the speech itself (logos), defined by Aristotle as "when we have proved a truth or an apparent truth from such means of persuasion as are appropriate to a particular subject" (p. 9).

Central to the study of rhetoric is the audience, which Aristotle classified and analyzed. Logic is established through audience participation in an interactive reasoning process. Known as the *enthymeme*, this practical device is regarded by many as a syllogism with some part or parts missing. In fact, the enthymeme enabled the persuader and persuadees to co-create reasoning by dialectically coming to a conclusion. It requires the audience to mentally fill in parts of the reasoning process, thus stimulating involvement. Aristotle regarded the enthymeme as a way of guarding truth and justice against falsehood and wrong. He believed that audiences could not follow close and careful logical reasoning related to universal truths but could participate in reasoning related to probability in the sphere of human affairs.

In his *Nicomachean Ethics*, Aristotle dealt with his expectations for high moral principles. With regard to persuasion, he indicated that a crafty person could artfully manipulate the instruments of rhetoric for either honest or dishonest ends. Depending upon which end is desired, the use of rhetorical devices is judged accordingly: "If . . . the aim be good, the cleverness is praiseworthy; but if it be bad, it becomes craft" (Browne, 1850, pp. vi, xii, 8). MacCunn (1906) interprets this to mean that the Aristotelian thesis postulates that "cleverness and character must strike alliance" (p. 298). MacCunn also sees Aristotle's general point of view as judging the means according to the ends sought: "He who would win the harper's skill must win by harping; he who would write, by writing; he who would heal the sick by healing them. In these, as indeed in all the arts, faculty is begotten of function, and definite proclivity comes of determinate acts" (p. 301).

Quintilian, the premier teacher of imperial rhetoric in Rome during the first century A.D., wrote the *Institutes of Oratory*, in which he advocated the necessity of credibility, arguing on behalf of Cato's definition: "An orator is a good man, skilled in speaking" (Benson & Prosser, 1969, p. 118). This concept was reiterated by St. Augustine in his fifth-century work on Christian preaching and rhetoric, *On Christian Doctrine*. Insistence upon truth as the overall objective of public speaking is the cardinal tenet of this treatise. Augustine was concerned about using rhetorical techniques for false persuasion, but he felt that the way in which it was used did not reflect upon rhetoric itself: "There are also rules for a more copious kind of argument, which is called eloquence, and these rules are not the less true that they can be used for persuading men of what is false, but as they can be used to enforce the truth as well, it is not the faculty itself that is to be blamed, but the perversity of those who put it to a bad use" (Shaw, 1873, pp. ix, 5).

Classical concepts of rhetoric, especially that of the good man speaking well, were revitalized throughout the Middle Ages, the Renaissance, and the Reformation. Neoclassicism held forth in theoretical works on persuasion despite the appearance of despot princes and authoritarian rulers in the same countries in which the rhetorical works were published. In the same century that Machiavelli wrote *The Prince*, advocating the use of dishonest methods to gain and maintain power, rhetorical theorists such as Phillipp Melanchthon, the humanist educator and religious reformer of Germany, Leonard Cox, the first to write a treatise on rhetoric in the English language, and Thomas Wilson, whose *Arte of Rhetorique* was published eight times in thirty years from 1553 to 1583, were turning out works that echoed Cicero and Quintilian.

Even after the *Sacra Congregation de Propaganda Fide* became an official organ of the Roman Catholic Church in 1622, no rhetorical theorist addressed its implications with regard to persuasion. The major rhetorical works of the seventeenth century were Francis Bacon's four treatises—adapting classical rhetoric to the needs of the scientist and affirming the value of ornamentation and imaginative coloring in rhetoric—and the early elocutionists, Robert Robinson and John Bulwer, whose works on delivery foreshadowed the rhetorical movement that placed major emphasis on delivery and pronunciation.

Rhetoric and Propaganda

The study of persuasion in the theories of rhetoric laid down throughout the centuries emphasized adherence to the truth in revealing the real intent of the persuader and a sincere concern for the welfare of the audience. These are the humanistic concerns of the classicists. It can be argued that the humanists were more concerned with eloquence than with truth and consequently preferred rhetoric to logic. There are no major rhetorical theories from nations whose governments have been totalitarian, thus the history of rhetoric hardly includes the study of propaganda except for allusions to misuse of rhetorical techniques for dishonest ends. The Bolsheviks had Eisenstein to describe and demonstrate the use of propaganda in film, and the Nazis had Hitler's *Mein Kampf* and Goebbels's diaries as guidelines for propaganda, but these have not been part of the history of rhetoric. The reason for this comes from the rhetorician's insistence upon a consideration of ethics in rhetoric. It was not until Kenneth Burke (1973), the American literary critic, wrote "The Rhetoric of Hitler's 'Battle'" in 1939 that a serious rhetoric critic tackled and analyzed propaganda while simultaneously contributing new ideas to rhetorical theory.

Drawing upon what he called the Dramatistic Pentad—five interrelated motivational or causal points of view—Burke analyzed the Act (what took place in thought or deed), the Scene (the background of the Act, the situation in which it occurred), the Agent (the actor or person or institution who performed the Act), the Agency or Agencies (the means or instruments used by the Agent), and the Purpose (the motive or cause that lay behind the Act). Burke determined that in *Mein Kampf* the Act was the bastardization of religious thought; the Agent was Hitler; the Agencies were unity identification such as "one voice", the Reich, Munich, the army, German democracy, race, nation, Aryan, heroism, and so on versus disunity identification such as images, ideas, and so on of parliamentary wrangle of the Hapsburgs, Babel of opinion, Jewish cunning, together with spiritualization and materialization techniques; the Scene was discordant elements in a culture weakened progressively by capitalistic materialism; and the Purpose was the unification of the German people. Burke's description of Hitler's strategies to control the German people is a masterful criticism of propaganda, yet it also is heavily flavored with moralistic judgement. It warns the reader about "what to guard against if we are to forestall the concocting of similar medicine in America" (Burke, 1973, p. 191).

Donald C. Bryant's seminal essay, "Rhetoric: Its Function and Scope" (1953) devotes a few pages to propaganda, which includes advertising and certain political discourse, as "partial, incomplete, and perhaps misused, rhetorics" (p. 413). He characterized propaganda by technique—exclusion of competing ideas, short-circuiting informed judgment, ignoring alternative ideas or courses of action, and in general, subverting rational processes. Although Bryant did not engage in propaganda analysis or add new insight into understanding propaganda, he acknowledged that the understanding of propaganda is grounded in the understanding of rhetoric. His stance is a classical one, for he said, "The major techniques of this propaganda are long known rhetorical techniques gone wrong" (p. 415).

Although few rhetorical theorists discussed propaganda, the study of persuasion blossomed in the twentieth century as an inquiry into behaviorism. This happened almost concurrently with the serious study of propaganda by social scientists. This development and synopsis of the resulting research is presented in Chapter 4. Now let us return to the model that differentiates propaganda from other forms of communication.

Propaganda as a Form of Communication

Propaganda may appear to be informative communication when ideas are shared, something is explained, or instruction takes place. Information communicated by the propagandist may appear to be indisputable and totally factual. The propagandist knows, however, that the purpose is not to promote mutual understanding but rather to promote his or her own objectives. Thus the propagandist will attempt to control information flow and manage a certain public's opinion by shaping perceptions through strategies of informative communication.

A persuader, likewise, shares ideas, explains, or instructs within the purpose of promoting the mutual satisfaction of needs. In fact, a persuader skillfully uses evidence to teach potential persuadees rather than to persuade them. Evidence itself does not persuade, but it can enhance a persuader's credibility (McCroskey, 1969). Persuaders, however, do not try to appear as informers. An effective persuader makes the purpose as clear as possible if he or she hopes to bring about attitude change. The explicitly stated conclusion is twice as likely to get desired audience response compared to the suggested one (Biddle, 1966; Hovland & Mandell, 1952).

Concealed Purpose

The propagandist is very likely to appear as a persuader with a stated purpose that appears to satisfy mutual needs. In reality, however, the propagandist wants to promote his or her own interests or those of an organization, sometimes at the expense of the recipients, sometimes not. The point is that the propagandist does not regard the well-being of the audience as a primary concern. The propagandist is likely to be detached from the recipients. Not only does the propagandist not care about the audience, he or she may not believe in the message that is being sent. In fact, concealment of purpose may not be the only deviousness. Often a propagandist does not want his or her or its identity known.

Concealed Identity

Identity concealment is often necessary in order for the propagandist to achieve desired objectives and goals. The propagandist seeks to control the flow of information, manage public opinion, and manipulate behavior patterns. These are the kinds of objectives that might not be achieved if their true intent were known or if the real source were revealed.

Control of Information Flow

Control of information flow takes the form of withholding information, releasing information at predetermined times, releasing information in juxtaposition with other information that may influence public perception, manufacturing information, communicating information to selective audiences, and distorting information. There are two major ways in which the propagandist tries to control information flow: (a) controlling the media as a source of information distribution and (b) presenting distorted information from what appears to be a credible source. Using journalists to infiltrate the media and spread disinformation is one way to present distorted information. Altheide and Johnson (1980) make a case for what they call "bureaucratic propaganda" in which organizations, ranging from the military to television networks to evangelical crusades, release official reports containing what appears to be scientifically gathered and objective information to influential groups with the purpose of maintaining the legitimacy of organizations and their activities. The information in the official reports is often contrived, distorted, or falsely interpreted. This information, according to Altheide and Johnson, may never be seen by the public but rather by a congressional committee or some citizens' group and may be used for some action or program.

When Chinese students demonstrated in Tiananmen Square in Beijing in 1989, the government blacked out news reports of the protest to smaller cities and the countryside. Chinese citizens in these areas never knew about the Beijing unrest and demands for reforms. The world saw the demonstrations because the media was in Beijing to cover Mikhail Gorbachev's visit there. When the government brutally massacred thousands of protestors fleeing from tanks and grenades, it distorted the truth by claiming that thugs and counterrevolutionaries had murdered soldiers of the People's Republic of China, who fired back in self-defense. Here the Chinese government successfully controlled information flow to its own people, but other people of the world knew about it.

The Management of Public Opinion

Propaganda is most often associated with the management of public opinion. Public opinion has been defined by Land and Sears (1964) as "an implicit verbal response or 'answer' that an individual gives in response to a particular stimulus situation in which some general 'question' is raised" (quoted in Mitchell, 1970, p. 62). Walter Lippmann (1922) regarded public opinion as that which emanated from persons interested in public affairs rather than a fixed body of individuals. He believed that the public opinion was effective only if those persons supported or opposed the "actors" in public affairs. Speier (1950) felt that public opinion exists when a unique "right" is granted to a significant portion of extragovernmental persons: "In its most attenuated form this right asserts itself as the expectation that the government will reveal and explain its decisions in order to enable people outside the government to think and talk about these decisions, or to put it in terms of democratic amenities, in order to assure 'the success' of the government's policy" (quoted in Altheide & Johnson, 1980, p. 7).

Mitchell gives four forms that public opinion usually takes: (a) popular opinion as generalized support for an institution, regime, or political system (as opposed to apathy, withdrawal, or alienation), (b) patterns of group loyalties and identifications, (c) public preferences for select leaders, and (d) intensely held opinions prevalent among a large public regarding public issues and current affairs (Mitchell, 1970). Mitchell likens the propagandist's management of public opinion to "a burning glass which collects and focuses the diffused warmth of popular emotions, concentrating them upon a specific issue on which the warmth becomes heat and may reach the firing-point of revivals, risings, revolts, revolutions" (p. 111).

The Manipulation of Behavior

Ultimately, the goal of propaganda is to manipulate behavior and behavior patterns; external rather than internal public opinion is sought. Voting, buying products, selecting entertainment, joining organizations, displaying symbols, fighting for a cause, and other forms of action responses are sought from the audiences who are addressed by the persuader and the propagandist. These are *overt* behaviors that can be observed as both verbal and nonverbal responses.

There are other categories of behavior according to Triandis (1977): *attributive* behavior, that which is derived from the conclusions drawn about the internal states of others from observations of their behavior; and *affective* behavior, emotional reactions to people and events. An example of an attributive behavior would be a manufacturer concluding, "consumers buy our product regularly; therefore they must like it." Affective behaviors could be cheering and yelling for a political candidate or experiencing a burst of pride when the national anthem is sung. Triandis (1977) points out that behaviors become habits or behavior patterns when they are performed repeatedly over a long period of time. Patterns in past behaviors or habits are fair predictors of future behaviors. In other words, they become "scripts" for behavior in similar situations. When a similar situation is encountered, it does not require a great deal of consciousness to carry out the same behavior (Roloff & Miller, 1980). Robert Coles 's (1986) book, *The Political Life of Children*, which is about how children learn about political loyalties from language, religion, and family, tells, for example, about the children of wartorn Northern Ireland. The Protestant children believe that God is on their side, and Cole relates how their parents sang "God Save the Queen" to them while rocking them to sleep in the nursery.

A propagandist or a persuader will have difficulty changing behavior if the audience already has habits to the contrary. This is especially true when a habitual behavior is triggered by emotion (Triandis, 1977). The point is that behavior change is not easy to bring about. Both persuaders and propagandists are well aware of this and actively seek information regarding the variables related to behavior change and predictors of behavior.

Thus, we have seen how propaganda is a form of communication and how it utilizes both informative and persuasive communication concepts to promote its own objectives by controlling the flow of information, managing public opinion, and manipulating behavior patterns. Propaganda is a subset of both information and persuasion. Sharing techniques with information and persuasion, but going beyond their aims, propaganda does not seek mutual understanding or mutual fulfillment of needs. Propaganda deliberately and systematically seeks to achieve a response that furthers the desired intent of the propagandist.

Overview of the Book

The modern study of propaganda came about after World War I and, interestingly enough, led the way to the social scientific study of persuasion. At the same time, as Doob (1966) points out, the word *propaganda* became less used and was replaced by words such as *communication, information,* and *persuasion* because they imply no value judgment and tend to embrace the development of new communication technologies as well as the "intricate perplexities inherent in developing societies and international diplomacy" (p. vi).

The historical development of propaganda and the developing media and audiences are the subjects of Chapters 2 and 3. Chapter 4 reviews the theories and research regarding persuasion and propaganda. Chapter 5 examines the use of propaganda in psychological warfare and the emerging fear of propaganda in mass society. The remainder of the book concentrates on modern propaganda methods of analysis (Chapter 6), case studies (Chapter 7), and a process model that depicts how propaganda works in modern society (Chapter 8).

2 Propaganda Through the Ages

The use of propaganda has been an integral part of human history, and can be traced back to ancient Greece for its philosophical and theoretical origins. Used effectively by the Roman Empire and the early Christians, propaganda became an essential activity in the religious conflicts of the Reformation. The invention of printing was quickly adopted by Martin Luther in his fight against the Catholic church and provided the ideal medium for the widespread use of propagandistic materials. Each new medium of communication was quickly adopted for use by propagandists, especially during the American and French revolutions, and later by Napoleon. By the end of the nineteenth century, the improvement in the size and speed of the mass media had greatly increased the sophistication and effectiveness of propaganda.

The use of propaganda as a means of controlling information flow, managing public opinion, or manipulating behavior is as old as recorded history. The concept of persuasion is an integral part of human nature, and the use of specific techniques to bring about large-scale shifts in ideas can be traced back to the ancient world. Many of the artifacts from prehistory and from earliest civilizations provide us with evidence that attempts were being made to use the equivalent of modern-day propaganda techniques to communicate the purported majesty and supernatural powers of rulers and priests. In a largely preliterate age, dazzling costumes, insignia, and monuments were deliberately created symbols designed to evoke a specific image of superiority and power that these early propagandists wished to convey to their audience.

As it was noted in Chapter 1, the first systematic attempt to use and analyze propaganda was in ancient Greece. The use of deliberate forms of speech carefully calculated to deliver a persuasive message can also be found in the writings of Confucius in his *Analects*, where he suggests that the use of the "good" rhetoric, together with the proper forms of speech and writing, could be used to persuade men to live meaningful lives. Bruce L. Smith (1958) has pointed out that this Platonic admonition is echoed today by the leaders of Communist China, only it is called "brainwashing" (pp. 579-80).

The history of propaganda is based upon three interweaving elements: First, the increasing need, with the growth of civilization and the rise of nation-states, to win what has been called "the battle for men's minds"; second, the increasing sophistication of the means of communication available to deliver propagandistic messages; and third, the increasing understanding of the psychology of propaganda and the commensurate application of such behavioral findings. Throughout history these three elements have combined in various ways to enhance and encourage the use of propaganda as a means of altering attitudes and for the creation of new ideas or perspectives. It is, however, only in comparatively modern times that scholars and scientists have begun to understand and assess the role of such mass propaganda techniques as an aspect of the social process. The history of propaganda is not necessarily a linear progression, but there are certain significant benchmarks that are worth examining as illustrations of how propaganda has been utilized at different times. In each case, those wishing to control or manage others (the propagandists) have made maximum and intelligent use of the forms of communication (the media) available to them, while also accurately gauging the psychological susceptibility of their audiences so that their messages can be tailored to ensure the best possible reception. The successful propagandist is always able to discern the basic needs or fears of the audience, and to play upon those.

Imperial Rome

The Imperial Roman Empire between 50 B.C and A.D. 50 applied systematic propaganda techniques that utilized all of the available forms of communication and symbology to create an extremely effective and extensive network of control. The resulting "image" of Imperial Rome remains strong even today, and has become an integral part of our popular culture as we can all identify with the trappings associated with this great empire. The Roman emperors developed their propaganda strategies to meet a very real need. The geographic extent of their far-flung conquests had created a difficult problem of control over their empire, and necessitated the development of a strong, highly visible centralized government. The wealth and power that had come with the conquests were used to maximum advantage as vast sums of money were spent on symbolizing the might of Rome through architecture, art and literature, and even the coinage. Coordinated from Rome, the policy of the Caesars was to combine all of these symbols into a form of "corporate symbolism" reminiscent of modern-day advertising plans, which projected the image of an all-powerful, omnipresent entity.

Whereas the Greek city-states had already discovered that judicious use of sculpture, poetry, building, and music and theater could project the desired image of sophistication, one historian has noted that "the skill of the Caesars was in expanding and mass-producing this means of communication so that it was projected successfully over a long period to a very large area" (Thomson, 1977, p. 56). There were other factors that contributed to the success of the Romans, for they were able to exploit a political and spiritual vacuum that made their imperial subjects much more susceptible to the sophisticated offerings of their conquerors. The Roman Empire was able to offer more than military protection—they provided both a moral philosophy and cultural aesthetic that was adopted by the local peoples. In this way the art and architecture of Rome was as much a symbol of imperial power as were the garrisons of armored legions; and the cultural legacy remained much longer.

Julius Caesar (100-44 B.C.) was particularly adept at utilizing sophisticated propaganda techniques throughout his rise to power and during his move to assert totalitarian power. Initially he used stories of his military exploits abroad, combined with actual terror tactics at home to put fear into the populace. One of the prime communication channels for conveying these messages were coins; they were widely used to boast of victories or to show the emperors in various guises such as warlord, god, or protector of the empire. Coins were the one social document that the Romans were certain would be seen by the widest possible range of subjects under their control. Caesar also made maximum use of the spectacle, spending lavishly on massive triumphal processions—more than four in one month at one point—each representing a victory in the civil war, and each different from the other. The cumulative effect of all this pomp and show of power helped to create an atmosphere that enhanced Julius Caesar's reputation and seemed to justify his careful hints that he was descended from the goddess Venus. It was no accident that he chose the phrase, "I came, I saw, I conquered," which in Latin is reduced to the alliterating and rhyming words *veni, vidi, vici.*

Julius Caesar was a master propagandist, equaled only by Napoleon and Hitler in his understanding of meaningful symbols and in his ability to understand instinctively the psychological needs of his audience. He understood the need to use such symbols of power and sophistication as a means of converting subject populations to the Roman way of life. This was far less expensive than maintaining elaborate garrisons of legionnaires, and induced obedience to the new regime through cooperation and identification rather than subjugation. Significantly, subject peoples were often granted the right to become Roman citizens under certain circumstances, thus increasing personal identification with the conqueror.

Caesar created his own legends out of ordinary events, and by making himself seem supernatural, he was able to set in motion the psychological changes in the minds of the Roman people that would lead away from republicanism and toward the acceptance of monarchical rule and the imperial goals. It is not surprising that throughout history there have been repeated evocations of the Caesarist image by those who aspire to leave their mark on the world. Thus not only Charlemagne, Napoleon, Mussolini, and Hitler have invested themselves in Caesarist trappings, but so has almost every parvenu monarchy in Europe. Whether it be the image of the eagle, the armored breastplate, the man-god on the white horse, or the powerful orator, the propagandistic legacy of the Roman Empire is still much in evidence in our own world.

Propaganda and Religion

When considering the effect of long-range propaganda activities, there have been no more successful campaigns than those waged by the great proselytizing religions of Buddhism, Christianity, and Islam. Although each of these great religions has used different strategies to achieve its purpose, they have all relied upon the use of charismatic figures, heavy symbolism, a simple and incessant moral philosophy, and an understanding of their audience's needs. In each case the new religion had to find a way to replace the existing religious beliefs, and to win over the minds and hearts of the populace.

It should also be made clear that the propagandistic aspects of religions change over time, and are subject to variations depending upon a variety of social and political factors at any point in time. The somewhat humane practices of proselytization of the early Christians were not followed in the coercive techniques of the Spanish Inquisition in the sixteenth century, and even today there are quite wide differences in the use of propaganda in different Christian denominations such as fundamentalist Southern Baptists or Methodists. In the case of Islam, in which religion permeates all aspects of life, including politics (Islam does not recognize the concept of a "secular" authority), there have been many shifts in the strict application of religious laws in various Islamic countries over the centuries. Today we are witnessing a renewed propaganda effort by fundamentalist Muslims to use Islam as a means of achieving both the cultural and political goal of creating unity among the Arabic nations. The fundamentalists see strict adherence to the religious (and therefore political) laws of Islam as being the only way to counteract the inroads made by more materialistic Western influences (Patai, 1983).

Religions can be used very effectively as propaganda vehicles for broader social or political purposes. Beginning with the Chinese-Japanese War (1894-1895), the Japanese military used the Shinto religion as one of the important elements in providing public support for their expansionist policies. This was done by turning the previously benign practice of Shinto into a suprareligious national cult. This allowed the cult of Shinto to be imposed on the entire nation, while still giving lip service to the modernistic notion of freedom of religious belief which the Japanese were eager to convey to the outside world. It was in the name of this Shinto cult of supranationalism that the emperor cult (worshiping of the emperor as a living god) was artificially devised, and a course in *shushin* (moral teaching) was made the basis of compulsory education for all. In this way Shinto was manipulated by the militarists and jingoistic nationalists as the spiritual weapon for mobilizing the entire nation to guard the safety and prosperity of the emperor's throne. Japanese soldiers were sent into battle propagandized in the belief that they were fighting "for the emperor!" After the defeat of Japan in 1945, the Allied powers prohibited the practice of State Shinto, although the pure religion was allowed to return, and today it continues to be an important part of Japanese life.

The use of religion continues to be a very important ingredient in modern propaganda practices. The Irish Republican Army, especially its military wing, the Provisional Irish Republican Army (PIRA), in its efforts to force the British out of Northern Ireland continues to emphasize the differences between the living conditions (such as housing, jobs, schooling, etc.) for the British-favored Protestants and its own followers in the Roman Catholic community (Wright, 1990). In South Africa, until very recently, the Dutch Reformed Church (DRC) provided a religious justification for the establishment of the government's policies of apartheid. The DRC used its interpretation of certain biblical texts to actively propagandize in favor of racial separation. As Allister Sparks (1990) notes:

> While the state has implemented the political philosophy, the church has supplied the theological justification for it. Thus has Afrikanerdom been largely relieved of what Leon Festinger [a psychologist] would call the "cognitive dissonance" of a devoutly religious people imposing a discriminatory, oppressive and manifestly unjust system on others of God's children. More than that, the church's endorsement gave a great impetus to the apartheid idea. It replaced the sense of guilt with a sense of mission, teaching not only that apartheid is not sinful but that it is in accordance with the laws of God. To implement it is therefore a sacred task which the Afrikaner people have been specially "called" to perform. (p. 153)

In one of the most dramatic shifts in South African history, the Dutch Reformed Church eventually renounced its theological position in the late 1980s, and apologized to those it had harmed by propagating these false interpretations of the Bible. This decision demolished the theological justification for political separation of the races, and removed one of the major stumbling blocks in the dismantling of apartheid.

The Rise of Christianity

To examine the propaganda tactics of a religion in no way demeans it; on the contrary, it provides a clear example that not all propaganda messages are negative, but are often aimed at some positive social or political purpose. The example of the rise of Christianity demonstrates how by skill and understanding of the audience, a specific appeal was made that eventually altered the shape of our world. Christianity was aimed to a large extent at the defeated, the slaves, and the less successful part of the Roman Empire. It had to compete with literally hundreds of other similar religions for this audience at the time of the dissolution of the Roman Empire, and considering that Christ and his followers did not have control over the existing communications media at the time, the ultimate level of adoption of Christianity must be considered one of the great propaganda campaigns of all time.

When the strategy of Christian techniques is broken down, we find a masterful use of images and emotion. The legacy of the Jewish synagogue preacher was well established, but Christ and his followers took what were basically traditional messages and put them into a new form. The use of parables, dramatic gestures on the floor of the Temple, the graphic use of metaphor—the seeds on stony ground, the eye of the camel, the shepherd and his flock—and the personal factor of singling out individuals as human metaphors—Peter, "the Rock" or Simon "the Fisherman"—combined to provide a powerful, emotional, and easily understood message. The keynote was simplicity and a promise of humanity and dignity for those who had often been denied such treatment. The early organizers of the Christian religion also developed the concept of cellular proselytization, later to be adopted and developed by Lenin in the Russian Revolution and other revolutionaries since then. This was exemplified by the choice of Twelve Disciples as the dedicated core who would carry the message to other groups, who in turn would spread the word through personal contact in a system resembling today's pyramidal marketing schemes. Each cell would have its own leaders, and the loyalty and faith of the cell members were solidified by the rituals of baptism and communion (Thomson, 1977).

It was nearly three centuries after the death of Christ that the cross became the symbol of Christianity, but during that time the use of the two curved intersecting lines symbolizing a fish was widely used.

Not only was this symbol easy to draw, it also had mystical overtones in that it derived from an acronym for the Greek words for "Jesus Christ, Son of God, saviour," *ichthus*, which means "fish!" The theme of the fish was particularly suited to a religion that relied upon recruitment; and the metaphor of the apostles as "fishers of men," which many of them were in real life, was most appropriate. Initially used as a secret sign during the time when Christians were persecuted by the Roman authorities, the fish symbolized the mission of the group it represented, and did so simply and effectively; and as a result it was found scrawled on walls, trees, in the dust, and any place where Christians wished to leave their mark to communicate their increasing numbers and strength to others. Even graffiti has a powerful propaganda value (Dondis, 1981).

The early Christians persevered against great odds, not only in the form of persecution and competition from other religions but also from dangerous internal schisms and heresies from dissident groups. One of the factors that eventually allowed Christianity to flower was the rejection of attempts made to absorb it into a universal world-religion (Gnosticism), or to restrict it to the select few (Montanism). From the outset, Christianity had asserted that it was catholic, or universal in its message and appeal long before it became Roman Catholic in fact. What helped was that Christianity was syncretic; it absorbed and utilized aspects from both Greco-Roman classicism and the new Germanic culture, as well as elements from ancient Oriental religions. When combined with the dramatic gospel of a saviour who had died to save the entire world, and told in the common Greek or Koine that was the universal literary language of the Roman Empire, the religion thus possessed identity as well as universality for its increasingly wider audience.

After Constantine I adopted Christianity for a mixture of personal and political motives about A.D. 313, Christianity became for all intents and purposes the official religion of the emperors and was eventually adopted by the Germanic tribes who inherited the remnants of the empire. It took several hundred years for the full panoply of Christian symbolism to develop, but aided by the resilience of the infrastructure and communications system developed during the Roman Empire, the religion spread remarkably quickly. Its theme of universal love and a promise that the humble and meek would inherit the earth, was a dramatic reversal of the established order, but it found a sympathetic ear and gained audience empathy. The success of Christianity must also be considered within the sociohistorical period of late antiquity. The period A.D. 100-300 was an extremely religious age, evidenced by an increasing interest in the "other world." The material world, beset by barbaric invasions, plagues, disintegrating governments, and incessant warfare, was increasingly considered to be a place of evil, and humans were regarded as strangers in this world. Christianity, more than other religions, emphasized mortification of the flesh and the spiritual separation from the material world, and also promised a glorious afterlife to the faithful (Forman, 1979).

In succeeding centuries the full symbolism of Christianity would be adopted—the cross, the lion and the lamb, the virgin and child, and even the horned and tailed figure (surely taken from pagan symbols) of the devil. These symbols have endured for nearly 1500 years, and today Christianity is practiced by several billion people. The success of Christianity is a testament to the creative use of propaganda techniques.

The Crusades

As was noted earlier, religious faith has been one of the most potent sources of propaganda in human history. Of all of the wars that have been fought in the name of religious faith, none have been so bloody or more protracted than the Christian Crusades of the Middle Ages. For nearly two hundred years, between 1095 and 1291, the forces of Christendom tried to wrest control of the Holy Land at the eastern end of the Mediterranean from the Islamic forces that controlled it. The origin of the Crusades can be traced directly to the exploitation of the almost mystical religious fervor of this period by a series of popes and monarchs seeking to consolidate their own powers in the ongoing controversy between church and state. In fact, the basic concern that the holy places of Christendom were in the control of Moslem "infidels" was not really a problem, for although Christian pilgrims were often taxed, the Moslems had seldom denied religious visitors access to these sacred sites.

It was more practical political and economic considerations that fueled the crusading impulse. The Roman Catholic church saw an opportunity to spread its influence eastward into the sphere of its archrival, the Eastern Orthodox church, from which it had been separated since 1054 as a result of a dramatic quarrel over doctrine. The feudal monarchs and lords of Western Europe dreamed of the riches that could be obtained from new lands and subjects. Also there was the promise of penance for all sins, and the forgiveness of debts for those going on Crusades. All of these factors were exploited in the Church's exhortations for people to take up arms to recover the soil where Jesus had trod.

The most significant propaganda events of the Crusades were the circumstances surrounding the original plea for the Crusades made by Pope Urban II in 1095. The Byzantine emperor, Alexius Comnenus, responding to increasing inroads made by the Seljuk Turks on his territory, appealed to Pope Urban II for military assistance to protect "Christianity." The pope carefully staged his response at the Council of Cleremont held in November 1095 in southeastern France. He had previously announced that he was going to make a great public speech, thus assuring a significant audience. The splendor of the convocation was impressive, with cardinals, bishops, and nobles resplendent in their robes, while the common folk gathered outside the church. After the ecclesiastical business had concluded, Urban moved outside to mount a large platform that had been specially built for this occasion. According to one version (Fremantle, 1965, p. 54), he began by saying: "It is the imminent peril threatening you and all the faithful which has brought us hither. From the confines of Jerusalem and from the city of Constantinople a horrible tale has gone forth . . . an accursed race, a race utterly alienated from God . . . has invaded the lands of those Christians and has depopulated them by the sword, pillage and fire." Urban then enumerated the atrocities that the Moslems had supposedly committed, including the ravaging of churches and their use in Islamic rites, the rape of Christian women, and the defiling of Christian alters.

He was graphic in his details, reporting that one technique used by the Turkish with their victims was to "perforate their navels, and dragging forth the extremity of the intestines, bind it to a stake; then with flogging they lead the victim around until the viscera having gushed forth the victim falls prostrate upon the ground." As the crowd stirred with emotion, Pope Urban II asked: "On whom, therefore, is the labor of avenging these wrongs and for recovering this territory incumbent, if not upon you? . . . Enter upon the road to the Holy Sepulcher; wrest that land from the wicked race, and subject it to yourselves." Urban skillfully balanced his appeal to the emotions with these atrocity stories, with a practical vision of what he was offering to those who would undertake this holy crusade. He reminded his audience that the land to which he was urging them to go "floweth with milk and honey . . . like another paradise of delights," whereas the land that they would be leaving was "too narrow for your population," and notably poor in food production.

Once Urban had announced the crusade, and even before he has completed his speech, individuals in the crowd were calling out *Deus volt! Deus Volt!* (God wills it!). Whether this was response was spontaneous, or the result of deliberate planning we will never know, but Urban lost no opportunity and declared then and there that *Deus Volt!* would become the battle cry against the heathen foe, and further, that each man embarking on the crusade would wear the sign of the cross on his clothing. Next the bishop of Puy, possibly briefed beforehand, stepped forward and shouted "I confess!" volunteers came forward, and before an emotionally charged crowd, the Christian crusade to liberate the holy city of Jerusalem was launched (Thomson, 1977).

Even before the crowds had dispersed, many had already ripped their clothing to make two strips forming a cross. This gesture was soon repeated by scores of thousands all across Europe. The cry for revenge on the infidels and in favor of a holy crusade was propagated by priests and preachers, and a significant number of written tracts was distributed describing the nature of Moslem atrocities on Christian people. Woodcuts of a monstrous Turk trampling the cross were circulated from village to village (Freemantle, 1965). All of these propaganda strategies would not have been so effective if there had not been an underlying mood of piety that had been established a century earlier. Significant numbers of people had already experienced lengthy religious pilgrimages to such places as Rome, Venice, or even the Holy Land. The concept of undertaking such an arduous trip in the name of God for a clearly devout purpose officially sanctioned by the Church was not as far-fetched as might be imagined.

While Pope Urban II and the feudal monarchs were organizing official expeditions, the common people, roused to a fever pitch, surged forth on their own with little preparation. It is at this point that one of the most significant figures of the Crusades mythology appears—Peter the Hermit. A priest of Amiens, a town in France, Peter was one of the preachers whose propagandistic eloquence attracted thousands of ordinary people to take part in what has been called the People's Crusade of 1096. Peter was very much like one of the Old Testament prophets with his wild hair, his rolling eyes and his torrential speech. He claimed to be carrying a personal letter from God, and was frequently subject to visions. He was so revered that the hairs of his donkey's tail were plucked to be kept as holy relics by worshippers. He arrived in Constantinople in July 1096 with only a remnant of the original ragtag band of almost 50,000 pilgrim-crusaders which had left France and Germany. There he joined the other band of commoners, led by Walter the Penniless, which had managed to make its way eastward. Despite the warnings of the Christians living in Byzantium, these unprepared pilgrims began hostilities against the Turks, and they were systematically cut to pieces. Peter eventually joined forces with the princes of the first official crusade, but his moment of glory had vanished, and in the end he returned to France where he died in 1151.

The People's Crusade may have failed, but the first crusade of the princes was a great success, and by 1097 four expeditionary forces converged on Constantinople by land and sea. The climax of a series of Crusader victories came on July 15, 1099, when, after a five week siege, they entered the city of Jerusalem to kneel in prayer at the site of the Holy Sepulcher. The crusader kingdoms maintained a strong presence in the Holy Land for nearly two hundred years afterward.

The entire crusading ethos fostered a new element of propaganda—the rise of chivalry. In the twelfth century, a series of epic poems, the *Chansons de Geste*, were widely spread along the pilgrim routes by wandering troubadours. These stories about the feats of valor of Roland and his friend Olivier, who sacrificed themselves in the service of their king, served to provide role models for the chivalric ideal of knighthood. These epic poems were a form of propaganda for the idea of combat in the noble cause, and helped to establish the romance of all of the attendant pomp and ceremony associated with chivalry. In many ways the romantic notion of chivalry was as dangerous as later beliefs in nationalism and race, in that it created a romantic ideal of knighthood in which young men were asked to prove themselves in war or combat.

The Crusades started with great religious fervor, and ended in disillusionment and political disarray, but in the end the propaganda that created the Crusades served a positive end. Despite the eventual loss of both Jerusalem and Constantinople, the contact with the civilizations of Byzantium and Islam brought many new ideas into Europe, such as glassmaking, silk weaving, and the use of sugar and spices in cooking. But an even greater consequence of the Crusades was the changes in the structure of feudalism brought about by the decline in wealth of the great feudal families. Towns now became wealthier and freemen more assertive in demanding their rights. Tradesmen and artisans prospered in this new climate of freedom, and the use of money began to replace the previous system of barter. Finally, the Roman church, the moral and propagandistic force behind the Crusades, was able to solidify its power in the face of declining feudalism.

The Reformation and Counter-Reformation

In the history of propaganda Christianity figures prominently, as both the proponents and adversaries of the various denominations have utilized every conceivable technique to maintain their power and spread their ideas. Development of the movable type printing press in the middle of the fifteenth century created a totally new form of communication that was almost immediately put to use as a major channel of propaganda in the titanic struggle for power between the Roman Catholic church and Martin Luther.

An explanation of the causes of the struggle between the Roman Catholic church and the "reformists"is beyond the scope of this book, but it essentially involved disagreements with increasingly corrupt practices in the established church—such as the sale of indulgences for vast sums of money—and a desire to establish direct contact with God without having to go through the priests. This latter desire ultimately manifested itself in a call for the establishment of a simplified liturgy and Bible in the vernacular German language rather than in Latin, which prevented full participation by the congregation. Martin Luther provided the first vernacular liturgies in 1526 (the *Deutsche Messe*), and his major literary achievement. the German language Bible, was first printed in complete form in 1534. (A translation of the New Testament had appeared earlier in 1522.) It was the printed Bible—which went through many editions in Luther's lifetime—that was the highest achievement of the Reformation, and was the direct result of the application of a new technology to the furthering of a specific cause. As noted Reformation historian A. G. Dickens (1968) has pointed out,

> between 1517 and 1520, Luther's thirty publications probably sold well over 300,000 copies. . . . Altogether in relation to the spread of religious ideas it seems difficult to exaggerate the significance of the Press, without which a revolution of this magnitude could scarcely have been consummated. . . . For the first time in human history a great reading public judged the validity of revolutionary ideas through a mass-medium which used the vernacular languages together with the arts of the journalist and the cartoonist. (p. 51)

The development of the printing press was a quantum leap in the speed of communication, and in the sixteenth century printing speeds increased from about 20 sheets per hour to over 200; although this was slow in comparison to modern printing presses, it was nevertheless an important step toward the evolution of true mass media. Luther's works were widely circulated by printers using aggressive sales tactics, but then their appeal for the increasingly literate population was enhanced by his vigorous, entertaining style as well as the use of woodcut illustrations by leading artists of the time such as Lucas Cranach. These early cartoons were able to convey in a simplified manner Luther's attack on the papacy and Catholicism, and greatly increased the effectiveness of his message.

As a study in propaganda, the Reformation, particularly the role played by Martin Luther and his followers, is a perfect example of how the channeling of the message, couched in an empathetic emotional context and provided with an effective means of delivery can bring about mass changes in attitudes. Luther used plain German language laced with the common idiomatic expression of Northern Germany and Austria, and based his sermons on metaphor and folk wisdom, which allowed effective communication over a wide area and with a heterogeneous audience of Germans of all social classes. Basing his operations in the small town of Wittenberg, he distributed his stirring pamphlets all over Northern Europe, taking advantage of the lack of effective censorship in the divided German states.

Using a novel and entertaining "dialogue" style in his printed sermons, he was able to attack precisely those aspects of the established church practices, such as the sale of indulgences, the buying and selling of church offices, the open hypocrisy of clerical celibacy, and papal corruption, all of which had already received wide attention among the general public. Luther used the basic strategy of widely disseminating and emphasizing information that had previously been a part of what can be called the "general public paranoia," thus confirming the public's fears and increasing the potential for attitude change on a mass scale. But he was also able to offer a positive message of hope as a counter to this aggressive negativity; now the people could control their own religious destinies, and using a language they understood they could now participate more meaningfully in the religious ceremony. What Luther encouraged in essence was the concept that individuals could communicate directly with God without the intervention of the church. Comparing the hold of the Catholic church over the German population to that of the Hebrews held in captivity in Babylon, he struck a very sympathetic chord with his audience.

Luther made sure that his religious activities were supported on the political front, once again demonstrating a masterful grasp of the elements of a successful propaganda campaign. Immediately after he had been condemned by the papacy in 1520, he penned a manifesto entitled *The Address to the Christian Nobility of the German Nation* (the first edition of four thousand was sold out within a week), which was pointedly aimed at the rulers of Germany, the princes, the knights, and cities, that under the young Emperor Charles V had a series of grievances against Rome. Although the emperor was himself a devoted Catholic, for political reasons (the Turkish menace was a constant problem) he seemed powerless to act against Luther, and Luther suddenly found himself swept along with the tide of national resentment against Rome. Luther was thus able to exploit the political disorganization in Germany at this time to serve his own purposes, pitting the German nobility, Protestant and Catholic, against each other.

Luther did not limit his propaganda strategies to the sermon or the pamphlet but used a range of other techniques. The dramatic public act of nailing his Ninety-Five Theses to the church door in Wittenberg on the eve of All Saint's Day in 1517 was a major propagandistic gesture. Luther knew that simply sending a copy of his document to the leaders of the Church would not have served his purpose. This very public act moved his action from one of persuasion to a deliberately planned propaganda strategy. Had it not been for the printing press, only a few copies of this protest may have circulated among the people of Wittenberg; but with the new technology this gesture was turned overnight into a manifesto that swiftly circulated throughout Germany, attracting an ever-widening audience, and eventually becoming the precipitating factor in the greatest crisis in the history of the Western church.

In the sixteenth century, despite the inroads of the printing press, most information was still obtained and circulated orally. Luther, recognizing the continued importance of the oral tradition, used not only the sermon (which he then had printed), but also the emotional power of music in the form of the vernacular hymn. Of special importance was the poetic version of Lutheran doctrine put to verse by Hans Sachs, the most prolific German poet and dramatist of his age. Propaganda activities in the form of theatrical presentation were also very influential in an age when most people could not read.

It was the work of artist and engraver Lucas Cranach (1472-1553) that was of most assistance to Luther's propagandistic efforts. His portraits of the reformers and the Protestant princes were widely circulated, thus giving them greater personal identification with the audience and turning them into visual embodiments of heroic proportion; however, it was Cranach's engraved caricatures satirizing the pope or depicting the Catholic church as the Babylonian woman of the Revelation that had the greatest propaganda value. These were easily identifiable and provided a measure of entertainment as well as underscoring political and religious tensions. From all accounts these caricatures and portraits sold extremely well in the Protestant sections of Germany.

The Protestant movement was not limited to the activities of Martin Luther in Germany. Other Protestant reformers such as John Calvin in Switzerland and John Knox in Scotland also used sophisticated propaganda techniques, extending the mere persuasive aspects of the pulpit by the judicious use of the printing press to refine their particular theological philosophies. In fact, one of the significant

Figure 2.1 "The Donkey-Pope of Rome," by Lucas Cranach, 1523. A major propaganda cartoon from the Reformation. Here the pope and the Catholic church are depicted as being a mixture of real and mythological animals such as the donkey and the gryphon. The devil is also shown emerging from the donkey's rump.

Figure 2.2. "The Devil With Bagpipes," by Erhard Schön, 1535. This colored woodcut is an explicit criticism of the clergy, showing a monstrous devil sitting on the shoulders of a friar, and playing his head as if it were a bagpipe. The meaning here is obvious: the clergy speaks the language of the devil. This is a particularly effective and direct form of visual propaganda, even for those who could not read the accompanying text.

features of the Protestant Reformation was the large number of different Protestant sects that came into existence. Though there were differences in the theological interpretations of these groups, their propaganda strategies were almost identical. First, their propaganda efforts had two main objectives, a negative one to emphasize and exploit the wide discontent with the practices of the old church; and a positive one, to associate themselves with the aspirations and expectations of a new religious order. Second, their propaganda was as much secular (especially political) as it was spiritual (Roelker, 1979). This latter strategy was especially effective in areas in which new political allegiances based upon territorial or cultural identifications were being formed. The end result of the Protestant Reformation was a fundamental restructuring of both secular and religious power in Western society.

The Counter-Reformation

The established Roman Catholic church did not quietly acquiesce to the demands and actions of the Protestant reformers. The Catholic church soon began its own propaganda campaigns to prevent further inroads on its powers. One of the most important figures of the Counter-Reformation was Ignatius Loyola, the founder of the Jesuits, who developed his own highly effective and instinctual propaganda techniques. The Society of Jesus, which was the official name of the Jesuits, was organized into a cellular structure, and Loyola created in his followers a highly emotional, almost mystical fanaticism. He understood the significant power of education as a means of altering and then fixing attitudes in the young, and he insisted on total obedience from those in his order.

The Jesuits became the major force in the Church's attempt to counter the Protestant reformation, and under Loyola they achieved some remarkable successes. Austria was restored completely to the Catholic position, and the Polish peasantry were converted to Catholicism in the face of strong opposition from the reformers (Thomson, 1977). Later, it was through the use of Jesuits that the Catholic church began to expand its missionary efforts in other continents, most notably South America and China. For his efforts, Ignatius Loyola was made a saint by Pope Gregory XV in 1622. The Society of Jesus continues as one of the major teaching arms of the Roman Catholic church today—a fitting tribute to the power of propaganda.

It was also in 1622 that Pope Gregory XV, after examining the state of the Church in Europe, decided to establish on June 22 of that year

the *Sacra Congregatio Christiano Nomini Propaganda*, or as it was more
commonly known, the *Sacra Congregatio de Propaganda Fide* (Congregation for the Propagation of the Faith), which was charged with
carrying "the faith" to the New World and with reviving and strength-
ening it in Europe as a means of countering the Protestant revolution.
This unified and centralized Roman Catholic church missionary
activities, and within a few years, in 1627, Pope Urban VII founded
the Collegium Urbanum, the seminary that served as the training
ground for the *Propaganda*.

It is interesting that the methods and strategies to be used by the
missionaries of the *Propaganda* were left to the discretion of those in
the field. The object was to bring men and women to a voluntary
acceptance of the Church's doctrines, not through coercion. It was
Pope Gregory's plan that laid the foundation for modern propaganda techniques in that it stressed the control of opinions, and
through them the actions of people in the mass. It also provided a
convenient term for the description of the practice of public opinion
control. At first the word *propaganda* was applied to any organization
that set out to propagate a doctrine; then it was used to describe the
doctrine itself, and finally it came to mean the techniques employed
to change opinions and spread the doctrine. Thus was born the
modern day usage of propaganda (Qualter, 1962).

In his study of propaganda, Qualter (1962) points out that the
Catholic origins of the word gave it a sinister connotation in the
Northern Protestant countries that it does not have in Southern
Catholic countries. He cites an English encyclopedist of the mid-
nineteenth century, W. T. Brande, as saying of Gregory's organization: "Derived from this celebrated society the name propaganda is
applied in modern political language as a term of reproach to secret
associations for the spread of opinions and principles which are
viewed by most governments with horror and aversion" (pp. 4-5).
This largely negative connotation, as we have seen in the first chapter, continues to cloud the discussion of propaganda.

After the development of the printing press, and the examples of
its judicious use in the Reformation, the adoption of propaganda
techniques became a normal part of the strategies devised by those
seeking to control or manipulate others. Now all major conflicts in
society, whether they were religious or territorial, provided an opportunity for the contesting forces to utilize whatever techniques
they could find for disseminating propagandistic information. As an
example, both sides in the Thirty Years' War (1618-1648), that titanic
struggle waged all over Germany and Northern Europe by competing

religious forces, turned out massive quantities of leaflets, pamphlets, and line drawings, including vicious caricatures of the religious and secular leaders. A new development of some importance in this conflict was the printing of posters from copper plates, which made possible a much wider distribution than was possible from wood-cuts. Both sides engaged in writing about the atrocities that the other had committed (a technique widely used even today), while the roving bands of uncontrolled soldiers produced printed materials warning towns of starvation if they resisted and promising booty to those who joined with them. Historians have noted about the Thirty Years' War that in spite of the low level of literacy, all classes of the population were reached by one or more of the various propaganda techniques (Davison, 1971; Thomson, 1977).

The Emergence of Propaganda

The eighteenth century was one of revolution, and much of the increasing political agitation as subject populations sought to march toward a greater degree of political freedom was fueled by the developments in printing and improved transportation. As the century progressed, so did the technology of printing and paper making, and with improved efficiency and speed in transportation, it was possible to disseminate messages to increasingly wide audiences. The availability of printed materials provided an impetus for the increase in the rates of literacy among the general population of most countries, and written propaganda messages became quite sophisticated in their appeal to the reader.

It is also interesting to note that the path to literacy has not always been a smooth progression, for at various times there have been political, economic, or social reasons for discouraging literacy in a society. Those in power may wish to prevent literacy as a means of controlling the flow of information; or there may be no real economic incentive to devote the time to acquiring literacy skills. Also, the internal values of the society itself may not encourage the need to read and write in the majority of the population. As an example of the danger of generalizing about literacy, in certain countries women were not encouraged to become literate, whereas in others there were far more literate women than men (Graff, 1981).

The use of political cartoons and other visual material that established direct communication with the audience became quite common, and satirical prints were a staple part of most eighteenth-century propaganda campaigns, creating a new visual "language." In his detailed historical study of the use of print in propaganda Robert Phillipe (1980) notes that

> caricature is the most usual and familiar mode of this language. It was by means of such distortion that prints appealed to a wider public and gained universal popularity. The metamorphosis of the political print was linked, as indeed was its first appearance, to the developments in printing techniques. The spirit and general tendency of this form of visual expression have remained steadfastly the same for five hundred years. The print is a mass medium—universal, direct, immediate, and pithy. (p. 9)

But how do such cartoons and satirical drawings work, and why do they have such strong propagandistic potential? Phillipe suggests a possible answer when he notes that

> prints are partisan. They espouse causes. Exaggeration is second nature to them. Their methodology is accumulation and synthesis—and hence events, places, moments and people acquire an extraordinary intensity and power. A print is neither historic evocation nor narrative, but rather a conjunction of symbols and allusions. It enlarges, shrinks, or disguises people, to reveal their many facets at a glance. The synthesizing power of the print expresses both what is visible and what is concealed. To what is, it adds what has been and what will be. The image is thus liberated from the grammar of space and time and the print remains dynamic, aggressive, fertile and creative. (p. 9)

This was the age of the great English graphic satirists and propagandists William Hogarth (1697-1764), James Gillray (1757-1815), and Thomas Rowlandson (1756-1827), whose drawings were sold to bolster rival political activities or to make telling moral points for their eager audiences. It was Gillray who became the most obvious propagandist, devoting his entire output to creations of social or political satire, many of which were circulated widely throughout Europe and even in North America. King George III—"Farmer George"—and his family suffered widely at Gillray's hands; and after Gillray's conversion to conservatism as a result of his dismay at the French Revolution, he launched a long series of political attacks ridiculing Napoleon and the French, while glorifying John Bull and the common Englishman.

Gillray's work was very influential on nineteenth-century political satirists such as the American Thomas Nast (1840-1902). Nast was

Figure 2.3. A seller of leaflets during the Thirty Years War, 1631. The advent of printing made the leaflet seller a common sight in European cities at this time. These leaflets, in which the illustrations were a vital part, were used to inform the public about the events of this religious war, as well as spreading propaganda messages for each side.

Figure 2.4. "The Three Estates," sixteenth century. The development of printing encouraged the distribution of propagandistic engravings such as this one which graphically represents the inequities of the social pyramid in France. In this illustration the clergy and the nobility are supporting the country on the back of the peasantry. Note the plow yoke around the neck of the peasant, as well as the other implements of work at his feet. It is unclear whether the hands of God are helping to lift the burden up, or pushing them down.

most famous for his crusade against the political machine of William Marcy Tweed in New York City. Tweed was reported to have said, "Stop them damn pictures. I don't care so much about what the papers write about me. My constituents can't read. But, damn it, they can see pictures" (Hess & Kaplan, 1975, p. 13). The members of the Tweed Ring were eventually driven from office, and many of them were tried and sentenced to prison. Tweed himself escaped to Spain, where he was recognized five years later, thanks to a Nast cartoon showing him in prison garb with two young urchins in tow. Nast had drawn the cartoon as an indication that Tweed was apprehending minor criminals while major criminals went unmolested. The Spanish police, however, interpreted it to mean that Tweed was wanted for kidnapping and the word *Reward* also caught their eye. Tweed was promptly extradited to the United States, where he died in the New York City jail in 1878 (St. Hill, 1974). This propaganda campaign has now become a historical legend and constitutes the most dramatic instance of deliberate propagandistic cartooning in American politics. However, Nast was only one of several American cartoonists whose work was influential in shaping political opinions in an age when journalism was not required to be objective, and politically biased reporting was normal.

The American Revolution

Historians agree that the philosophical underpinnings of the revolution of the American colonists against their British rulers can be found in a variety of sources, most notably the series of political writings beginning during the seventeenth century, including the work of John Locke (1632-1704), especially his *Treatises on Government* (1690), in which he refuted the divine right of kings, and the absolutist theory of government. Written in defense of the coming to the British throne of King William III, in the place of the deposed and beheaded Charles I, these documents had a significant effect on subsequent political action in the American colonies. Essentially Locke suggested that the people are the ultimate sovereign, and that they always have the right to withdraw their support and overthrow the government if it fails to fulfill its trust. (During the Vietnam War period of the 1960s-1970s, many opposed to the war espoused a similar philosophy.) Such ideas had a profound influence on the writers and pamphleteers whose propagandistic work was so instrumental in helping to foment and sustain the energy of the American

Figure 2.5. This cartoon by Thomas Nast caused William Marcy "Boss" Tweed to be arrested in Spain. The Spanish police misinterpreted the illustration to mean that Tweed was wanted for kidnapping. The word *reward* on the bottom left also caught the eye of the police. First published in *Harper's Weekly*, July 1, 1876.

Figure 2.6. "A Group of Vultures Waiting for the Storm to 'Blow Over'—Let Us Prey." It was Thomas Nast's cartoons such as these that caused "Boss" Tweed so much anguish and eventually resulted in his downfall. First published in *Harper's Weekly*, September 23, 1871.

Revolution. Bernard Bailyn (1967), in his important book *The Ideological Origins of the American Revolution*, notes that

> the American Revolution was above all else an ideological, constitutional, political struggle and not primarily a controversy between social groups undertaken to force changes in the organization of the society or the economy . . . intellectual developments in the decade before Independence led to a radical idealization and conceptualization of the previous century and a half of American experience, and it was this intimate relationship between Revolutionary thought and the circumstances of life in 18th-century America that endowed the Revolution with its peculiar force and made it so profoundly a transforming event. (pp. vi-vii)

The American colonists were remarkably literate and well informed on political matters; therefore, the spread of ideas through the printed word was a major factor in the development of a revolutionary ideology. In particular, the ideas contained in Richard Price's *On Civil Liberty* (1776), which sold 60,000 copies in hardback and 120,000 unbound, and Thomas Paine's *Common Sense* (1776) which sold nearly as well, were widely distributed throughout the colonies (Wish, 1950). Thomas Paine (1737-1809) can be considered to be the first great propagandist of the American Revolution, and George Washington claimed that *Common Sense*, an emotional pamphlet that contained persuasive arguments for independence from England, had been a powerful influence on the minds of many men prior to the war. The son of a Quaker corset maker from Norfolk, England, Paine came to America in 1774 and worked for Benjamin Franklin editing the *Pennsylvania Journal*. Paine used a simple, forthright writing style, not unlike Luther's, and shocked his readers by his boldness, while also using wit and satire to bring opposing ideas into sharp ridicule. His appeals were equally balanced between the head and the heart, and he noted that his aim was to "fit the powers of thinking and the turn of the language to the subject, so as to bring out a clear conclusion that shall hit the point in question and nothing else."

The newspaper provided the major vehicle for the dissemination of propagandistic information, and there had been a steady development of these after 1740 despite various attempts to tax such periodicals by the British. When the war began on April 19, 1775 with the battles of Lexington and Concord, there were thirty-seven newspapers being published in the colonies. However, at the highest point, there were seventy papers being published during the Revolutionary War. When the war concluded six-and-a-half years later thirty-five newspapers were in business. The war had taken its toll on some papers, but others had been established in their place. No sooner did a newspaper close down than it would reappear under another name, and precisely because of this, newspaper editors were willing to print inflammatory material, knowing that they could restart anytime they wished. Also, printing attacks on the colonial powers was sure to increase circulation among an audience primed to accept such information.

The demand for news during the war increased newspaper readership to 40,000 households, but this did not include multiple readers for each copy, and the extent to which such information was then further disseminated by word-of-mouth. One problem faced by editors was that there was no way to organize systematic newsgathering. The principal means of obtaining news was through exchanges with other newspapers, or chance letters and official messages. Even when reports of major events were picked up, they often constituted little more than a short paragraph. Worst of all was the slowness of message dissemination during this crucial period. It took more than six weeks for the news of Lexington and Concord to reach Savannah in South Carolina (Emery & Emery, 1984). In the absence of fast, hard news, it was no wonder that false information and rumors spread quickly and widely. Printing materials were also in short supply, and fearing that the patriotic newspapers would not be able to continue their important role, special pleas were made to contribute rags for paper making.

A classic example of newspaper propaganda was the so-called Boston Massacre, which took place in 1770. British troops had been quartered in Boston for a year and a half, against the wishes of the citizens, and they were forced to face continuous harassment, a situation that was not helped by the historical aloofness of British troops toward the colonists. On March 5, 1770, a crowd looking for trouble started pelting snowballs, sticks of wood, and oyster shells at ten soldiers outside the Boston customshouse, daring the soldiers to fire. Eventually they did fire, and eleven of the unarmed rioters were injured, four of them fatally (a fifth died later). This event provided the impetus for numerous propaganda attacks on the British in which the facts of the event were totally blown out of proportion or exaggerated to emphasize British tyranny. The most famous of these attacks was Paul Revere's engraving, which, masquerading as a realistic portrayal of the event, was in fact a political cartoon deliberately created as propaganda for the anti-British forces. Revere's engraving included a sign "Butcher's Hall" above the British customshouse, and interestingly he also changed the race of one of the victims, Crispus Attucks, who was, in reality, a towering black man. The cartoon was considered to be so inflammatory that when the soldiers were brought to trial, their lawyer warned the jury to not be swayed by drawings that add "wings to fancy" (Hess & Kaplan, 1968). This cartoon was widely reprinted in the colonial press, and was followed by other Revere efforts including an engraving of four coffins, above which were the initials of the American dead.

The political cartoon proved to be a potent propaganda weapon throughout the Revolutionary period. As early as 1754, Benjamin Franklin had drawn his famous snake, severed into eight pieces to symbolize the separate colonies, with the legend "Join, or Die." This was the first cartoon to appear in an American newspaper. Published first on May 9, within a month it had been reprinted by virtually every newspaper on the continent. Although the snake was ridiculed by those loyal to the British side, the serpent won out in the end, and in his equally famous cartoon James Gillray, the British satirist sympathetic to the American side, drew the defeated British camp completely surrounded by a large rattlesnake.

There was a macabre fascination with the symbology of death in American political cartoons, as we have noted with Paul Revere's work. The most obvious example took place on October 31, 1765, when eight newspapers being shut down as a result of the imposition of the notorious Stamp Act, used black mourning border and symbols from tombstones on their front pages to symbolize their death. William Bradford's *Pennsylvania Journal* included the masthead motto "EXPIRING: In hopes of a Resurrection to Life again." The association of death with the lack of freedom was a simple one for the colonials to grasp, and as individual freedoms were restricted by the British powers, these were symbolized as "deaths." The restriction of the freedom of the press was a particularly galling one for the Americans, as this was the chief means of dissemination of both political and commercial information, and in binding the colonists together into a cohesive opposition to British tyranny.

Samuel Adams was considered to be the chief architect of the anti-British propaganda activities, and he based all of his plans on the achievement of five main objectives: The aims of the revolution needed to be justified; the advantages of the victory needed to be advertised; the masses needed to be aroused to action by creating hatred for the enemy; logical arguments from the opposition needed to be neutralized; and all issues needed to be stated in clear black and white terms to ensure that even the common laborer could understand (Emery & Emery, 1984). Adams devoted his life to the Revolutionary

Figure 2.7. Paul Revere's famous engraving, entitled "Boston Massacre," from March 5, 1770. While masquerading as a depiction of the actual events, this was in reality a propagandistic cartoon. The words *Butcher's Hall* have been added above the British Customs House. Note also, that the artist has depicted the African-American, Crispus Attucks, as a white man. This cartoon was widely reprinted in the colonial press.

SOURCE: The Metropolitan Museum of Art, Gift of Mrs. Russell Sage, 1909. (10.125.103)

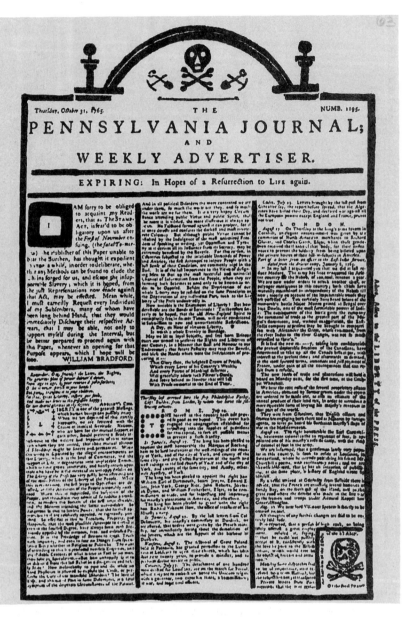

Figure 2.8. A facsimile of the front page of the *Pennsylvania Journal* of October 31, 1765, showing the black mourning border and other emblems of death symbolizing the death of freedom of the press as a result of the imposition of the Stamp Act.

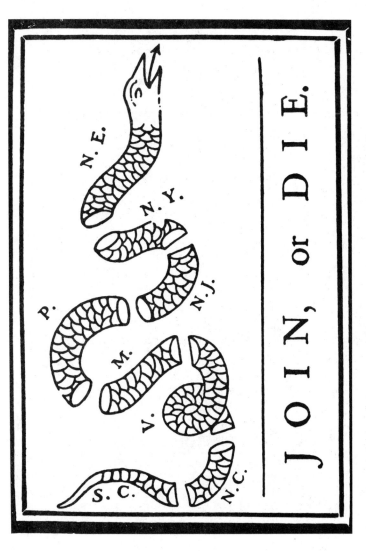

Figure 2.9. Benjamin Franklin's famous cartoon in support of a "Plan of Union" for the colonies. It first appeared in the *Pennsylvania Journal* on May 9, 1754, and was based upon the superstition that a snake that had been severed would come back to life if the pieces were put together before sunset. Each segment represents one colony. This cartoon was revived at the time of the Stamp Act Crisis in 1765 and again at the start of the American Revolution in 1774.

67

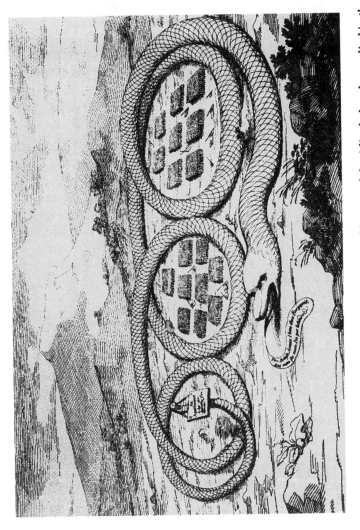

Figure 2.10. Benjamin Franklin's "snake" cartoon (Figure 2.10) had been widely ridiculed and parodied in the British press. However, in October 1776, when General Cornwallis surrendered at Yorktown, the famous English caricaturist, James Gilray, who opposed British policies in the American colonies, drew this cartoon, which showed the defeated British camp completely encircled by a rattlesnake. Franklin's snake had the last laugh.

cause and became known as the "master of the puppets" because of his ability to orchestrate and manipulate others. Nor was he the most scrupulous individual, and many of his numerous attacks on the British, printed under a variety of names, painted the actions of governors, customs men, and judges in the darkest possible colors.

Adams was also a master of organization, helping to elect men who were sympathetic to his cause, and procuring the passage of resolutions that he favored. Operating from his base as a journalist with the *Boston Gazette*, Adams put together his Committee of Correspondence in 1772, and this group became the propaganda organization for the Revolution. He had his agents cover every important meeting and gathering to collect "news" that was immediately relayed back to Adams's central committee, where the information was processed and disseminated to the appropriate areas.

Perhaps Adams's greatest individual propaganda coup was the organization of the Boston Tea Party, which symbolized the opposition to the Tea Act of 1773, although he took no personal part in the dumping of the tea into Boston Harbor. The incident was a classic example of provocation, which was turned into a major item of propaganda when the British predictably retaliated, as Adams knew they would, by the passing of the Boston Port Bill, which closed the harbor and ruined trade. This just served to increase the hostility of the colonists, particularly after more troops were dispatched to the city; the stage for open revolt was being carefully set. Eventually it would come at Concord in 1775, when the British troops sent to confiscate weapons and ammunition stored by the skeleton colonial army engaged in a skirmish that eventually led to a full-scale war. It was also this incident that served as the background to another great American legend—Paul Revere's famous ride to warn the inhabitants of Concord, "The British are coming! The British are coming!"

During the Revolutionary War itself incidents such as the skirmish in Lexington were turned into major victories, and events such as Paul Revere's ride took on an almost mythical status. Adams, Benjamin Franklin, Thomas Jefferson, and even George Washington wanted to instill into the colonists a belief that not only was their cause just, but that their "native" skills were more than a match for the trained soldiers and mercenaries of the British army. To this end they became skillful propagandists by manipulating (and even creating) information to their advantage, or making appeals to the emotions. Washington had Tom Paine's *American Crisis* read to his troops; words written on a drumhead that have survived through the centuries as inspiration in the darkest times in a nation's history:

These are the times that try men's souls. The summer soldier and the
sunshine patriot will, in this crisis, shrink from the service of his country. . . . Tyranny, like hell, is not easily conquered; yet we have this
consolation with us, that the harder the conflict the more glorious the
triumph. What we obtain too cheap, we esteem too lightly. (Emery &
Emery, 1984, p. 82)

Written on December 19, 1776, these words were broadcast widely
during the difficult period in the early days of World War II. It is also
to Washington's and Paine's credit that a week after hearing those
inspirational words, the frozen and tattered colonial forces won a solid
victory in Trenton. Jefferson was a master propaganda strategist, with
his draft of the Declaration of Independence one of the great propaganda statements in all of history. Based upon a combination of the
ancient Greek and Roman philosophy of the rationalist "laws of nature"
earlier expounded by Locke, and the modern philosophy of a secular
natural law derived from Isaac Newton's scientific work, Jefferson was
able to write a document in which he emphatically declared, "We hold
these truths to be self-evident, that all men are created equal." Dropping
all pretense at the fiction that a good king had been misled by evil
advisors, Jefferson listed a long series of charges against King George
III, and suggested that because all appeals for redress had been re-
buffed, there was now no alternative but to "alter or abolish" a government destructive of the principles of freedom. The Declaration thus
became the legal and philosophical justification for the Revolution
sought by Adams as one of his objectives.

Benjamin Franklin also proved to be an instinctual master of
propaganda, using his talents as journalist, scientist, and diplomat
to great advantage. In his role as diplomat he was assigned to the
French court to plead the colonist's case. Dressing in a fur hat and
openly wearing spectacles, he became a living symbol of the unso-
phisticated nobility of the New World seeking to free itself from its
feudal masters. His portrait began to appear on a wide range of
popular culture objects, from snuff boxes to chamber pots, and his
company was eagerly sought by scientists, politicians, and fashion-
able ladies in whose company he revelled. Going out of his way to
promote his new status as a cult figure, he used these contacts to
enormous advantage, pleading for both financial and military assistance in the fight against the British, and he was so successful that
his personal popularity endured in France for many generations.

In his role as a journalist, Franklin had, of course, many years of
experience both as an editor and as what we would today call a

publicist, having promoted a wide variety of schemes and ideas during his lifetime. He was particularly famous for his series of *Poor Richard Almanacs*, which contained a collection of maxims and proverbs culled from throughout the world's literature and given a pragmatic American flavor—"Early to bed, early to rise, makes a man healthy, wealthy and wise." He became a master of both white and black propaganda during the Revolutionary War. He published *The Sale of the Hessians*, which dealt with the British press gangs in Germany forcibly recruiting mercenaries, and later was responsible for a fake issue of the *Boston Independent* in which the British appeared to be boasting of scalp-hunting, a practice which was particularly repugnant to the American colonists (Thomson, 1977). In many respects, Franklin was a man ahead of his time, including his clear grasp of the rudiments of the psychology of modern propaganda techniques.

With the end of the Revolutionary War, the press had proven itself as an indispensable factor in the creation of the public opinion leading up to the war, and an important rallying point during the fighting. (As an example, the Declaration of Independence appeared in print in colonial newspapers before it was issued as an official manifesto. It was included in its entirety in the *Pennsylvania Evening Post* on July 6, 1776, just two days before it was adopted by the Continental Congress. As soon as it was ratified it appeared in most of the other newspapers in the colonies.) Now that the colonists had won their freedom from Britain, it would be necessary to implement the new democratic political philosophy. Although the press had won their own freedom from the restraints of the British Crown, it was uncertain how this freedom would be institutionalized by the new government that had not yet taken shape.

Once the Revolutionary War was over, the young nation was faced with developing its own propaganda campaigns to ensure its commercial and political survival in the face of a skeptical world. All the trappings of rampant patriotic nationalism were required to give the new nation a clear identity of its own, separate from the mother country, and thus were created the military uniforms, the flags, the patriotic songs and slogans, and the diplomatic stances such as the Monroe Doctrine, which proclaimed the United States sphere of interest in the New World. The development and international publicity attendant upon the framing of the "democratic" Constitution was perhaps the greatest propaganda vehicle of all for gaining the attention of the rest of the world. Eventually the image of the United States would be most successfully propagandized though its industrial and commercial achievements, together with the enormous output of material from its developing mass communication industries.

The French Revolution and Napoleon

The French Revolution was a complex political event that has had wide political and philosophical implications for the course of modern Western history. Taking their inspiration from the American patriots' revolution against their colonial masters, the French overthrew their despotic monarchy in an attempt to establish an entirely new form of government. Such action meant denying the concept of the "divine right of kings" and overturning the "natural order," and required a major shift in the philosophical underpinnings of French society. In order to accomplish this change the leaders of the Revolution resorted to a massive propaganda campaign, the purpose of which was to "sell" these new ideas and the resulting alterations in the structure of French society and culture.

By 1788 there was a well-developed newspaper readership in France, and pamphlets were appearing at the rate of 25 a week; this reached a climax of information in 1789 when more than 60 new newspapers were started. Although much of the information offered was contradictory, the tone was becoming steadily more radical and critical of the monarchy and government. Many of the critics were the skilled propagandists known as the Encyclopedists, who had worked on Diderot's famous compendium of human knowledge. The key events of the eventual revolution were themselves all carefully orchestrated pageants of propaganda. The storming of the Bastille—the dreaded symbol of oppression full of tortured prisoners—has remained with us until today as an archetypical image when, in fact, the prison was almost empty, containing only seven individuals. Further, the destruction of the building (which took place two days after the "storming") has assumed mythical proportions. Total demolition was still incomplete in 1792. However, the destruction of the physical edifice was symbolic of the overthrow of the old regime.

The adoption of specific forms of dress was a major propaganda device during the ebb and flow of the course of the French Revolution, as were other symbolic devices. The national colors of red, white, and blue were seen everywhere, as was the Phrygian stocking cap and the tricolor sash. Crowds were manipulated by fireworks displays, the burning of effigies of hated politicians and aristocrats, and especially patriotic music, in which the great theme of the Marseillaise remains even today a stirring tribute to the power of musical propaganda. The Revolution even had its own official propagandist artist, the great Jacques Louis David (1748-1825), whose works had been an incitement to revolution before 1789 and who served in this capacity through the reign of Napoleon. David was far more than a painter, directing the artistic affairs of the new Republic, until he too fell out of favor at the time of the downfall of Robespierre in 1794. He was later restored to his former glory by Napoleon for whom he created a very specific imperial image. David's style utilized a sense of realism that sought to create art for the middle classes, and was entirely appropriate to the revolutionary context of the times. His work continues to serve as an inspiration to later political regimes seeking to glorify their exploits through works of art. The French revolutionaries used a wide variety of media to export their doctrines throughout the world at the end of the eighteenth century. W. Phillips Davison (1971) points out that even their style of dress was worn by revolutionary sympathizers throughout Europe. This form of symbolic propaganda was countered when "a conservative German prince, the Langraf of Kassel, seeking to combat these subversive styles, ordered that all prisoners be dressed in them and sent out to sweep the streets" (p. 2). This provides an excellent example of counterpropaganda. Despite small victories of this sort, the French Revolution was so devastating to the existing social and political structure of Europe that entirely new forms emerged, and these required that new myths and heroes be created to provide the necessary social and cultural cohesion.

It was out of the chaos of the destruction of the old French society that the "man on the white horse" emerged—Napoleon Bonaparte, who must be considered one of the great masters of the use of propaganda in history. He recognized the power of manipulation of symbols early in his career as an army officer, and throughout his life he learned to glory in his victories while placing the blame for his failures at the feet of others. Like Caesar before him, he wrote self-congratulatory accounts of his military exploits, and created for himself a swashbuckling image of the dashing commander. Napoleon was among the first of the modern propagandists to understand the need to convince the population that the rights of the individual were less important than the willingness to sacrifice one's life for emperor and nation. In this way he was able to gather large, populist armies even in the worst of times.

The visual image of the romantic hero was created with the assistance of the artist Jacques Louis David, who helped design the clothes, hairstyle, and other accoutrements that have come down to us today as an unmistakable symbol of the diminutive French leader. Napoleon's portrait appeared everywhere, accompanied by his ubiquitous eagles, and he took the lead in designing a specific form of imperial architecture that was a mixture of Roman, Etruscan, and Egyptian styles—all great empires of the past. Triumphal arches and massive victory columns were erected, again evoking images of the Roman Caesars.

It was at his coronation at Notre Dame Cathedral on December 2, 1804, that Napoleon achieved one of his great propaganda triumphs when he took the imperial crown from the hands of Pope Pius VII, and placed it on his own head, symbolizing that he owed allegiance to no one, and that he was a self-made emperor. The imperial regime that followed his coronation had its own symbols, with the Roman eagle figuring prominently above the tricolor flag, and the use of princely titles was brought back for members of Napoleon's family.

Napoleon quickly learned to exploit the power of the press to his advantage as a political weapon, devising new propaganda techniques that caught his opponents by surprise. Like most European governments of the time, he maintained domestic censorship, but he went out of his way to plant pro-French items in foreign language newspapers on the continent. Several papers were even founded by the French in occupied German territories, while in Paris there appeared a newspaper called the *Argus of London*, which was allegedly edited by an Englishman, but was, in actuality, produced by the French Foreign Office. Supposedly written from an English viewpoint, the newspaper attacked the "war mongering journals" back in London, and was widely distributed throughout the West Indies and to British prisoners of war in places such as Verdun (Thomson, 1977). Napoleon also made wide use of leaflets distributed before his invading armies; he projected a promise of French "liberty" to countries such as Italy where oppression had been the normal political way of life, and a hint of freedom was bound to create widespread excitement. Even the Napoleonic Code, an easily translated volume of law, was an impressive demonstration of revolutionary imperial power that could be readily transported to other European countries. One of his major internal propaganda weapons was the use of the plebiscite, in which the population were asked to vote on an issue, the outcome of which was already clearly decided, and then publicizing the results as an unequivocal indication of his popularity. As an example, in May 1802, the French people were asked to vote on the following question: "Shall Napoleon Bonaparte be consul for life?" The result was an overwhelming majority of 3,500,000 votes in favor against less than 10,000 opposed. Two years later he became emperor when another plebiscite approved the change. The use of such predetermined plebiscites has been a favorite technique of

Figure 2.11. At an early stage in his career Napoleon is shown as the heroic leader. Note the stormy setting in the background, with the implication that Napoleon, pointing forward, would lead the country through this troubled period. The romantic imagery was consistent with the general public mood in France at this time.

Figure 2.12. Napoleon shown as the "Emperor of Europe." Once Napoleon had consolidated his power in France and begun his conquests, his propagandistic image changed to that of a near-Greek god. This fanciful engraving shows him astride the world, with the light of the gods shining down on him as he leads the way forward to further conquest.

modern dictators and political regimes such as Hitler and the Soviet Union, who are eager to give international recognition to the apparent popularity of their internal programs. This type of staged plebiscite was also used by the Baltic nations of Lithuania, Latvia, and Estonia to clearly demonstrate the level of internal cohesion and support in their attempts to become independent from the Soviet Union.

So successful were Napoleon's propaganda techniques in creating his imperial image that his legend became even stronger after his death in 1821. Hundreds of books appeared, some attacking, but most praising him, and finally in December 1840 his body was returned from the remote island of St. Helena to a magnificent funeral in Paris. Nearly a million people watched as his remains were conveyed through the Arc de Triomphe to his specially built tomb in the Place de l'Etoile. Napoleon left behind an enormous legacy of important institutions, such as his legal Code, the French internal administrative system, the national banking system, the military academies and universities, and, most important of all, a dramatic symbol of French might and glory so deeply ingrained into Western popular culture that it continues to have useful propaganda value even today.

Propaganda in the Nineteenth Century

The main development in propaganda techniques during the nineteenth century was the increase in the speed in which messages could be conveyed to increasingly urban-based audiences. The importance of printing, especially after the introduction of steam and later electricity, created new opportunities for refining propaganda as a political and economic weapon. The ability to print engravings and, after 1880, photographs added further impact to the printed word. As each new form of mass communication found an audience, it was immediately seized upon as a vehicle for conveying propaganda. Thus newspapers, then magazines, and later motion pictures were each used by propagandists in their attempts to capture the public's attention.

The development of democratic political institutions was the single most important impetus to the growth of the use of propaganda in the nineteenth and twentieth centuries. As Qualter (1962) so eloquently states it,

Even those whose attitude toward the role of public opinion in politics did not change found that of necessity they had to learn the mechanics of peaceful persuasion by propaganda. With an extended franchise and an increasing population it was becoming too expensive to do anything else. Where at one time voters could be bought, they now had to be persuaded. Politicians had, therefore, to become interested in propaganda. (p. 33)

It was the combination of the demands created by democratic political institutions and the increasing sophistication of propaganda techniques used in warfare that marked the emergence of an awareness of propaganda as a ubiquitous force in the late nineteenth and early twentieth centuries. We must also not overlook the increasing importance of advertising as an integral part of economic development and the emergence of consumerism, for many of the techniques developed to persuade customers to purchase products were later adopted by other propagandists. One significant aspect of twentieth-century propaganda is the symbiotic relationship between advertising and other forms of propaganda, particularly as techniques for reaching audiences become more sophisticated and reliable. Propaganda began to emerge as a modern force in the nineteenth century; it has become an integral part of the social, political, and economic life of the twentieth century.

3 Propaganda Institutionalized

The late nineteenth and early twentieth centuries were periods of great expansion of propaganda activities. The growth of the mass media and improvements in transportation led to the development of mass audiences for propaganda, increasing its use and effectiveness. Each of the mass media—print, the movies, radio, and then television—contributed its unique qualities to new techniques of propaganda. Radio, in particular brought into existence the possibility of continuous international propaganda, whereas television has increased the problem of "cultural imperialism," in which one nation's culture is imposed upon another nation's. This has led to a call for a New World Information Order by many Third World countries. Since the nineteenth century, advertising has become the most pervasive form of propaganda in modern society.

The nineteenth and twentieth centuries saw an unprecedented explosion in the field of communication and transportation. Initially, the limitation on both the speed of communication and the difficulties experienced in transportation in an age of rough roads and horse-drawn traffic severely restricted the flow of information between geographically separated points. Even within the growing urban centers, which were now a common manifestation of the push toward industrialization, there were problems in circulating and controlling information to a large number of people within a short period of time. The newspapers and commercial newssheets of the early nineteenth century did not have wide circulations, and despite the increase in the literacy rate among the middle classes, books were not yet as widely available for the general population as they would be later in the century. Public oratory, though important, also had the inherent handicaps of a limited size of audience and irreproducibility. The result was that rumor and gossip continued to be an important means of maintaining communication links between groups and individuals wishing to circulate specific messages.

The major problem with rumor as a means of communication is that it lacks the necessary control to ensure that the message content is not distorted. As Shibutani (1966) explains, "content is not viewed as an object to be transmitted but as something that is shaped, reshaped, and reinforced in a succession of communicative acts. . . . In this sense a rumor may be regarded as something that is constantly being constructed; when the communicative activity ceases, the rumor no longer exists" (p. 9). Clearly this is not a useful means of disseminating propaganda; it may work splendidly if the rumor continues to take the direction intended, but rumors have a life of their own, and they could just as easily turn on the propagandist. We have recently witnessed the difficulties that one of the world's largest manufacturers of household products, the Procter and Gamble Company, has had fighting a rumor that their trademark of the moon and stars was, in reality, a satanic symbol. Despite the enormous sum of money they had spent on advertising trying to create a specific public image, this rumor was widely circulated, largely by fundamentalist Christian groups. Ultimately, because of their failure to halt the economic damage caused by the continuance of this rumor, the company has decided to change its trademark (Kapferer, 1990).

Before the practice of propaganda on the mass scale could proceed, new forms of communication, which provided a greater degree of message control and targeting of audiences, had to emerge. This is exactly what did happen in the nineteenth and twentieth centuries, and propaganda became increasingly more sophisticated, widely practiced, and accepted as part of modern society.

The New Audience

The introduction of new forms of communication also created a new historical phenomenon—the mass audience. For the first time in history, the means now existed to disseminate information to large, heterogeneous groups of people within a relatively short period of time. With the introduction of the *New York Sun* on September 3, 1833, the era of the "penny press" was begun and the entire shape of news was altered. The penny press was not so much a revolutionary development, but the inevitable result of the gradual shift away from selling newspapers only through monthly or annual subscription. The founders of the penny press, such as Benjamin Day of the *Sun* and James Gordon Bennett of the *New York Herald* recognized that there was a growing audience of middle- and working-class readers willing to pay for a newspaper on a daily basis (Crouthamel, 1989). Whereas the earlier commercial press had disdained much interest in everyday events, the penny press deliberately sought to cultivate the audience's interest in local events and everyday occurrences. Also, as Schudson (1978) notes, "The new journalism of the penny press . . . ushered in a new order, a shared social universe in which 'public' and 'private' would be redefined. . . . With the growth of cities and of commerce, everyday life acquired a density and a fascination quite new" (p. 30).

The formation of these new mass publics came about at the same time as democracy as a political process was gradually being introduced into many countries; and although the United States had been founded on entirely democratic principles, the young nation was still struggling to internalize exactly how this rather novel experiment of "government by the people" would work in practice. Historians have often labeled the 1830s the era of *Jacksonian Democracy* because of the emergence of a clear populist sentiment at this time. It is against this historical-political background that we must view the introduction of the mass press. Schudson (1978) after examining this important historical event suggests that the penny press was a response to what he calls the emergence of "democratic market society," created by the growth of mass democracy, a marketplace ideology, and an urban society. He notes that "the penny press expressed and built the culture of a democratic market society, a culture which had no place for social or intellectual deference. This was the groundwork on which a belief in facts and a distrust of the reality, or objectivity, of 'values' could thrive" (p. 60).

As the newspaper assumed a larger and more consistent role in the dissemination of information, the public came to depend upon such daily information to a much greater degree than ever before. There were several reasons for this. First, there were, as yet, few competing voices besides the remaining commercial newsletters and the occasional book. Second, even those competing news sources could not match the newspaper for timeliness and consistency. Third, newspapers made no pretense at being politically neutral in this early period, and therefore they appealed directly to the biases of their readers. Fourth, the demands of a democratic political system required that the electorate have a continuous knowledge of the workings of the political system, and only newspapers were able to provide this continuity. Fifth, the average working-class or middle-class citizen did not have the time nor the organization at his or her disposal to keep up with political or economic developments, and therefore was forced to rely upon the newsgathering abilities of the newspaper. Last, the newspaper provided more than just political and economic information; it also offered entertainment and local news that created a sense of social cohesion in an increasingly fragmented world. The reader was made aware that he or she was part of a wider world sharing and reacting to the news.

It was the existence of this shared experience that made it possible for propaganda to work, for propaganda can only be successful when it is targeted toward specific groups, without having to diffuse the message through a variety of channels. The gradual increase in importance of the mass media throughout the nineteenth and into the twentieth century not only brought into existence viable and reachable publics, but the media themselves began to assume the mantle of "expertise." This proved to be a potent combination, for now the media were both collectors and disseminators of information, and this placed them in a powerful position to act as the channel for all types of persuasive messages, from merely informative advertising to the most blatant forms of propaganda for specific causes.

The Emergence of Mass Society

What was more important than the real power of these new media was their perceived power, for politicians and others reacted to what they assumed this power to be. This was an age when the study of the psychology of human communication was still in its infancy, and it was naturally assumed that the audience would react in a homogeneous manner to whatever stimulus was exposed to them. Much of the concern for the power of the media stemmed from the growing body of sociological literature in the nineteenth century that suggested that the shift from a rural society to an urbanized, industrial society was creating something known as "society." Bramson (1961) notes that European sociological pessimism on the subject of mass society stems from the nineteenth-century notion of the breakdown of the traditional community. Thus European sociology of this period had a preoccupation with "social disorganization" and "social disintegration" caused by the emergence of an industrialized and urbanized, large-scale society. The end result is that

this perspective of nineteenth century sociology is recapitulated in the twentieth century theory of mass society, particularly in its view of the past. By contrast with the anarchic individualism of life in the cities, the impersonality of social relationships, the peculiar mental qualities fostered by urban life with its emphasis on money and abstraction, theorists of mass society idealized the social aspects of the traditional society of the later middle ages. (p. 32)

The role of the emerging mass media in this shift from the traditional type to the modern type of society was seen as crucial, for it was through the popular media that the public was acquiring new ideas. It was also suggested that the media encouraged a cultural blandness that satisfied public tastes at the lowest possible level, and thereby severely hampered attempts to elevate humankind to its full potential. Further, from the perspective of the socialist and Communist thinkers whose ideas were beginning to gain some credence at the turn of the century, the mass media were seen as the handmaidens of the capitalist system, lulling the populace into a political lethargy that prevented them from realizing their true plight as victims of the capitalist system.

The dominance of the negative concept of mass society in intellectual circles in the first part of the twentieth century was a salient factor in shaping the attitudes and subsequent attempts to control the perceived power of the mass media. It is within this intellectual context that subsequent developments in propaganda must be examined, for early propaganda efforts utilizing the new mass media seemed to justify all the fears and doubts surrounding these new channels of information, and their potentially dangerous ability to manipulate their audiences.

The Emergence of the Propaganda Critique

One of the major concerns that emerged at the end of the nineteenth century was for the future of the democratic process in the face of the new possibilities of manipulation of public opinion through increasingly skillful propaganda techniques. The potential for such manipulation led many theorists to even reject democracy as a viable political system. Qualter (1962) cites the case of the English philosopher Graham Wallas, who in his book *Human Nature in Politics* (1908) suggested that men were not entirely governed by reason, but often acted on "affection and instinct" and that these could be deliberately aroused and directed in a way that would eventually lead to some course of action desired by the manipulator. Qualter notes of Wallas:

Given a greatly expanded franchise, with its corollary of the need to base authority on the support of public opinion, political society invited the attention of the professional controller of public opinion. When to the demand for new methods of publicity there were added revolutionary advances in the techniques of communication, and the latest discoveries in social psychology, mankind had to fear more than ever "the cold-blooded manipulation of popular impulse and thought by professional politicians." (p. 51)

Although he never used the word *propaganda,* preferring the phrase "the manipulation of popular impulse," (the word *propaganda* did not become part of common useage until after 1918), Graham Wallas was but one of many concerned with the future of democracy in a world in which propagandistic manipulation seemed to be increasing (Qualter, 1985).

In the United States the concerns in the early part of the twentieth century for the increasing potential of mass media to manipulate human emotions and behavior took a different form than those of the European philosophers who had developed the "mass society" theories. The important revisionist work of Michael Sproule (1987; 1989; 1991) provides us with a useful overview of the emergence of what he calls "Propaganda and American Ideological Critique." Sproule points out that the American intellectual tradition was to treat public opinion as "enlightened discussion," rather than as the European intellectuals' concern about the "rise of the masses." This was because in the United States there was far less alienation between the government and its citizens than found in European countries. Also, inherent in democracy was the faith that public opinion would be ultimately rational, because it would be judged by an educated citizenry. Whereas European Marxist-based theories tended to treat social class and the political state as the prime shapers of ideology, the major concern of the propaganda critique that emerged in the United States in the Progressive Era was for "the implication for democratic social organization of the new marriage between private institutions and the emerging professions of mass communication" (Sproule, 1991, p. 212).

The widespread and potent use of propaganda in the First World War was clearly a watershed moment in the history of propaganda studies, in Europe as much as in the United States. Sproule suggests that

while progressive propaganda criticism did not begin with the state as the archetypal source of ideological manipulation, the Great War did show that the American government was capable of pursuing an ideological hegemony. However, unlike Marxists, progressive critics treated state propaganda in the Great War as less a central problem and more a harbinger of how various private institutions and interest groups would compete after the war. Working from this perspective, American progressives developed a body of criticism focused on the array of social forces that competed for control of what Marxists would call the ideological apparatuses of civil society: education, news, religion, and entertainment. (1991, p. 214)

In the period immediately after 1918, the concerns of the progressive propaganda critics were articulated in Walter Lippmann's *Public Opinion* (1922), and *The Phantom Public* (1925). Lippmann gradually shifted his concerns away from the potential for institutional manipulation to a more general concern about the ability of the public to be able to make decisions in the complex modern era. The philosopher John Dewey in his books *The Public and Its Problems* (1927), and *Liberalism and Social Action* (1935) also examined the new complexities of social interaction brought about by the increasing importance of the mass media in modern society. There were many others (see Sproule, 1989, 1991, for example) who were part of this movement. As Sproule notes:

During the 1920s and 1930s, the progressive propaganda critics developed a wide-ranging program to combat the problem of partisan ideological diffusion through news, religion, entertainment, education, and government. In contrast to Marxist scholars, however, progressives were optimistic about the public's ability to withstand propaganda, especially since progressives believed they would turn the ideological apparatuses, particularly education, into weapons against the powerful propagandas. . . .

With its wide popular audience, progressive critique became the dominant school of thought on propaganda during the years between the two world wars. . . . Progressives had faith in the essential cognitive competence of the public, believing that all that was necessary to combat propaganda was to inform the public about how modern institutions diffused their ideologies through news, religion, entertainment, education, and government. (1991, pp. 219-20)

Propaganda analysis was both an important journalistic and scholarly activity in the interwar period. (The role of propaganda analysis in the interwar period will be examined in greater detail in Chapter 5.) Much of this scholarly activity was devoted less to pure theorizing, than to analyzing the methods by which propagandists worked, often making this knowledge public in the hopes of affecting some type of reform. In one famous study, using Federal Trade Commission data, Ernest Gruening exposed the propaganda activities of the National Electric Light Association (NELA). The NELA had co-opted educators, subsidized the writing of textbooks, bribed news reporters and editors, and supplied classroom material for schools all in the hope of developing a favorable impression of the monopolisitc activites of their member companies (Gruening, 1931).

One exception to this activist position was the political scientist Harold D. Lasswell (1927; Lasswell & Blumsenstock, 1939) an important pioneer in the scholarly analysis of propaganda activites. Although he did eventually take political positions, particularly during World War II, in this early period Lasswell was much more concerned with developing a theoretical perspective of propaganda, and less interested in public policy. As an example, his case study (in Lasswell & Blumsenstock), *World Revolutionary Propaganda: a Chicago Study* (1939), is a meticulously assembled collection of data on the precise methods of propaganda used by Communist groups in Chicago in the Depression years to instill in that city's workers a concept of "world revolution." He states his aims quite clearly "We are interested in the facts. We have taken care to find them. But we are chiefly concerned with the meaning of the facts for an understanding of the future" (p. v). For Lasswell, understanding and discerning patterns in the propaganda process would reveal its strategies and ultimate effectiveness. He also took the position that manipulation of the mass public was possible because individuals tend to react to emotional impulses rather than sober analytic statements. As the various forms of mass communication developed into their powerful institutional structures, employing skillful manipulators of information, such views as Lasswell's would increase, particularly after the apparent spectacular success of propaganda in World War I.

The New Media

Each of the major forms of mass communication that emerged in the nineteenth and twentieth centuries have their own peculiar set of strengths and weaknesses. What they had in common was their ability to establish direct contact with the public in such a manner as to bypass the traditional socializing institutions such as the church, the school, the family, and the political system. Because of this historically unique and very significant ability, the media were feared by those concerned with the moral welfare of society, but welcomed by those who sought to use this "direct contact" in order to present their own cases to the mass audience, whether it be an advertiser trying to convince the public to purchase a new product or a politician "selling" policies.

The Print Media

We have already noted earlier in this chapter how significant the penny press was in the early part of the nineteenth century in the creation of the first modern media publics. Throughout the rest of the century and into the twentieth, the mass press continued to grow both in size and in significance as a purveyor of information and as a shaper of ideas. During the fight for abolition of slavery and the American Civil War newspapers on both sides played significant roles as propaganda agents, and in the postwar years the newspaper business grew spectacularly. Emery and Emery (1984) note that

> between 1870 and 1900, the United States doubled its population and tripled the number of its urban residents. During the same 30 years the number of daily newspapers quadrupled and the number of copies sold each day increased almost sixfold. . . . The number of English-language, general circulation dailies increased from 489 in 1870 to 1967 in 1900. Circulation totals for all daily publications rose from 2.6 million copies in 1870 to 15 million in 1900. (p. 231)

Another feature of the last half of the nineteenth century was the spectacular rise of magazines as important sources of information. Spurred on by cheap postal rates established by Congress in 1879, magazines such as *Ladies' Home Journal* and *Saturday Evening Post* soon had circulations that exceeded half a million. These popular periodicals, while not blatantly propagandistic, nevertheless presented a particular perspective that proved to be a major influence in shaping domestic life in the United States. Particularly after 1899, under the editorship of George Horace Lorimer, the *Saturday Evening Post* became one of the major vehicles of mass culture in the United States (Cohn, 1989). As an example, in World War I the *Saturday Evening Post*, which was read by nearly 10 million a week, took a decided anti-German editorial perspective, and "the constant repetition of these themes in editorials, articles, fiction, and cartoons worked to create a broad-based acceptance for the terms of Lorimer's Americanism. As Will Irwin, a major Post writer during the war years, cynically expressed it, 'In pouring the plastic American mind into certain grooves, [Lorimer] had a great social influence'" (Cohn, 1989, p. 103). Smaller "literary" publications, such as *Harper's Weekly* (1857), *Atlantic Monthly* (1857), and the *Nation*, although limited in circulation, nevertheless had a profound influence on public opinion. There were many other magazines of political and social opinion that also contributed to the shaping of the public agenda on issues such as poverty, immigration, business corruption, and public health (Tebbel, 1969). Magazines were and continue to be a very personalized medium, creating strong reader identification and association with the editorial tone and content. It was in magazines that most of the political and social muckraking took place.

By the beginning of the twentieth century the major daily newspapers in the United States had clearly established themselves as leaders and shapers of public opinion on a wide range of issues. This was the era of yellow journalism in which the major New York dailies, Joseph Pulitzer's *World* and William Randolph Hearst's *Journal*, competed with each other for the coveted circulation by seeing who could cover or create the most spectacular news. One famous example of the increasing potential of the press to create propaganda in this period was the battleship *Maine* incident. As a result of their direct intervention in a series of incidents fomenting the Cuban insurrection (1895-1898) the major daily newspapers in America have been accused of having created an extreme war psychosis in the minds of the American people, leading up to the mysterious sinking of the *Maine* in Havana harbor in 1898, and the subsequent Spanish-American War of the same year. There has never been a satisfactory answer as to why the *Maine* sunk, but this did not stop Hearst's New York *Journal* from offering a $50,000 reward for information leading to the arrest of the alleged criminals, while the paper's headlines screamed for war (Wilkerson, 1932; Wisan, 1934). Once war had been declared, the newspapers spent enormous sums of money covering it, with the *Journal* proclaiming, "How do you like the *Journal*'s war?" (Emery & Emery, 1984, p. 295).

Although newspapers have declined in readership in the twentieth century, they provide a continuous source of propaganda in our society. During both World Wars, newspapers were the major source of information for the general public, and as such were used for propaganda purposes rather extensively. Despite the significant inroads made by broadcast journalism, newspapers are still read for in-depth information and perspectives on news and events, and, as such, under the guise of both straight newsreporting and editorializing, they do carry propaganda messages. There is nothing in the

Constitution of the United States that forces a newspaper publisher to be totally neutral and objective in reporting the news, and thus whether it be in clearly labeled editorial opinion, or the particular slant of an "innocent" newsreport, or in paid advertising, newspapers are a prime source of propaganda in our society. This is equally true for the large newsmagazines such as *Time* and *Newsweek* in which both the selection of the specific stories to be featured and the manner in which those stories are treated can be considered to be propaganda. Even an apparently harmless publication such as the *Reader's Digest* can, in fact, be carefully constructed to be a propaganda vehicle for the values and politics of the owner (Schreiner, 1977).

In 1988, more than two billion books (81.4 million hardback, and 138.1 million paperback) worth more than $18 billion were sold in the United States (Statistical Abstracts, 1991). Although books are still an important source of propaganda, they are somewhat limited in their circulation, and seldom have a mass audience. Nevertheless, they can and do have an impact far beyond their primary readership circle, as the opportunity to develop specific ideas in-depth makes the book a particularly potent source of propagandistic information. Throughout history books have played a very pivotal role in the shaping of ideas and attitudes on a large scale—certainly beyond their actual primary readership. The Bible, even for those who do not read it, continues to provide the source of social and cultural values that shapes a great portion of our lives. Depending upon the specific theological interpretation, the Bible also serves as the source of a great deal of religious and political propaganda on such issues as abortion or the public acceptance of homosexuality. In the past, books such as Charles Darwin's *Origin of the Species* (1859) or Harriet Beecher Stowe's *Uncle Tom's Cabin* (1852) were the sources of major conflicts in our society. Even closer to our present day, the unexpected popularity of Rachel L. Carson's *Silent Spring* (1962) was really instrumental in gaining public attention for the damage done to the environment by pollution.

Although not deliberately propaganda, we cannot ignore the work of Sigmund Freud as an important factor in shaping twentieth-century thought about the nature of human beings. Unfortunately, one of the most significant propagandistic books in this century was largely ignored when it was first published. In fact, had the world taken Adolf Hitler's *Mein Kampf* (My Struggle) seriously in 1926, when it appeared in Germany, rather than waiting until the first English edition in 1939, the international diplomatic approach to Hitler's conquests throughout the 1930s might have been quite different.

The Movies

It is rather surprising that despite the enormous inherent appeal of the motion picture, this medium has never become the powerful vehicle of "direct" propaganda that its critics feared it would be. In fact, it might be precisely because of its popularity as one of the world's great entertainment forms, rather than as a medium of conscious information dissemination, that it has failed to fulfill its initial promise as both an educator and as a channel for the propagandist. Of all the mass media, the motion picture has the greatest potential for emotional appeal to its audience, offering a deeper level of identification with the characters and action on the screen than found elsewhere in popular culture. The motion picture can also make audiences laugh, cry, sing, shout out loud, become sexually aroused, or fall asleep—in short, they have the ability to evoke an immediate emotional response seldom found in the other mass media. Yet systematic attempts by governments or other groups to use the motion picture as a channel for the delivery of propagandistic messages have not, on the whole, been very successful.

On the other hand, the motion picture has been extremely successful in influencing its audience in such areas as courting behavior, clothing styles, furniture and architectural design, speech mannerisms, and eating and drinking habits (Jowett, 1982). In these and other areas the motion picture is an excellent shaper of subtle psychological attitudes and can under the right circumstances be a potent source of social and cultural information. In his famous study *Movies and Conduct* social psychologist Herbert Blumer (1933), after examining hundreds of diaries kept by young moviegoers, noted that

> for many the pictures are authentic potrayals of life, from which they draw patterns of behavior, stimulation to overt conduct, content for a vigorous life of imagination, and ideas of reality. They are not merely a device for surcease; they are a form of stimulation . . . motion pictures are a genuine educational institution . . . in the truer sense of actually introducing him [the student] to and acquainting him with a type of life which has immediate, practical and momentous significance. (pp. 196-97)

One could argue that movies do, in fact, succeed as propaganda vehicles in a much more subtle way, by presenting one set of values as the only viable set. Over a period of years, these values can both reflect and shape society's norms.

Immediately after projected motion pictures were introduced in 1896, they were used for propaganda purposes in a variety of ways.

Raymond Fielding (1972) in his history of the newsreel recounts fake news films of the Dreyfus affair in France in 1896, while actual political events were also the subjects of early films, including fake footage of the charge up San Juan Hill, and the sinking of the Spanish Fleet in Santiago Bay in the Spanish-American War. The pure visual power of the motion picture can be seen in one of the first films to be made after the declaration of war against the Spanish. Made by Vitagraph studios, it was entitled *Tearing Down the Spanish Flag,* and simply showed a flagpole from which a Spanish flag was flying. The flag was abruptly torn down, and in its place an American flag was raised. In the words of Albert E. Smith, one of the founders of the Vitagraph Company, "Projected on a thirty-foot screen, the effect on audiences was sensational and sent us searching for similar subjects. . . . The people were on fire and eager for every line of news. . . . With nationalistic feeling at a fever pitch we set out to photograph what people wanted to see" (Fielding, 1972, pp. 29-30).

The fear of the motion picture's power both to communicate and educate resulted in early and consistent attacks on it from all those institutions and individuals who had the most to lose from its inherent appeal. Thus throughout the world the clergy, social workers, educators, and politicians were all involved in trying to make the motion picture more responsive to their call for social control of this obtrusive new form of information (Jowett, 1976). In the United States the Supreme Court refused to allow the motion picture the right of free speech granted by the First Amendment to the Constitution. In the landmark case of *Mutual vs. Ohio* (1915), Justice McKenna, speaking for the unanimous Court, noted that motion pictures were

> not to be regarded, nor intended to be regarded as part of the press of the country or as organs of public opinion. They are mere representations of events, of ideas and sentiments published or known; vivid, useful and entertaining, no doubt, but . . . capable of evil, having power for it, the greater because of their attractiveness and manner of exhibition. (Jowett, 1976, p. 120)

Thus of all the various forms of mass communication that have been introduced into the United States, only the motion picture has been subjected to systematic legalized prior-censorship. This situation continued until the mid-1970s, at which time the Supreme Court began to strike down the various censorship restrictions against the medium (Randall, 1968).

During World War I there were crude attempts made to utilize the motion picture as a propaganda device, including such films as *The Kaiser, The Beast of Berlin*, and *My Four Years in Germany*, but the most important of these propaganda efforts, aimed at molding public opinion in favor of the United States entering the war, was *Battle Cry of Peace* (1915) produced by J. Stuart Blackton (whose hand had earlier ripped down the Spanish flag in 1898). This film showed the Germans attacking New York by sea, and reducing the city to ruins, but it also had a reverse effect, in that the pacifist movement used the film to expose the war profiteers and armament manufacturers who would benefit from American entry into the war (Campbell, 1985). Before 1916, most American films were decidedly pacifist in tone, reflecting the mood of the American people; as an example in *War Brides* (1916) the peace-loving heroine committed suicide rather than give birth to a future soldier (Furhammer & Isaksson, 1971). Once America declared war in 1917, encouraged by public sentiment there was a flurry of anti-German films.

All of the Allied countries made propaganda films, the British government going so far as to import the great American director D. W. Griffith to direct *Hearts of the World* (1918), featuring the Gish sisters in a plot that was set against authentic war-shattered backgrounds from the western front (Reeves, 1986). In the United States, the Committee on Public Information (CPI), formed by the government to become the propaganda agency for the war effort, worked with the film industry in making films with patriotic content, including offering suggestions for stories and military expertise and props as required by the studios. The significant role of the movies in World War I did much to establish and legitimize the movie industry as an important part of American society. By the end of the war, President Wilson, and other high government officials were not adverse to be seen in the company of movie stars at war bond drives and other social occasions—something that would have been unthinkable before 1916. This testified to the increased awareness of politicians about the potential power of the motion picture (Ward, 1985) .

In Germany in 1917, Chief of Staff General Ludendorff sent a letter to the Imperial Ministry of War, in which he noted:

The war has demonstrated the superiority of the photograph and the film as means of information and persuasion. Unfortunately our enemies have used their advantage over us in this field so thoroughly that they have inflicted a great deal of damage. . . . For this reason it is of the utmost importance for a successful conclusion to the war that films should be made to work with the greatest possible effect wherever any German persuasion might still have any effect. (Furhammer & Isaksson, 1971, p. 11)

By the time the German government got around to setting up its film propaganda arm the war was nearly over, but this same organization, Universium Film Aktiengesellschaft (UFA) survived to become a major propaganda agency for the Nazis during the 1930s and through World War II.

The period between the two world wars was known as the "golden age" of the commercial cinema, as the medium achieved heights of popularity that had not been thought possible for an entertainment that had started out in cheap storefront nickelodeons. The Hollywood product dominated world screens as the European film studios were still recovering from their devastation from the war. Audiences were so used to seeing commercial escapist material that it was extremely difficult to get them to view anything that appeared to be educational. The only propaganda films that were ever seen in the commercial theaters were the often innocuous newsreels and the occasional documentary such as *Nanook of the North* (1926), which was a surprising commercial success despite the fact that it had originally been made as a propaganda film for a fur company. If audiences were being propagandized, then it was under the guise of entertainment, and they numbered in the hundreds of millions every week.

In 1928, the Motion Picture Research Council was given over $200,000 by the philanthropic Payne Fund to conduct the most extensive research into the influence of the movies on American life ever undertaken. This research was conducted by a distinguished group of social scientists on a nationwide basis, and was aimed at determining the degrees of influence and effect of films upon children and adolescents. The research was carried out over a four-year period, 1929-1933, and was eventually published in ten volumes. The origins of the Payne Fund Studies point out the shift that was then taking place in assessing the significance of media in shaping the lives of their audiences. The Reverend William Short, the man most responsible for setting up the studies, wanted to have scientific evidence that he could use to foster his campaign to place the motion picture industry under a more stringent form of social control. By the late twenties, it was no longer acceptable to present evidence that could not be empirically verified (Jowett, 1992). The research itself became the center of a propaganda campaign when a popularized version of some of the research findings was published in the book entitled *Our Movie-Made Children* by journalist Henry James Forman in 1933. Forman had been employed to simplify and in some cases distort the research so as to arouse public concern in favor of the establishment of a national film censorship commission. Although this ploy did not work in the end, the Payne Fund Studies (usually as interpreted by Forman) were widely quoted in all types of media and formed the platform for the launching of many critical essays on the state of the motion picture industry (Jowett, 1976).

It was in the Soviet Union that films were controlled more firmly by the political authorities than anywhere else in the world (Taylor, 1979). The theme of revolution was fundamental to almost all Soviet films, with Lenin as the central figure. In order to achieve the maximum emotional impact, Soviet filmmakers developed a visual technique called *montage*, in which the various film images were juxtaposed to create a specific response from the viewer. The idea was that the skill of the director could create a reality from the different pieces of film that would almost assault the visual sensibilities of the audience and achieve the desired psychological effect. The great Russian propaganda films such as Sergei Eisensteins's *Battleship Potemkin* (1925), Vsevolod Pudovkin's *Storm Over Asia* (1928), and Alexander Dovzhenko's *Earth* (1930) all used montage as a central technique for eliciting the proper audience response. But even in the Soviet Union, despite the achievements of the filmmakers of the early revolutionary period, the authorities were not satisfied with the medium's role, and with the coming to power of Josef Stalin in the late 1920s the Soviet cinema began to concentrate on socialist realism. This meant that "all films were to be comprehensible to and appreciated by the millions, and their one aim was to be the glorification of the emerging Soviet state" (Furhammer & Isaksson, 1971, p. 20). As a result of this edict, Soviet films were drained of their vitality, and they only regained their original powers of propaganda in the mid-1930s after Hitler had come to power and several successful antifascist films were produced. These included Eisenstein's *Alexander Nevsky* (1938), which used the theme of a thirteenth-century battle as an obvious prophesy of what was to come. After the war, the Soviet film industry turned its attention to making blatant anti-American propaganda films up until the death of Stalin (1953), at which time there was a change in tone. Up until the very recent period of glasnost, the Soviet cinema continued to be a mixture of politics and art, and there was little pretense about trying to achieve propagandistic goals. In the last few years, with the relaxation of government control, the Soviet cinema industry has begun to explore themes (poverty, sexual dysfunction, domestic violence, political corruption) that it would not have been allowed to examine during the previous hardline Communist regime.

The enormous Hollywood film industry has never lent itself to overt propaganda on any grand scale, but there have been times when even the commercial filmmakers have used their entertainment medium for putting forward a specific idea. As an example, after several years of conspicuous silence, motivated no doubt by international marketing considerations and not wishing to alienate the important German market, Hollywood finally produced its first anti-Nazi film in 1939, more than six years after Hitler had come to power. (In fact, the Nazi menace was already surfacing in Germany by 1928.) This film, *Confessions of a Nazi Spy*, was based upon the exploits of a former FBI agent who had cracked a spy ring inside the German-American Bund. Once war broke out in Europe in 1939, Hollywood countered with films such as *Devil Dogs of the Air, Here Comes the Navy,* and *Miss Pacific Fleet,* which were deliberately designed as recruiting films for the still neutral U.S. armed services by presenting this as an attractive life-style. These became known as the "preparedness films" and they immediately aroused the suspicion and anger of those who did not wish to see the United States become involved in a European war.

In 1941 the isolationist senator from North Dakota, Gerald P. Nye, recognized the potential power of the movies in a famous radio speech when he criticized the Hollywood studios for their role in bringing America "to the verge of war." He was perceptive in his assessment of the movies' potential for successful propagandizing when he noted:

> But when you go to the movies, you go there to be entertained. You are not figuring on listening to a debate about the war. You settle yourself in your seat with your mind wide open. And then the picture starts— goes to work on you, all done by trained actors, full of drama, cunningly devised, and soft passionate music underscoring it. Before you know where you are you have actually listened to a speech designed to make you believe that Hitler is going to get you if you don't watch out . . . the truth is that in 20,000 theaters in the United States tonight they are holding war mass meetings, and the people lay down the money at the box office before they get in. (Nye, 1941, p. 722)

Once the United States entered World War II in December 1941, the movie industry did contribute toward the total war effort, but not only by making war films, for less than one-third of all the films released in the United States in the period 1942 to 1944 actually dealt with the war (Jowett, 1976). What the Hollywood industry did so well was to provide morale-building films for consumption on the home front and overseas, for during the war entertainment was not only a luxury but also an emotional necessity. American films managed to develop a most potent combination of being able to entertain and propagandize at the same time, thus "getting the message across" while also attracting the large audiences that obvious propaganda and documentary films were seldom able to do.

In November 1941 a prominent and articulate Hollywood producer, Walter Wanger, noted that motion pictures should be used in the upcoming conflict "to clarify, to inspire and to entertain." He continued, "The determination of what ought to be said is a problem for our national leaders and our social scientists. The movies will make significant contributions to national morale only when the people have reached some degree of agreement about the central and irrefutable ideas of a nation caught in the riptide of war" (Wanger, 1941, p. 381). Wanger was stressing the fact that although movies were merely a medium of entertainment, they were very popular and therefore had a powerful potential to gain the public's attention. For this reason, it was essential that the content of the propaganda "messages" carried in movies during this time of crisis should be based upon national interests and not left up to the patriotic whims of the heads of the studios. Once the war did begin for the Americans in 1941, that is precisely the dictum that was followed.

Film was an important medium for propaganda during World War II, but seldom in the manner in which the official propagandists intended. In many cases audiences were far more sophisticated than expected, and the result was a rejection of obvious, blatant efforts to bring about changes in existing opinions. When film propaganda was most successful it was usually based upon a skillful exploitation of preexisting public emotions, eliciting an audience response that closely matched public sentiment. A good example is the Nazi film *Baptism of Fire* (1940), which was a skillful compilation of documentary footage dramatically illustrating the supposed invincibility of the German armed forces as they battered the Polish army out of existence in under three weeks. When this film was screened in those countries threatened with German invasion, it had a definite intimidation effect. American films, on the other hand, were most successful when they stressed positive themes, particularly as they depicted normal life on the home front. The Hollywood studios, because of their prior experience at developing strong characterizations, were particularly adept in their war films at depicting the inner strength of the ordinary fighting men—usually in groups carefully balanced to underscore the various ethnic origins of Americans such as Irish, Italians, Jews, and so on. In fact, many of the most successful American films during the war did not concern themselves with the fighting at all.

In a 1945 study of the contribution made by movies to the war effort, Dorothy Jones of the Office of War Information (OWl) found that between 1942-1945, only about 30% of Hollywood films actually dealt with the war itself. Although she was critical of the movie industry for "lacking a real understanding of the war" she ignored the established fact that by 1943, having grown tired of war films, not only the home front audience but also the combat forces preferred to see the spate of musicals, comedies, and escapist romances that the movie industry was only too happy to turn out. This blend of war films and escapist material, most of which tended to emphasize the positive aspects of the "American way of life," combined to create a potent propaganda source for morale building during this difficult period in American history. Of equal significance was the appeal that these domestic films had among both America's allies and conquered enemies, where their popularity was exceeded only by the demand for American food. Recognizing this fact, at the end of the war the U.S. government made serious efforts to make available to the occupied countries only those films that showed the United States and its democratic institutions in a favorable light.

Since the end of World War II, there has been little systematic use of film for propaganda purposes on a large scale. There are occasional commercial films that propagandize in the sense that they espouse a particular point of view about a controversial subject. Examples of such films would be *The China Syndrome* (1979), which was about the dangers of nuclear power; *Missing* (1982), which dealt with American complicity in the overthrow of the Chilean government; *Salvador* (1986), which detailed U.S. complicity in the political upheaval in El Salvador; and *JFK* (1991), which put forward director Oliver Stone's personal vision of the assassination of President Kennedy. However, these are not part of an organized campaign on behalf of a recognized propaganda agency. This was not always so, for in the cold war period (roughly 1947-1965) the American film industry was actively solicited by the U.S. government to make commercial films that pointed out the dangers of Communism. This contrasted wildly with the pro-Russian films that Hollywood had turned out once Hitler had marched into Russia in 1942, and the American public had to be convinced that we were all now allies. Previously exposed to films such as *The North Star* (1942), *Mission to*

Moscow (1943), and *Song of Russia* (1944), the American film audience was now treated to *The Iron Curtain* (1948), which confusingly starred Dana Andrews, who only a few years before had been featured in a sympathetic role in *The North Star* as a Russian partisan; *The Red Menace*, which cataloged the methods of Communist subversion in the United States; *Whip Hand* (1951), which dealt with Communists running a prison camp in a small town in the United States to test biological weapons; *I Was a Communist for the FBI* (1951), which later became the basis of a television series; *My Son John* (1952), which examined the reaction of patriotic parents when they discover that their son has become a Communist; and *Big Jim McLain* (1952), which featured John Wayne hunting Communists in Hawaii. (It was no coincidence that the name McLain was used to identify the hero closely with noted anti-Communist Senator Joseph McCarthy.)

The fate of the film *North Star* in the postwar period is particularly interesting. The film was produced by Sam Goldwyn from a script by Lillian Hellman and distributed by RKO studios with a big name cast and major studio production values, ostensibly to solidify Soviet-American relationships at the height of the war. The story dealt with a Russian village defending itself against the invading German forces, and while the inner strength of the Russian peasants was stressed, nowhere in the film were the words *Communist* or *Communism* mentioned. But even this was too much in the hysteria of cold war red scare. When the film was shown on television in 1957 the title was changed to *Armored Attack*, and comments were inserted into the film to repudiate the original sentiments, innocent though they may have been. A new ending was added showing Russian tanks invading Hungary in 1956, with the voice-over reminding the viewer that the heroism of the Russian peasants in World War II should not obscure the brutality of the Communist leaders in the postwar period. At the very end, another voice-over apologized for any pro-Soviet impressions that the film may have given (Whitfield, 1991).

It was no coincidence that much of the focus of the House Un-American Activities Committee on Communist subversion in the United States in the period after 1947 was on ferreting out potential Communists in the Hollywood community. Not only did the committee gain national media attention by questioning entertainment personalities who were widely recognized public figures (who cared about anonymous government employees?), but there was a genuine fear that because the film industry was very powerful, it would be dangerous to allow Communist sympathizers to use it as a propaganda tool. Much the same could be said for the attention given to both radio and television, for the commercial media were considered to be potent sources of propaganda disguised as entertainment, as Senator Nye had pointed out in 1941.

Since the breakup of the large Hollywood studios and the emergence of largely independent producers, there has been little attempt to use the motion picture industry for organized propagandizing. On the other hand, show business personalities are increasingly using their media-obtained popularity to espouse political causes. The majority of the public seems clearly able to distinguish the on-screen persona of the actor from the off-screen political causes with which he or she might be identified. As an example, there was and continues to be considerable hostility toward Jane Fonda for her activities during the Vietnam War, and subsequent support of liberal causes, but she still has an enormous number of fans who are willing to ignore her political stances and pay money at the box office to see her in such films as *Nine to Five* (1980), or to buy her workout videos. (It is interesting to note that this film was a political film, dealing with significant issues of feminism; however, audiences did not really perceive it as such.) The propaganda value of such personalities lies mainly in their ability to gain media attention for their favorite causes; however, the public seldom sees them as credible sources. Jane Fonda can create public interest in the issues of Vietnam, but she was not considered an expert in foreign policy.

There is a subtle, but important difference between a star deliberately pushing a personal cause, and merely being associated with a politican or a political campaign. Richard Brownstein in his detailed examination of the relationship between Hollywood and politics, *The Power and the Glitter* (1991) notes that the specific image a star projects can lend an aura to the politician that associates with him or her, and that this association sends out a cultural message to the audience. Brownstein continues:

> For their fans, these entertainers embody memories, lifestyles, places and times, shared experiences. They suggest a way of looking at the world, symbolizing not only experiences but also values; you can often tell a lot about someone by how they feel about John Wayne or Sylvester Stallone, or whether they prefer Bob Dylan to Elvis Presley. They are all part of the code people use to recognize others like themselves. . . .
>
> These cultural messages can help politicians make themselves more three-dimensional, particularly to the many voters who pay little attention to elections. . . .

To play these cultural roles, stars need not be personally credible messengers on public policy, the way they must to push individual causes; what matters instead is how their image affects the way voters see a politician who associates with them. (pp. 369-70)

When Hollywood attempted to make so-called message films in the period after World War II, it quickly became obvious that most people do not go to the movies to have their consciences disturbed. Subsequent research has clearly demonstrated that movies, like other mass media, rarely bring about a major change of opinion; however, we also know that consistent exposure to a specific point of view when the audience has none of its own stands a good chance of making some impact. Thus the cumulative effect of filmic propaganda is greater than any individual film. Foreign audiences, often knowing little about the United States, will after years of exposure to American films develop very specific attitudes about the American way of life. On the other hand, no single film can change an individual's racial attitudes ingrained after years of socialization.

The U.S. government is still very concerned about the potential for filmic propaganda both from within and from outside of the country. In 1983, the U.S. Justice Department labeled three documentary films produced by the National Film Board of Canada "propaganda." One of these films, *If You Love This Planet*, about the nuclear arms race subsequently won the Academy Award (Rosenberg, 1983). This issue was challenged in court, and on April 27, 1987, the Supreme Court upheld the Federal Law under which this decision was made, stating that the labeling was "neutral and evenhanded," and did not constitute an infringement of freedom of the press. (For an excellent, full account of this important case, see Gustainis, 1989.) American films going out of the country are also subject to censorship for propagandizing. Through a little-known program, under the Beirut Agreement adopted by the United Nations in 1948 to "facilitate the international circulation of visual and auditory material of educational, scientific and cultural character," the United States Information Agency provides "Certificates of International Educational Character" to all films wishing to be exempt from export duties. Over the years the many films which have been denied such certificates fall into one of three categories: blatant promotion of a specific product or service; offensive religious proselytizing; or political propaganda. In 1983, "The Killing Ground," an Emmy-winning ABC News documentary on toxic wastes was denied a certificate on the basis that it was "emotional rather than technical," and because "the primary purpose or effect of the film appears to be less to instruct or inform in an educational sense than to present a special point of view" (Rosenberg, 1983, p. 40). John Mendenhall, who ran the program at the USIA at the time said, "if we feel that the purpose of the film is to advocate a cause or is persuasive of one point of view, that's one type of propaganda, and we deny it a certificate" (Rosenberg, 1983, p. 41).

The motion picture is still a highly effective form of information dissemination, but its use as a propaganda vehicle is severely restricted by several factors. First, audiences worldwide have become used to large-budget films with high quality production values, and this works against the use of low-budget productions. Second, the concept of the fictional story complete with acknowledged stars as the basic attraction in commercial films is so well established that it is very difficult to generate a mass audience for anything else. Third, the distribution system for commercial films is tightly organized and extremely difficult to break into for those outside of the mainstream filmmaking community. Last, filmmaking technology has now been superseded by new video technologies that offer greater opportunities for dissemination of propaganda messages without the need for a large audience base to justify cost. Thus the motion picture's effectiveness as a propaganda medium is largely limited to the values and ideologies that are an integral part of the plot structure. Such content, although subtle, is in its own right an extremely potent source of modern propaganda, and is certainly more powerful in the long run than the deliberate and often clumsy attempts in the past.

Radio

The invention of radio in the late nineteenth century totally altered for all time the practice of propaganda, making it possible for messages to be sent across borders and over long distances without the need for a physical presence. Ultimately radio has become the major medium of full-scale international "white" propaganda, in which the source of the message is clear and the audience knows and often eagerly expects to hear different political viewpoints. Despite the inroads made by television viewing on leisure-time activities in most industrialized countries, there is no indication of any decline in the use of radio for propaganda purposes, and large sums of money are currently spent on the worldwide dissemination of information from a variety of political ideologies.

The first known use of radio for international broadcasting was in 1915 when Germany provided a daily news report of war activities, which was widely used by both the domestic and foreign press that was starved for up-to-date news. Although these broadcasts were in Morse code, and therefore not available to all, they served their purpose. Radio was used dramatically by the Soviets in 1917, when under the call sign "To all . . . to all. . . . to all. . ." the Council of the People's Commissars' Radio put out the historic message of Lenin announcing the start of a new age on October 30 (Hale, 1975). The message stated that

> the All-Russian Congress of Soviets has formed a new Soviet Government. The Government of Kerensky has been overthrown and arrested. . . . All official institutions are in the hands of the Soviet Government. (p. 16)

This was an international call to all revolutionary groups throughout Europe as well as those inside of Russia, and later broadcasts would be aimed specifically at foreign workers to "be on the watch and not to relax the pressure on your rulers." Soviet radio was quickly placed under the control of the government, for Lenin noted that radio was a "newspaper without paper . . . and without boundaries," and a potentially important medium for communicating his Communist ideas to the dispersed workers and peasants in both Russia and the rest of Europe, and, ultimately, the world. By 1922 Moscow had the most powerful radio station in existence, followed in 1925 by a powerful shortwave transmitter, which soon began broadcasting in English.

The interest in radio grew rapidly during the 1920s, and turning the radio dial in the hope of picking up foreign stations became the pastime of millions of listeners in many countries. In the United States much of the pioneering credit can be given to station KDKA in Pittsburgh, which started the first regularly scheduled radio service in 1920. By the end of 1923 the station had successfully transmitted a special holiday program to Great Britain, which was picked up and rebroadcast from a Manchester station; and later in 1924 and 1925 it broadcast programs to South Africa and Australia, respectively. These early broadcasts set the scene for a regular exchange of radio programs between countries during the late 1920s and early 1930s and shortwave radio listening became a fascinating hobby for enthusiastic radio fans. It was the Dutch who inaugurated the first regular shortwave broadcasts in 1927, sponsored by the giant electrical engineering company Phillips; by 1930 this station was broadcasting to most parts of the world in more than twenty languages.

Radio Moscow started broadcasting in French in 1929, and this action caused an outcry from the French press, which questioned the right of the Soviets to broadcast in a language other than their own, and the League of Nations was asked to consider the matter. Within a year the French had seen the light and began their own international broadcasts. In 1930, the English language broadcasts from Moscow had caused sufficient concern to warrant the British Post Office to monitor these on a regular basis. The success of these foreign broadcasts was not lost on the BBC, which in 1929 proposed to the Imperial Conference (where all parts of the British Empire were represented) that a worldwide service be established to maintain the links of the empire. In proposing this service, the BBC submission noted that in presenting national cultures to other parts of the world, "boundary between cultural and tendentious propaganda is in practice very indefinite" (Bumpus & Skelt, 1985, p. 13). The Empire Service was begun in 1932, in English only. One week after it opened, King George V delivered a Christmas message to his subjects throughout the world, and the *New York Times* ran a banner headline, "Distant Lands Thrill to his God Bless You!" The BBC gained enormous publicity and prestige from this broadcast.

In 1929, Germany also started broadcasting to its nationals abroad from a shortwave transmitter outside of Berlin, and Italy set up its service in 1930, broadcasting at first only Italian domestic programs. By 1932 even the League of Nations had its own station broadcasting new bulletins in three languages: English, French, and Spanish. Only in the United States did the government steer well clear of any involvement with international broadcasting, preferring to leave this to the large commercial networks then being established. These stations, of course, broadcast in English only, and therefore did not have the same direct propaganda value in foreign countries.

With the coming to power of the National Socialist government in Germany in 1933, the role of international broadcasting was dramatically elevated to major prominence. (The use of radio by the Nazi regime will be discussed in more detail in Chapter 5.) Both Hitler and his Propaganda Minister Josef Goebbels had been impressed with the Soviet Union's German language service and the development inside Germany of widespread and powerful listener groups for these propaganda broadcasts. By August 1934 the Nazi administration had reorganized German broadcasting, and programs were now being beamed to Asia, Africa, South America, and North America. The Germans pioneered in the use of music as a means of attracting listeners, and by all accounts the quality of the music was superb, with news bulletins and special programs interspersed. One German radio expert was quoted as saying, "Music must first bring the listener to the loudspeaker and relax him" (Grandin, 1939, p. 46). The 1936 Olympic Games in Berlin provided the impetus to construct the world's largest shortwave radio transmitter facilities, and by the end of 1938 the Germans were broadcasting more than 5,000 hours a week in more than 25 languages. The Nazis also introduced medium-wave broadcasts for the neighboring European countries, especially those with pockets of German-speaking minorities.

Italy followed Germany's lead, increasing foreign and Italian broadcasts to both Europe and the Americas, including the provision of Italian language lessons that cleverly used many passages from Mussolini's speeches as texts. Listeners were asked to send their translations to Rome for correction, and by 1939 more than 35,000 people had done so (Grandin, 1939, p. 30). Japan also began its own foreign language radio service in June 1935 as a means of informing the large number of Japanese living on the Pacific rim about activities in the home country. This soon changed, for after Japan found itself internationally isolated following its invasion of Manchuria in 1936, Radio Tokyo was used as a propaganda medium for putting across the Japanese government's position on Japan's role in creating a new Asian alliance. Broadcasts were aimed at the United States and Europe, but the quality of these broadcasts was hampered by a lack of personnel trained in foreign languages. Interestingly, the Japanese government did all that it could to discourage the ownership of short-wave radio sets to diminish the impact of broadcasts from outside.

By the beginning of World War II in the summer of 1939, there were approximately 25 countries that were broadcasting internationally in foreign languages. The outbreak of war once again brought about an enormous expansion of international radio services. In particular, the BBC was charged with becoming a major arm of the Allied propaganda effort, so that by the end of 1940, 23 languages had been added and more than 78 separate news bulletins were being offered everyday, with special attention given to Germany and Italy. Governments in exile in London were also given the opportunity to broadcast to their home countries. By the end of the war the BBC was the largest international broadcaster by far, programming in more than 43 languages, and because of its earned reputation for total accuracy, even the German troops were tuning in to find out what was happening.

In the United States at the time of the attack on Pearl Harbor, there were only 12 shortwave transmitters in action, all owned by private broadcasters. Under the guidance of the Office of War Information, these stations became collectively known as the Voice of America. Eventually the U.S. government rented the stations and all programs were prepared by the foreign operations unit of the OWI, under the control of playwright Robert Sherwood. By 1943 the number of transmitters had risen to 36, and the VOA was broadcasting in 46 languages for some 50 hours a day. (A useful history of the early years of the VOA is Shulman, 1990; a detailed examination of the later period is found in Alexandre, 1988.) There was some uncertainty about the future role of VOA once the war was over, for there has always been a nervousness in the U.S. Congress about propaganda activities, whether domestic or foreign. (This fear stems largely from the concern that the administration in power will eventually utilize such activities to serve its own domestic ends.) Immediately after the war ended, VOA was severely cut back, but with the start of the cold war Congress, feeling that American response to increasing Soviet propaganda actions was inadequate, voted in 1948 to create a permanent role for VOA as part of the information activities of the State Department.

It was in the decades following World War II that the unprecedented expansion of international broadcasting activities took place. Immediately after the war the main thrust of such broadcasts was toward Europe, but gradually during the 1950s, 1960s, and 1970s more attention was given to India, the Arab countries, Africa, Latin America, and Asia. As the dynamics of world politics were being played out, international radio broadcasts became a prominent weapon in the arsenal of propaganda. With the Communist takeover in China in 1949 a new major world and radio power appeared, while the Soviet Union, threatened with defections in the Soviet Bloc, steadily expanded its broadcasts in an increasing number of languages. The non-Communist countries retaliated, with West Germany expanding its facilities, as did all three of the United States operations. (Radio Free Europe had begun in 1951; Radio Liberation started broadcasting in 1953.) By the end of the 1970s, the use of radio as a major medium for international propaganda was greater than it had ever been.

Current International Radio Propaganda

No field of international propaganda has been so affected by the dramatic changes in world politics since the collapse of Communism in Eastern Europe than international shortwave broadcasting. However, there are still several distinct kinds of international broadcasting systems that can be said to be clearly propagandistic. The most important by far are the national broadcasting organizations that are usually state funded, or supported by a group of politically or religiously active citizens eager to reach a specific audience, usually in other countries. More than 80 nations are currently involved in this type of activity, some operating more than one such service (Bumpus & Skelt, 1985). The United States has the Voice of America (VOA), which is the main international service, Radio Free Europe (RFE), which transmits to 5 countries in Central and Eastern Europe, Radio Liberty (formerly Radio Liberation), broadcasting to the USSR, and has recently added Radio and TV Marti as a special service aimed at Cuba and other Caribbean countries. The USSR has one main station, Radio Moscow, the national service, as well as many regional outlets. The Federal Republic of Germany has two, Deutsche Welle and Deutschlandfunk; and although the United Kingdom has only one official station, the British Broadcasting Corporation's World Service, it has an extensive rebroadcasting network throughout the world.

It is not really the number of stations that is important, for these national organizations have access to extremely high-powered transmitters that ensure a wide reception, and there is constant technological improvement. Of greater significance is the number of languages in which these international services are offered. The USSR broadcasts nearly 2,100 hours a week in more than 80 languages. (The number of hours differs for each language.) The Chinese People's Republic Radio Peking broadcasts more than 1,400 hours in 45 languages; the combined American services broadcast more than 2,000 hours in 45 languages, the German stations broadcast more than 780 in 39 languages, and the BBC broadcasts more than 720 hours in 37 languages. Even such minor world powers as North Korea (593 hours), Albania (581 hours), Nigeria (322 hours), and South Africa (205 hours) all transmit their messages over the world's airwaves.

There are other kinds of international broadcasters, but their impact as direct propaganda media is far less. First are the commercial stations, which garner large audiences by targeting their broadcasts to specific listening groups attracted to popular commercial programming. The use of pop music (in a variety of languages) forms the staple content for such stations as Radio Luxembourg, Radio Monte Carlo, and Sri Lanka's All Asia Service. These stations perform a subtle but valuable propaganda role in the international transmission of popular culture. The United States has found that its popular music broadcasts on VOA, particularly jazz, have wide appeal throughout the world, especially in the Soviet Bloc countries.

In recent years a third kind of international broadcaster has begun to make a significant impact on the propaganda scene: the religious broadcaster. Broadcasting more than 1,000 hours a week in a variety of languages, these stations seek to promulgate their own brand of religion to as wide an audience as their transmitters will allow. Usually financed by subscriptions, much of it raised in the United States, they have brought a new type of propaganda to the international scene. Listening to these broadcasts, it is often difficult to separate out the political content from the religious. Vatican Radio began its worldwide service in 1931, the first of the international religious services, and this number has grown to more than 40 (Hale, 1975, p. 124). In the United States there are seven worldwide religious operations, including Adventist World Radio, World Radio Gospel Hour, and the Voice of the Andes. One of Radio Cairo's channels was given over entirely to Islamic teaching—the Voice of the Holy Koran—which used to break off for one hour a day to broadcast the Palestine Liberation Organization's propaganda program. (This service has since been discontinued—a further example of the changes in propaganda priorities brought about by shifting political alliances.) Even the BBC uses the powerful lure of Islamic devotion to attract listeners in Arabic countries by broadcasting readings from the Koran in its Arabic service.

Who is listening to all of this international flow of propaganda information, and what effect is it having? Here we must be careful to examine the effects of international broadcasting within the specific historical, social, and cultural context in which it takes place. There are over 600 million radios in the world outside of the United States, two-thirds of which can receive shortwave broadcasts. In the United States there are over 300 million sets, of which only 3 million can tune into the shortwave band. The transistor revolution and subsequent development of printed circuits have made it possible for radios to be made available in the smallest and poorest villages in the most remote parts of the world. From the rural areas of Latin America to the outback of Siberia and Australia, radio is the major source of outside communication and information. We must also keep in mind that much of the radio received in these areas is of the domestic variety; however, there is still a great deal of international broadcasting that can clearly be labeled *propaganda* attracting audiences.

The main attraction for audiences listening to foreign language broadcasts in the past was to get something they could not get from their domestic radio services. The most important of these alternatives seemed to be the desire for timely, accurate, objective information that the domestic media of many of these countries failed to provide. Often internal control of communications for political reasons forced the population to seek outside sources of information, such as occurred in Brazil after censorship was imposed in 1968. At that time, the VOA and the BBC became the most reliable source of news on events in Brazil itself (Ronalds, 1971). The BBC in particular has earned a reputation for being fair and unbiased in its reporting of events, so much so that during the British-Argentinian conflict British Prime Minister Thatcher became angry because the service reported the truth about casualties and other information that she considered to be harmful to British domestic morale.

In August 1985, members of the news service of the BBC went on strike to protest government interference in the showing of a television documentary on terrorism, which included an interview with a reputed leader of the Irish Republican Army. The government called the interview "dangerous propaganda"; the television news team called it "pertinent information." This strike gained worldwide attention because of the BBC's vaunted reputation for being unbiased. This reputation, earned during World War II, has continued to make the BBC a major international information source for hundreds of millions of listeners who have come to rely upon its daily news reports. The VOA also has a reputation for objectivity, and this accounts for the strong reaction whenever presidents attempt to interject their personal political philosophies into the operations of the VOA. Only by maintaining an unblemished history of fairness do these stations carry any weight with their listeners.

In the United States, where there is an enormous variety of available news sources, all of which is unrestricted by government censorship, there is no clearly perceived need to listen to outside news broadcasts. For this reason there has never been a history of massive shortwave listening, and shortwave radio receivers are not normally found on domestic radio sets. Currently it is estimated that about half-a-million people in the United States regularly listen to shortwave broadcasts, mainly the BBC and Radio Canada International. Those who do listen on a regular basis do so more out of curiosity and as a hobby than to seek out alternative news sources. Thus international radio propaganda is essentially ineffective when aimed at the U.S. population, but such propaganda broadcasts are nevertheless routinely monitored by the government because they can, with careful analysis, reveal the strategies and political maneuvering of the originating countries.

International radio propaganda covers a wide spectrum: on one end there is the osmotic effect of the BBC, which has with patience and professionalism carved a very special niche for itself as a reliable source of information, and all the other nonaggressive national news and cultural services; somewhere in between we find the more propagandistic broadcasts of the VOA, Radio Free Europe, Radio Moscow, Radio Peking, and other nationalistic services deliberately aimed at promoting a specific political perspective to audiences in other countries; at the far end are the aggressive, sometimes vitriolic broadcasts found on Arab language stations in the Middle East, certain African countries, Radio Moscow at times, and wherever there is a need to proclaim "a struggle for freedom."

It is difficult to measure the exact impact of all of this international propaganda broadcasting. Clearly some of it is very effective, particularly when the domestic population is denied access to a variety of alternative news sources, and they turn to outside channels of information. By all accounts most listeners to international broadcasts are sophisticated enough to be wary of blatant propagandizing, although here again the emotional circumstances providing the content of such broadcasts must be taken into consideration. If the message is too much at odds with what the audience believes or suspects to be true, then the end result is less effective than it would have been had it concentrated on a modicum of reality. As Brown (1963) pointed out, "The main lesson to be drawn . . . is how very resistant people are to messages that fail to fit into their own picture of the world and their own objective circumstances, how they deliberately (if unconsciously) seek out only those views which agree with them" (p. 309).

However, despite the caution in claiming success for international propaganda broadcasts, the fact is that many governments in the recent past were concerned enough about the provision of alternative news sources to resort to highly costly jamming of signals. (The People's Republic of China still jams the VOA broadcasts aimed at its population.) The jamming of signals has been around since the beginning of radio itself, and many sophisticated and expensive techniques were developed. But in the end these proved to be largely wasteful exercises, and were not always successful, especially in trying to cover large geographic areas. Thus the USSR, despite its most strenuous efforts, could not prevent some of the signals of the VOA, Radio Free Europe, and Radio Liberty from reaching target audiences. The United States has never had to resort to jamming signals because, as indicated above, the domestic audience for such broadcasts is not very large or likely to be negatively influenced.

International radio broadcasts have at times been a potent force in shaping the world of propaganda in this century, and they are likely to remain so in the foreseeable future, but with a different emphasis. Clearly the battle for the "hearts and minds" of listeners will not be the epic battles of the past between Communism and Capitalism, but probably on a larger world scale between the conflicting cultures of the industrially advanced countries and the less advantaged Third World countries. Between the start of the cold war in the late forties, and the collapse of Communism in the late eighties, the total number of listeners to foreign radio stations rose, partly as a result of the increase in radio sets, but also because of larger populations and the increasing frustration with the inadequacy of the local media in many Third World countries (Hale, 1975). In recent years the use of VCRs has cut into shortwave listening, while local stations in the former Russian satellite countries such as Czeckoslovakia, Hungary, and Poland are now free to broadcast whatever they wish.

Since the collapse of Communism in Europe, the future for international shortwave broadcasting is very uncertain. All jamming of the VOA and RFE in Eastern Euorpe has stopped, and the VOA has even opened an office in Moscow! The sudden change of the world's political configurations in the late eighties caught the propaganda broadcasters by surprise. While the VOA, RFE, and RL each stepped forward to take credit for having contributed significantly to the collapse of Communism by providing an alternative "truth" to its listeners, they were unprepared for a peacetime role. This was particularly true of RFE and RL, both of which had been specifically created to undermine Soviet influence in Eastern Europe. The VOA, (which falls under the umbrella of the United States Information Agency) with its worldwide mandate was less affected, and has already begun to change the basis of its operations away from direct broadcasting to include a major effort at distribution of radio and television material through its "placement" program. This includes sending several hundred hours of original programs via satellite to local radio and television stations throughout the world, especially in Spanish-speaking countries and East Asia (VOA, 1989). These programs range from popular music to question and answer sessions with U.S. government officials. In all of this the VOA adopts a strategy of reflecting the culture of target areas in order to best explain the culture of the United States. A great deal of research is conducted to discover what audiences in these countries need, and as a result this has led to programs with an increased emphasis upon how democracies work, the fundamentals of business enterprises, the workings of capitalism and even on export promotion (Short, 1990).

The future of VOA is still uncertain, and a presidential commission was created in 1990 to examine the state of U.S. government international broadcasting. One of the agenda items is whether VOA radio broadcasts are still needed in view of the new political configurations in the modern world. Kenneth Short, in his analysis of the potential for the future of U.S. international broadcasting efforts, suggests that the VOA should be separated from the USIA. Short (1990) also recommends that

> what the United States must do is to more clearly separate its international broadcasting from domestic politics and foreign policy. The new and comprehensive Voice of America, which is what any recognized radio will be called, must truly speak for the United States and not for the policies of the government in power, howbeit democratically elected. It is essential that a clear and unambiguous voice, one carrying accurate and timely information, be established for the United States. The United States cannot afford to have the "Voice's" impact and credibility undermined amongst listeners by having to speak on behalf of the Department of State. (pp. 28-29)

The U.S. government continues to propagandize against Communism where it still exists. Radio Marti went on the air May 20, 1985, broadcasting to Cuba from studios in Washington, D.C., and relayed from a transmitter in Marathon Key in Florida. Named after a famous hero of the Cuban Revolution against Spain, Jose Marti, thus further angering the Cuban government, this station broadcasts continuously on both medium (AM) and shortwave. The Cubans jam the AM, but 90 percent of the Cuban population has access to shortwave. The idea for Radio Marti originated in the Presidential Commission on Broadcasting to Cuba, which was established by President Reagan in 1981 to make recommendations on how the Reagan administration could "break the Cuban government's information monopoly" and "satisfy the Cuban people's thirst for reliable information about their own country" (Presidential Commission on Broadcasting to Cuba, quoted in Galimore, 1991, p. 2). The U.S. government was determined to undermine Fidel Castro's censorship barrier by making available to the Cuban people news about world affairs as well as news about what was going on in Cuba itself. In 1989 Radio Marti's Office of Audience Research confirmed that 85% of the Cuban population over age 13 were regular listeners to the station.

Radio Marti has proved to be a particularly difficult internal propaganda problem for the U.S. government, in that factions within the large Cuban expatriate community in Florida have continuously pressured for Radio Marti to become more aggressive in encouraging a Cuban revolution against Castro. This would violate the specific guidelines that were established by the advisory board, which stated that Radio Marti "must not encourage defections nor offer assistance to do so and that its broadcasts must avoid unattributed polemic, argumentation and sweeping generalizations and evaluations, and there must not be incitement to revolution or violence." The aim of the station was to present "the truth, hard facts and dispassionate analysis" (Advisory Board for Cuba Broadcasting, 1989, p. 7). The power struggle for the ideological control of Radio Marti continues as the political situation within Cuba itself becomes more unstable with the collapse of international Communism. (TV Marti is discussed below.)

Future technological developments such as Direct Broadcasting Satellites (DBS), which will enable both listeners and viewers to receive signals directly into their homes from satellite dishes parked in space, pose additional problems that have already been the subject of international rancor. (For a detailed discussion of this issue see Nordenstreng & Schiller, 1979.)

Television

Because television is essentially a domestic medium, it has not been extensively used as a means of direct international propaganda (with the exception of TV Marti discussed below). This may change with the introduction of the DBS technology indicated above, but it is unlikely that many countries would allow the cultural disruptions caused by such daily doses of foreign propaganda. Of far greater current danger is the immense amount of indirect propaganda presented under the guise of entertainment that forms the basis of the worldwide trade in television programming. Much like the motion picture industry has done, the giant television industries of the United States, Great Britain, and Germany have dominated the international market for television programs. Most Third World countries are unable to produce sufficient programming to meet their own needs, and the voracious appetite for television entertainment is met by importing programs from elsewhere. The United States alone sells more than 150,000 hours of television programs annually. (This problem is analyzed in some detail in Lee, 1980 and Negrine & Papathanassopoulos, 1990.)

The content of these programs clearly carries ideological messages, and often they create what is called "the frustration of rising expectations" in viewers from less developed countries by presenting an attractive life-style that is beyond their economic means. Ultimately, it is theorized, constant exposure to such a divergence in living conditions will bring about hostility toward the originating country. Schiller (1970) noted, "To foster consumerism in the poor world sets the stage for frustration on a massive scale, to say nothing of the fact that there is a powerful body of opinion there which questions sharply the desirability of pursuing the Western pattern of development" (p. 114). There has been much discussion that one of the major contributing factors in the collapse of the wall between West and East Germany was the daily dose of television images of "conspicuous consumption" that the East Germans could view in the context of their own relatively drab life-styles (Hanke, 1990).

In more sanguine times, it was often thought that the worldwide exchange of television programs would lead to greater international understanding and tolerance, but this has not proved to be the case. Today we have the anomalous situation in which American television programs (such as *Dallas*) are followed with almost religious devotion in many countries, while at the same time there is intense political hostility toward the United States as a symbol of capitalist oppression expressed by those same audiences.

Where television does have a major propaganda function is in the area of news reporting. There have always been complaints about misrepresentation in the reporting of international (as well as domestic) news, but this issue has recently received an unprecedented amount of attention as a result of complaints from Third World countries that their images are being distorted in the Western press. The issue of the imbalance in the "free flow" of information between the industrialized and developing countries became a major topic at international meetings, and a significant issue on the agenda of the fundamental political and economic issues in contemporary society. In particular, UNESCO has been the arena of many ardent discussions on the necessity to develop what has been called the New World Information Order (NWIO). At the General Conference of UNESCO in Nairobi in 1976, it was decided to undertake a major study of the problem of international communication flows. Known as the McBride Commission (Irish statesman Sean McBride was the president of the Commission), the subsequent report *Many Voices, One World* (1980) detailed the extent of the difficulties in reconciling widely differing philosophies on the issue of what constitutes a free flow of information. As the commission report noted, "It has been frequently stated . . . that due to the fact that the content of information is largely produced by the main developing countries, the image of the developing countries is frequently false and distorted. More serious still, according to some vigorous critics, it is this false image, harmful to their inner balance, which is presented to the developing countries themselves" (McBride, 1980, p. 36).

Predictably, the response in the United States to a call for government involvement to ensure a more balanced flow of communication was negative, and was based upon the historical notion of freedom of the press from all government interference. The issues are complex and easily open to misinterpretation depending on one's political philosophy (see Nordenstreng, 1982, for a discussion of this issue). By the early 1990s, UNESCO had begun to downplay the great push for a NWIO in the face of more serious problems, such as worldwide famine and AIDS; this was also a deliberate political decision aimed at allaying any fears that the United States had about the organization. Ultimately, the concept of developing a new world information order, which would provide more balanced coverage to news from developing countries, has not had wide acceptance in the West, and images of famine, corruption, and conflicts still predominate on our nightly news broadcasts. It is in this way that the powerful visual images are presented to television viewers—in broadcasts that seldom have enough time to develop the stories to provide adequate explanations. The "shorthand" nature of television news lends itself to such distortion, thus creating a form of indirect propaganda affecting our perceptions and shaping our attitudes toward a wide variety of issues. We learn to rely on the news media for information, and repeated frequently enough, these images become fixed beliefs, shaping our understanding of the world around us.

There is no clear-cut solution to this problem of distortion; it is an inherent part of a free media system in which market forces dictate the content of the media. The difficulties in reconciling this free market media system—in which the commercial mass media allow audience preferences to shape content—with the understandable desire by countries and individuals to present their "best" images are almost insurmountable. Clearly everyone would like to use the media to propagandize favorably on their behalf, but if the news agencies and television networks in the West feel that their audiences are more interested in learning about political coups, wars, and corruption in Third World countries rather than increases in food production, educational advances, and stable political regimes, then that is what will be featured on the news. This type of indirect and unconscious propaganda is a major product of modern media systems.

Television by its visual nature is vulnerable to misuse as a propaganda medium because it places a premium on using only material with great visual interest to broadcast. The use of "talking heads" to provide expert analysis is only relied upon as a last resort when there is little visual support. Thus in the infamous TWA 847 hostage crisis in Beirut in 1985, the American television networks were forced to rely upon visual material largely generated by the Lebanese hijackers, almost all of which was aimed at presenting the case for the Shiite Moslems in a favorable light. The networks therefore served as unwitting propagandizers, caught by their desperate need to present whatever visual material they could find and in their desire to compete with each other for the viewing audience. The American public, as we have noted before, is not always receptive to such blatant propaganda messages, and the networks were constantly apologizing for presenting them. Here again we witness the differences in conditions favoring successful propaganda in two cultures; for the Moslem terrorists, in a heightened emotional state of conflict and influenced by years of propaganda for their cause, were naive to think that American television viewers would uncritically accept the images emanating from Beirut. It is also important to note that despite the public nature of the propaganda generated by the terrorists, this did not result in any shift away from the "no concessions to terrorists" policy of the Reagan administration. How much this has to do with the decline in the number of such deliberate-staged propagandistic TV events in the period since 1988 is unclear.

The most blatant example of television propaganda is the recent introduction of TV Marti, which started beaming programs into Cuba in August 1990. A specially designed antenna was constructed that guaranteed that the signals could not be picked up within the United States, or interefere with existing domestic or Cuban television reception. The antenna is housed in an aerostat balloon hovering at 10,000 feet above the Florida Keys, and aimed at delivering a "Grade A" signal into the heart of Havana. The Cuban government immediately retaliated by jamming the signal into Havana, but according to reports, the station is received on the outskirts of the city and in outlying areas. It has been reported that 28% of the households in the potential viewing area receive the signals from TV Marti "at least occasionally." If the station is not seen by the majority of the population, then why is so much money being spent on it? The 1991 *Special Report on TV Marti* suggested several reasons for the need for both Radio and TV Marti.

For example, wise contingency planning leads us to believe that unforseen events causing instability in the Cuban government may precipitate a disruption of state broadcasts and/or jamming efforts, causing a disoriented Cuban society to be even more reliant on TV and Radio Marti as credible sources of news and information. . . . And still further in the future, both Radio and TV Marti will be indispensable elements in the U.S. government's efforts to educate Cuban citizens on the ways of democracy and its institutions following a democratic transition in Cuba. (pp. 7-8)

Both of these stations are bombarding the Cuban people with propaganda in the guise of entertainment as well as deliberate political messages. The use of these two broadcasting units by the U.S. government is as much a form of psychological warfare, as it is a threat to Cuba's economy. The Cuban government is forced to spend a great deal of its already depleted cash reserves on the very expensive jamming operation; and has declared that the watching of TV Marti or listening to Radio Marti is "an act of civil disobedience" (*Special Report*, 1991, p. 10).

During the Gulf War Crisis (1990-1991), the emergence of the Cable News Network (CNN), and the invaluable role it played as the major disseminator of news throughout the world took a great number of people by surprise. The Gulf War was the first major conflict of a global nature since the introduction of worldwide television satellite services, and the potential of these systems was dramatically illustrated by the instantaneous broadcasts of events from the embattled area. When CNN reporters remained in Baghdad after the war had actually begun, the world was witness to an unprecedented series of live broadcasts from within the enemy's capital city while it was actually under bombardment. CNN was criticized by some politicians and members of the public for playing into the hands of enemy propaganda, but on the whole, these broadcasts were well received and widely viewed. The question of CNN's unwitting role in "giving aid and comfort to the enemy" by showing the damage to civilian life within Iraq was widely debated at the time, with no clear public consensus emerging, except that viewers found the service almost indispensable.

The reporting of the Gulf War also raised new questions about the relationship between the media and the military; it was obvious that the instantaneous technologies available for disseminating news from the battlefields had clashed with the military's need and desire to control what images would actually be seen. The result was that the military denied access to all but a few reporters whom it could control through the use of official "pool" coverage, with military escorts. While this system was introduced in the name of safety (for troops and reporters), the end result was a great deal of dissatisfaction on the part of the media, and a large segment of the public, with the appearance of deliberately manipulated coverage. These are essentially political questions that will take many years to sort out satisfactorily. What was clear by the end of the Gulf War was that new communication technologies had fundamentally altered the way that all future wars would be reported.

It is difficult to predict exactly how much of a role television will play in direct international propaganda in the future. It is doubtful that the use of DBS will be allowed in the same fashion as international radio broadcasting, and the methods of technological control (going so far as to destroy offending satellites), are much easier. It is very likely that we will see a continuation of the argument surrounding the misrepresentation of countries and groups in those countries in which the media are not too tightly controlled by the government. On the other hand, where governments do have control of the media systems, television will continue to play a major role in propagandizing activities, as much through the ideological perspectives of so-called entertainment as through the management of the images presented in the news. The potential use of the VCR and the Mini-Cam for the circulation of taped material in a "closed network" is another medium that has just begun to be explored for propaganda purposes. It was widely acknowledged that the circulation of illicit underground tapes in Eastern Europe, even though the number of privately owned VCR's was small, was a significant factor in coalescing opposition groups. We are only now beginning to realize the enormous potential for television as a major propaganda medium in modern society.

Advertising: The Ubiquitous Propaganda

There is little doubt that under any definition of propaganda, the practice of advertising would have to be included. Advertising is a series of appeals, symbols, and statements deliberately designed to influence the receiver of the message toward the point of view desired by the communicator and to act in some specific way as a result of receiving the message, whether it be to purchase, vote, hold positive or negative views, or merely to maintain a memory. Also, advertising is not always in the best interest of the receiver of the message (refer to Figure 1.3).

It is the deliberateness of the intention and the carefully constructed nature of the specific appeal that distinguish advertising from other forms of persuasive communication; also, in our society advertising is generally communicated at a cost to the communicator. Whether it be paid advertising in the traditional sense or the production of leaflets or handbills on a small duplicating machine, advertising usually involves the cost of production and distribution. The advertiser (communicator) in turn hopes that this cost will be returned eventually in the form of some benefit such as the purchase of a product, the casting of a vote, or positive or negative feelings. In fact, advertising is the most ubiquitous form of propaganda in our society. It is found everywhere we look, almost everywhere we listen, and its pressure is felt in every commercial transaction we make. The use of advertising as a means of informing the public about the choices and availability of goods and services is an integral part of the free-enterprise capitalist system. Although there have been some exceptions (the Hershey Chocolate Bar became a big seller, although it did not do consumer advertising until the early 1970s), advertising is the primary means of stimulating the sales of the products of our consumer-oriented society, and as such has a direct influence in the economy. However, there are many critics of advertising who point out that vast sums of money are spent on promoting an increasingly wider range of choices for an already overburdened market—after all, does our society really need to choose from more than thirty brands of toothpaste? The debate about the actual economic utility of advertising is also echoed by economists, who disagree about whether of not advertising increases the costs of goods by creating a larger potential market, and thereby lowering unit costs, or merely adding to the cost of producing and selling these goods. These arguments have existed ever since advertising became an essential part of modern capitalist economies in the nineteenth century (Pope, 1983).

Advertising also serves as the financial base for our vast mass communications network, for the structure of our commercialized media system is totally dependent on the revenues from advertising. Even our public broadcast systems depend to some extent on being underwritten by funds from the business sector. Although advertising may be considered an intrusion into our television viewing, magazine or newspaper reading, or enjoyment of the radio, we accept its existence because we understand its role in making possible our enjoyment of these media. If we really consider the actual structure of the commercial media system, it is the audience that is being delivered to the advertiser and not the other way around.

Institutional Propaganda

In our society advertising is institutional propaganda at its most obvious level. It serves as a constant reminder that we are being bombarded with messages intended to bring us to a certain point of view. Yet we can only absorb so much of what we are expected to, and so we have learned to cope with this enormous information overload. We may look, but not really see the television commercial; we may listen, but not really hear the radio jingle; and we leaf by print ads without paying attention. But every so often we do see or hear or read, and this is what is intended by the creators of advertising. From the more than 1,600 "messages" we are exposed to every day, we remember at most only about 80 (Heilbroner, 1985).

In 1990, more than $120 billion was spent on advertising expenditures in the United States; this was for all types of advertising, from $850,000 commercials on the Superbowl telecast to the classified ads in the local neighborhood paper. There are more than 28,000 nationally advertised brands for sale in the United States (Heilbroner, 1985). It is the job of the advertisers (and their appointed advertising agencies) to make their brand stand out from the rest, and so we are inundated with advertising campaigns extolling the specific virtues of individual products, services, institutions, or individuals.

The Science of Advertising

It is in this process of product differentiation that advertising propaganda is selective and often distortive in what it tells the consumer. The desire to appear to be different, or to be considered a superior product, or to provide faster, more reliable service encourages the use of hyperbole and exaggeration, and this in turn has created a nation of skeptical consumers. To overcome this growing scepticism, and to increase the chances of success in an already overcrowded marketplace, advertisers have resorted to a wide range of techniques from the most obvious to the very subtle to attract attention to their specific propaganda strategy. In the act of gaining the consumers' attention we are all too familiar with the blatancy of the bikini-clad woman on the car hood, but most of us are unaware of the effectiveness of the psychologically tested and then readjusted copy for a headache remedy seen on the nightly network news. Increasingly advertisers are resorting to a variety of scientific testing methods to maximize the expenditure of their advertising budgets by increasing the potential of their message getting through the morass, and this includes close demographic analysis of their target audience; an understanding of the psychological framework of receptivity for their message and whatever adjustments might be necessary to improve this; a study of the effectiveness of one specific message versus another specific message; and even the application of the psychology of color to shape the mood of the audience.

Despite all of this expensive scientific analysis, much of advertising remains ineffective and the list of failed products continues to grow. As we have noted many times in this book, not all propaganda is successful, for a variety of reasons. The message may not be convincing enough to warrant the consumer to change existing behavior (or purchase) patterns; or the product may not be seen as utilitarian or cost effective; or there might just be plain, old scepticism, for after all, advertising has a long history of being deceptive or distortive. Of course, advertising can also be extremely effective when the right combination of circumstances comes together, and there are many examples of advertising success stories. However, despite its proven effectiveness as a "mover of goods," or perhaps because of it, public attitudes toward advertising are often very negative. In many ways the consumer's experience with advertising has made him or her suspicious of all propaganda, and this might prove to be a healthy trend in our society. It will force advertisers and other propagandists to improve the quality of their messages and diminish the possibility of negative propaganda influence. If consumers are aware that they are being propagandized, the choice to accept or reject the message is theirs alone.

The Role of Advertising

In his book *Advertising: The Uneasy Persuasion* the sociologist Michael Schudson (1984) suggests that advertising in the capitalist system serves the same function as the poster-art of authoritarian socialism, the state-sanctioned art which was pervasive in the former Soviet Union. We are all familiar with those realistic posters of sturdy men and healthy women, working in wheat fields or factories and affirming the joys of socialism; in Schudson's interesting metaphor, advertising serves the same function, depicting equally healthy capitalists driving cars, smoking cigarettes, drinking beer, or wearing designer jeans, and essentially enjoying the materialist fruits of the free-enterprise system. As Schudson (1984) notes,

American advertising, like socialist realist art, simplifies and typifies. It does not claim to picture reality as it should be—life and lives worth emulating. . . . It always assumes that there is progress. It is thoroughly optimistic, providing for any troubles that it identifies a solution in a particular product or style of life. It focuses, of course, on the new, and if it shows signs of respect for tradition, this is only to help in assimilation of some new commercial creation. (p. 215)

Advertising in our society, therefore, has a symbolic and cultural utility that transcends the mere selling of merchandise, but "the aesthetic of capitalist realism—without a masterplan of purposes—glorifies the pleasures and freedoms of consumer choice in defense of the virtues of private life and material ambitions" (Schudson, 1984, p. 218).

Schudson's unique perspective on advertising provides us with insightful confirmation of precisely why advertising is the most plentiful form of propaganda found in today's society. Like the socialist-realist art it emulates, advertising serves as a constant reminder of the cultural and economic basis of our society. We do not always respond to all of the messages we receive, but its pervasiveness provides a sort of psychic comfort that our socioeconomic system is still working.

In the final analysis, advertising as propaganda has been largely responsible for the creation of the massive consumer culture in the twentieth century, as well as fundamentally altering the nature of political practices in democratic societies. (This theme is developed at length in Qualter, 1991.) Together with the growth of the mass media and improvements in transportation and communications, it is one of the forces that have contributed to the emergence of the mass culture discussed earlier in this chapter. Good or evil, honest or dishonest, economically vital or wasteful, advertising is with us as long as we choose to live in a capitalist economic system, the ultimate success of which is dependent upon a high level of consumption of the products and services of this system. Where the real danger lies is in the increasing use of the tactics of this consumer advertising to market political figures and ideologies. This has resulted in a public that is increasingly ill-informed to make important political decisions on a rational basis, but which is instead, becoming more reliant upon the sophisticated manipulation of images and symbols.

4 Propaganda and Persuasion Examined

A seventy-five year history of social science research has yielded much valuable insight into propaganda and persuasion. Researchers began to investigate propaganda after World War I, and by World War II major studies were being conducted in attitude research. Recent research has included new insights into attitude formation and the study of behavior. It is believed that effects are highly conditional, depending upon individual differences, the context in which propaganda and persuasion take place, and a variety of contingent third variables.

The Modern Study of Propaganda and Persuasion

Studies of propaganda in the early part of the twentieth century were antecedents to the social scientific study of persuasion. After World War II, researchers stopped referring to their subject of study as "propaganda" and started investigating various constructs of "persuasion," which has become a highly developed subject in communication and social psychology. Today, the research tradition started in the 1920s continues with various analyses of mass-mediated information about politics, international issues, and trends in news coverage as well as studies of media content that are related to public concerns. Although many books date the modern study of propaganda and persuasion in the 1930s and 1940s with the beginnings of the scientific study of persuasion, interest in the use of propaganda in World War I prompted earlier investigation.

Propaganda in World War I

The period during World War I was the first time that the populations of entire nations were actively involved in a global struggle.

The citizens of Europe and America were asked to forego their own pleasures for the sake of the war effort. Money had to be collected; material comforts had to be sacrificed. All-out public cooperation was essential. To accomplish these ends, attempts were made to arouse hatred and fear of the enemy and to bolster the morale of the people. Mass media were used in ways they had never been used before to propagandize entire populations to new heights of patriotism, commitment to the war effort, and hatred of the enemy. Carefully designed propaganda messages were communicated through news stories, films, photograph records, speeches, books, sermons, poster, rumors, billboard advertisements, and handbills to the general public. "Wireless" radio transmission was considered to be the new medium for shaping public attitudes. It was believed that radio propaganda could weld the masses into an amalgamation of "hate and will and hope" (Lasswell, 1927, p. 221).

Nationwide industrial efforts were mounted with great haste, and the support of civilians who worked in industry was enlisted. Propaganda was developed and used to bring about cooperation between the industrialized society and the fighting armed forces. Posters depicting workers and soldiers arm-in-arm were plastered over walls in factories throughout America. The Committee on Public Information (CPI), under the direction of George Creel was commissioned to "sell the war to America." Creel established a division of labor publications with former labor organizer Robert Maisel as its head. Maisel's task was to produce and distribute literature to American workers. Another organization, the American Alliance for Labor and Democracy, was formed under the leadership of Samuel Gompers of the American Federation of Labor (AFL) to maintain peace and harmony in the unions in connection with the war effort.

The CPI sponsored a national speakers bureau on behalf of Liberty Bond sales drives and distributed more than 100 million posters and pamphlets. Wartime propaganda in America and abroad turned out to be very skillful, highly coordinated, and was considered by its audiences to be quite powerful.

Although much of the propaganda was factual and accurate, some of it was deceptive and exaggerated. Both the Allies and the Germans circulated false atrocity stories. The Allies told the story of Germans boiling down corpses of their soldiers to be used for fats. The story's inventors deliberately mistranslated *kadaver* as *corpse* instead of *animal* and circulated the story of a "corpse factory" worldwide in an effort to destroy pro-German sentiments. They knew that the German word *kadaver*, which literally means "a corpse," is used in

German to refer only to the body of an animal and never to that of a human, but the non-German-speaking audience did not know this. The story was invented in 1917 and was not exposed as false until 1925 during a debate in the British House of Commons (Qualter, 1962). Atrocity stories along with other more tasteful propaganda efforts were considered to be quite effective.

Aftermath of World War I and the Growing Concern About Propaganda

After the armistice, in the early 1920s, the experts who were involved in the development of wartime propaganda began to have second thoughts about their manipulation of the public. Some of them experienced guilt over the lies and deceptions that they had helped to spread.

George Creel recounted his experiences with the CPI in *How We Advertised America: The First Telling of the Amazing Story of the Committee on Public Information, 1917-1919*, published in 1920. In his book, Creel tells of the congressional attempt to suppress his report of the CPI's propaganda activities. Creel, who was proud of his activities, discussed in detail the history of the CPI's domestic and foreign activities.

There was widespread concern about the power of the developing forms of mass media, for some people believed that the mass media had extensive, direct, and powerful effects on attitude and behavior change. Harold Lasswell (1927) stated in grandiose language the belief that the media could sway public opinion and the masses toward almost any point of view in *Propaganda Technique in the World War*.

> But when all allowances have been made, and all extravagant estimates pared to the bone, the fact remains that propaganda is one of the most powerful instrumentalities in the modern world. It has arisen to its present eminence in response to a complex of changed circumstances which have altered the nature of society.
>
> . . . A newer and subtler instrument must weld thousands and even millions of human beings into one amalgamated mass of hate and will and hope. A new flame must burn out the canker of dissent and temper the steel of bellicose enthusiasm. The name of this new hammer and anvil of social solidarity is propaganda. (pp. 220-221)

Lasswell expressed his awe of propaganda in this pioneer work, noting that the people had been duped and degraded by propaganda during the war.

Works such as Lasswell's and Creel's expressed a fear of propaganda; whereas, others saw the need to analyze propaganda and its effects. Lasswell based his work on a stimulus-response model rooted in *learning theory*. Focused on mass effects, this approach viewed human responses to the media as uniform and immediate. E. D. Martin expressed the approach simply: "propaganda offers ready-made opinions for the unthinking herd" (Choukas, 1965, p. 15). Known as the "magic bullet" or "hypodermic needle theory" of direct influence effects, it was not as widely accepted by scholars as many books on mass communication indicate (Hardt, 1989; Lang 1989; Sproule, 1991).

Research concerning important intervening variables—for example, demographic background of the audience, selective perception, and other social and mental states of receivers—disputed the idea of direct influence. Such research led to "limited effects" models that explained the impact of media as a function of the social environment in which they operate. Effects came to be understood as activating and reinforcing preexisting conditions in the audience. It was not, however, until the end of the 1920s that human individual modifiability and variability began to be demonstrable through research.

The Social Sciences and the Study of Propaganda

After World War I, social psychology began to flourish as a research field and an academic discipline. In 1918, Thomas and Znaniecki defined social psychology as the study of attitudes. Other social sciences such as sociology and psychology were also stimulated by the need to pursue questions about human survival in an age in which social strain grew heavy with concerns about warfare, genocide, economic depression, and human relationships. These questions were about influence, leadership, decision making, and changes in people institutions, and nations. Such questions were also related to the phenomena of propaganda, public opinion, attitude change, and communication.

Marketing research also began to be developed in the 1920s. Surveys of consumers to analyze buying habits and effectiveness of advertising were refined by sampling techniques in the 1930s and were used to poll political as well as consumer preferences.

Public opinion research also began to develop. Walter Lippmann's (1922) *Public Opinion* voiced a concern that people were influenced by modern media, especially by the newspapers. In 1937, *Public Opinion Quarterly* began to be published. The editorial foreword in the first issue proclaimed, "For the first time in history, we are confronted nearly everywhere by mass opinion as the final determinant of political and economic action. . . . Scholarship is developing new possibilities of scientific approach as a means of verifying hypotheses and of introducing greater precision of thought and treatment" (1937, p. 3).

The Payne Fund studies, discussed in the previous chapter, assessed the effects of films on children and adolescents in the 1930s with respect to individual differences such as economic background, education, home life, neighborhood, gender, and age.

In 1933, the President's Research Committee on Recent Social Trends called the fields of research in propaganda analysis, public opinion analysis, social psychology, and marketing research "agencies of mass impression" (Czitrom, 1982, p. 126). Mass media, then, was considered to be a common denominator from which questions of behavioral and attitudinal change were to be studied. The media industries provided funding for research along with easily quantifiable data to be analyzed. Applied research also became the by-product of industrial and governmental institutions and centers, institutes, and universities. A substantial body of behavioral and social scientists turned their attention to communication studies.

Research in Persuasion: The Study of Attitudes

Although the flurry of research following the end of World War I was related to evaluating propaganda messages, much of the subsequent research had to do with persuasion, specifically the study of attitudes. During the 1920s and 1930s, research in persuasion was attitude research. Emphasis was placed on conceptually defining attitudes and operationally measuring them. Gordon Allport's (1935) definition of attitude was one of the most important: "An attitude is a mental and neural state of readiness organized through experience, and exerting a directive influence upon the individual's response to all objects and situations with which it is related" (p. 784). The concept of attitudes was so central to research that Allport said, "attitude is probably the most distinctive and indispensable concept in contemporary American social psychology" (p. 784).

Bogardus (1925), Thurstone (1929), and Likert (1932) developed three measures of attitudes. The Likert scale has been one of the most widely used attitude-measurement techniques and is still being used. It is a scale consisting of categories indicating attitude strength with a "strongly approve" answer graduating down to a "strongly disapprove" response on a five-point linear scale. The Thurstone scales, which weighted a series of attitudinal statements of equal intervals, were used in some of the Payne Fund studies. A representative study that used attitude-measuring scales to determine propaganda effects was done by Rosenthal (1934), who found that Russian silent propaganda films changed socioeconomic attitudes of American students. He also found that stereotypes were easier to arouse than to eradicate.

Another widely used attitude-measurement instrument was developed by Osgood, Suci, and Tannenbaum (1957). The semantic differential focuses on the meaning that people give to a word or concept. This procedure allows people to reveal an attitude by rating a concept on a scale of verbal opposites, such as good and bad with several blank spaces in between the poles. The midpoint in the blank spaces can be an indicator of neutrality. The semantic differential reveals the particular dimensions that people use to qualify their experience, the types of concepts that are regarded as similar or different in meaning, and the intensity of meaning given to a particular concept.

The study of attitude and attitude change has received more attention than any other topic in social psychology or communication, yet scholars are still far from achieving conclusive links between attitudes and behavior. One of the early studies of behavior and attitudes was done by Richard Lapiere in 1934 who toured the United States with a Chinese couple. They stayed at hotels and ate at restaurants, keeping records of how they were treated. After the trip, Lapiere wrote to all of the places they had visited and asked if they accepted or served Chinese persons as guests. A great majority wrote back and said that they did not. From this, Lapiere concluded that the social attitudes of the hotel and restaurant managements had little correspondence with their behavior.

World War II and Research in Communication

When World War II broke out in Europe, researchers turned their attention to studies of propaganda, counterpropaganda, attitudes, and persuasion. The studies conducted during and after the war were primarily undertaken by social psychologists and psychologists who used careful controls to measure effects. The war caused intense concern about the persuasive powers of the mass media and their potential for directly altering attitudes and behavior. Wartime research was conducted by the American government which was greatly concerned with the nature of German propaganda, the British communication system in wartime, and the means by which the

U.S. Office of War Information bolstered civilian morale as well as how to make commercial media fare more relevant to the military struggle (Lazarsfeld & Stanton, 1944).

Paul Lazarsfeld, professor of Sociology at Columbia University and head of the Bureau of Applied Social Research, along with other behavioral scientists, produced "Research in Communication" in 1940. This memorandum was a review of the state of the art of research at the time. He reduced the subject of communication research to four categories: (a) who, (b) said what, (c) to whom, and (d) with what effect. Lazarsfeld regarded the last category as the most crucial one.

The four-question scheme ("who said what to whom with what effect?") became the dominant paradigm defining the scope and problems of American communication research. It restricted communication to a narrow model of persuasion that guided research into the postwar era. Lazarsfeld's approach represented European positivism, the scientific approach of the Vienna Circle influenced by Albert Einstein and Ernst Mach. The Frankfurt School of critical theory was represented by Theodor Adorno and Max Horkheimer who were also in exile in America. These scholars were concerned with the values and ideological images reflected in media content. Less concerned with immediate effects, they addressed the more subtle and long-term implications of the underlying structure and the implicit themes in the media. Adorno was based in the Princeton Office of Radio Research. Lazarsfeld recalled in his memoirs the hope to "develop a convergence of European theory and American empiricism" (Fleming & Bailyn, 1969, p. 324). Lazarsfeld perceived critical research in opposition to his practice of administrative research, however, as Hardt (1989) points out, he failed to consider the role of culture and media in society. Lazarsfeld's focus was on mass media effects that were predictive, thus his methodology was empirical.

Some of the wartime research, however, could not measure effects. A study by Speier and Otis (1944), *Radio Research*, is representative of the content analyses of newscasts to determine the functions of such newscasts. They content-analyzed German radio propaganda to France during the Battle of France and found that the function of propaganda to the enemy in total war is "to realize the aim of war—which is victory—without acts of physical violence, or with less expenditure of physical violence than would otherwise be necessary" (p. 210). Speier and Otis also found that when actual fighting had not yet begun, the propagandist used propaganda as a substitute for physical violence; whereas, when actual fighting was going on, propaganda changed into a supplement to physical violence. For example, before fighting began in France, the Germans attempted to terrorize with words, threatening physical violence in order to get France to negotiate rather than fight. Once fighting actually began, the Germans changed their tactics and chronicled their acts and victories over the radio.

Merton and Lazarsfeld summarized the nature of effect studies in "Studies in Radio and Film Propaganda" (1968). These studies used content analysis and response analysis of pamphlets, films, and radio programs. Response analysis was derived through the "focused interview" and a "program analyzer", a device that enabled the listener of a radio program to press a button to indicate what he or she liked or disliked. Responses recorded on tape synchronized with the radio program, registering approval, disapproval, or neutrality, and were plotted into a statistical curve of response. Through response analysis, the researchers were able to determine (a) the effect aspects of the propaganda to which the audience had responded, (b) the many-sided nature of responses, (c) whether the expected responses had occurred, and (d) unanticipated responses. For example, a radio program designed to bolster American morale shortly after Pearl Harbor contained two dominant themes: the first stressed the power and potentiality of the United States in order to combat defeatism; the second emphasized the strength of the enemy in order to combat complacency and overconfidence. Response analysis revealed that the emphasis on the strength of the United States reinforced complacency of those who were already complacent, and, correlatively, references to enemy strength supported defeatism of those who were already defeatist (Merton, 1968).

The benchmark for the initiation of sociobehavioral experiments in the area of attitude change, communication, and the acquisition of factual knowledge from instructional media came from studies conducted by a group of distinguished social and behavioral scientists who had been enlisted into service by the U.S. Army. Working within the Information and Educational Division of the War Department, the Research Branch assisted the army with a variety of problems, involving psychological measurement and evaluation of programs. Some of their experiments were among the first to determine how specific content affected particular audiences. The best known of these experiments was the research that tested the effects of the army orientation films, a series called *Why We Fight*.

Frank Capra, the well-known Hollywood director, had been commissioned by the army to make a series of training films for recruits.

He produced seven films that traced the history of World War II from 1931 to Pearl Harbor and America's mobilization for war. As they trained to fight in the war, hundreds of thousands of Americans saw these films. The army wanted to find out whether the films did an effective job of teaching the recruits factual knowledge about the war and whether the factual knowledge shaped interpretations and opinions in ways necessary to developing an acceptance of military roles and related sacrifices.

The main team that conducted the studies consisted of Frances J. Anderson, John L. Finan, Carl I. Hovland, Irving L. Janis, Arthur A. Lumsdaine, Nathan Macoby, Fred D. Sheffield, and M. Brewster Smith. The results were published by Hovland, Lumsdaine, and Sheffield in 1949 in a work entitled *Experiments on Mass Communication*, which also included other experiments on communication issues. This work touched off considerable interest in the experimental study of persuasion during the postwar years.

Four of the seven *Why We Fight* films were included in the study. Several research procedures were used, including sampling, control groups, matching, pretesting, and measurement. The results showed that the films were not effective in achieving the goal of motivating the recruits to serve and fight in the war. The films were also not effective in influencing attitudes related to the army's orientation objectives, for example, deepening resentment toward the enemy, giving greater support to the British, and demanding unconditional surrender. They were, however, somewhat effective in shaping a few attitudes related to the interpretation of the content of the films, for example, that the failure of Germany to invade England during the Battle of Britain was a Nazi defeat. On the other hand, the films were markedly effective in teaching the subjects factual knowledge about the war. In fact, the majority of the recruits tested retained the same, correct answers when retested one week later. Although the films failed to influence attitudes and motivation of the recruits, they were most successful in presenting information to enhance learning.

Other research on the *Why We Fight* films tested the subjects' attitudes toward the films themselves. Results showed that the recruits liked the films, accepted the information in them as accurate, and did not perceive them as untruthful propaganda (Lowery & DeFleur, 1988). Several characteristics of the audience were tested including intellectual ability and how it related to learning from the films.

There were other studies to determine if a one-sided argument was more effective than a two-sided argument. After the German surrender, soldiers in training camps listened to radio speeches that attempted to persuade them to continue the war against Japan. Results indicated that the two-sided message produced greater attitude change than the one-sided message, especially among those who initially opposed prolonging the war. In contrast, the one-sided message brought about greater attitude change among those who initially supported prolonging the war. In addition, it was found that the better educated respondents were more favorably affected by the two-sided message, whereas the less well-educated were more responsive to the one-sided message.

The results of the research conducted by the Information and Education Division during the war were very important to the development of communication research. No longer were the media considered to be an all-powerful shaper of attitudes because the effects of films and radio broadcasts were clearly limited. Now the effects of mass communication were understood to be strongly influenced by individual differences in the audience.

Another research breakthrough occurred during the same era along with the development of new survey techniques for studying the interrelationship between the media and persuasion in natural settings over time. Lazarsfeld and his associates conducted a panel study during the presidential election of 1940 to determine whether mass media influenced political attitudes. What they found instead, as the interviews progressed from month to month, was that people were receiving information and influence from other people. Face-to-face discussions were a more important source of political influence than the media. The finding was a serendipitous one that had not been anticipated.

When they discovered what was happening, the researchers revised their plans and gathered as much data as they could about interpersonal communication during the campaign. They discovered that people were actually being influenced by *opinion leaders* who had received their information from the media. From this they developed the "two-step flow" model of communication effects through discussion with their peers (Lazarsfeld, Berelson, & Gaudet, 1948). This model was later revised to become a "multistep flow" model that has people obtaining ideas and information from the media, but seeking out opinion leaders for confirmation of their ideas and forming their attitudes. Later research indicated that a highly variable number of relays can exist between the media, the message receivers, and attitude formation (Rogers & Shoemaker, 1971).

Lazarsfeld et al. also found that when the political campaign persuaded at all, it served more to activate and reinforce voter predispositions than to change attitudes. They concluded that "exposure is always selective; in other words, a positive relationship exists between people's opinions and what they choose to listen to or read" (1948, p. 166).

Kurt Lewin, psychologist and German expatriate, was instrumental in wartime research on how to persuade Americans to change their food buying and eating habits to accept eating nutritious organ meats such as liver and kidney in times of meat shortages. His studies showed that discussion among shoppers when followed by a group decision was a more effective strategy to produce change than lectures by experts. This led to Lewin's conceptualization of a *gatekeeper*, someone who controls the flow of information. The gatekeeping function of the media has since become a significant factor that determines what gets into print or on the air (Lang, 1989).

The Yale Studies

After the war, Carl Hovland returned to Yale University, gathered a group of thirty colleagues, and developed what has since become known as the "Yale approach" to persuasion. The Yale group examined attitude change in a variety of experimental contexts. Working from a learning theory perspective that was based on stimulus-response, they investigated effects of many variables in persuasion. They were among the first researchers to examine the effects of source credibility on information processing. They found that source credibility had no effect on immediate comprehension, but it had substantial effect upon attitude change, although it was a short-lived effect.

Kelman and Hovland (1953) found that because people tend to disassociate source and content over time, the effects of source credibility were not as pervasive as they thought, and they called this a "sleeper effect." After people have forgotten the name and qualifications of a persuader, the influence of source credibility in changing their attitude disappears, leaving the people with the message content that provides the basis for their attitudes. Contemporary researchers call this a "dissociation hypothesis" rather than a true sleeper effect, which would be the case when a persuasive message results in little initial change followed by a delayed increase in impact on attitude or behavior change (Pratkanis & Greenwald, 1985).

Other variables that the Yale group investigated were personality traits and susceptibility to persuasion, the ordering of arguments (primacy-recency), explicit versus implicit conclusions (see Chapter 1), and fear appeals. The results on fear appeals were surprising to the researchers and of great interest to anyone studying propaganda because weak fear appeals turned out to have more influence on subjects than moderate and strong fear appeals did (Hovland, Janis, & Kelly, 1953). Over the next thirty years, researchers continued to study the impact of fear appeals on audiences with paradoxical results. In some instances, strong fear appeals were found to be persuasive; in others they were not. Boster and Mongeau (1984) did a review of fear-arousing messages since 1952, including a meta-analysis of 25 studies on fear appeals and attitude change. They concluded that a positive correlation between fear-arousing messages and attitude change might exist when certain potentially intervening variables are taken into account. These are as follows: age, certain personality traits, and whether the individual voluntarily has exposed him- or herself to the message.

The Yale group had wanted to discover governing laws of persuasion in laboratory settings. Many of the "laws" did not hold up over time, but their work led to a greater understanding of persuasion and stimulated subsequent research in persuasion for years to come.

Consistency Theories

One of the major groupings of laws that came out of the Yale group's research is known as *consistency theory*. Consistency theorists view the desire or drive for consistency as a central motivator in attitude-formation and behavior. Cognitive consistency is the mental agreement between a person's notions about some object or event. The underlying assumption is that when new information is contradictory or inconsistent with a person's attitudes, it will lead to some confusion and tension. This tension motivates a person to alter or adjust his/her behaviors. For example, most people, including those who smoke, have a positive attitude toward good health and longevity. Information about smoking as a cause of disease and death can create tension in smokers. When the tension due to inconsistency between attitude and behavior is no longer tolerable, smokers may adjust their behaviors by giving up cigarettes. The same inconsistency has produced new laws and ordinances about smoking in public places and on airplanes.

All consistency theories are based on the belief that people need to be consistent or at least perceive themselves as consistent. There is a human tendency toward balance, often called *homeostasis*. When there is imbalance in the human cognitive system, attitude and behavior change tend to result. Most consistency theories (Heider's balance theory, 1946, Osgood & Tannenbaum's congruity principle,

1955) attempt to predict the nature and degree of change that occur under conditions of inconsistency. The best known of the consistency theories is Festinger's *theory of cognitive dissonance.*

In 1957, Leon Festinger published *Theory of Cognitive Dissonance,* which generated a great deal of research, speculation, and argument over the long term. Festinger said that once a person has made an important decision, he or she is in a committed state. If alternatives are presented, the person is susceptible to cognitive dissonance or psychological discomfort. This is based on the need to have consistency among one's cognitive elements. For example, if a person was committed to working for a large corporation and was forced to make a negative speech about it, that person would be put into a state of cognitive dissonance because of the inconsistency. Dissonance can be alleviated in a number of ways including rationalization, avoidance, and seeking new support. The person could say that "it's only a job," or not think about the speech after it is given, or look for stronger reasons to support the commitment to the company. If there is a high discrepancy between the commitment and the inconsistent act, change will occur.

Festinger would say, in the case of wide discrepancy, that the person would change the commitment to the corporation after making a negative speech about it to bring attitude in line with behavior. This theory accounts for the practice of forced behavior producing attitude change. This influenced Daryl Bem's (1970) *theory of self-perception,* which states that an individual relies on external cues to infer internal states. Bem uses the example of the question, "Why do you like brown bread?" with its response "Because I eat it." This is an example of a self-attribution theory that will be discussed later in this chapter.

Theory of Exposure Learning

Social psychologists have amassed considerable evidence that affirms a truism about propaganda; that is, the more people are exposed to an idea, the more they are apt to accept to it. Robert Zajonc (1968) conducted a series of studies in which stimuli were exposed to viewers. Regardless of whether the stimuli were meaningful or not (Chinese characters, nonsense words), subjects who saw them more often liked them better. Zajonc (1980) suggested that there is comfort in familiarity. Zimbardo and Leippe (1991) extended this idea with their review of studies of subject exposure to stimuli that were previously liked or disliked. Frequent exposure intensified previous positive and negative attitudes. This "build-up" of attitude intensity is a factor in polarization of attitudes with repeated exposure.

Social Judgment Theory

Intensity is a key feature of social judgment theory, for it not only develops the concept of the direction of an attitude (like-dislike) but it also examines the level of ego-involvement. Ego-involvement is the degree of involvement of a person and how the person's life is affected by an issue. A linear scale is used to determine a subject's latitude of acceptance, rejection, or noncommitment. If a subject's perception of a message falls within the latitude of acceptance, he/she tends to perceive the message closer to his/her position than it actually is, which results in an assimilation effect. If the message lies in the latitude of rejection, it will be perceived much further from a person's position than it actually is, which produces contrast effects. The intensity of ego-involvement produces a wide latitude of rejection. Social judgment theory is used to predict attitudes on the basis of latitude of acceptance and ego-involvement and has been widely used to predict political election outcomes.

Resistance to Persuasion

Most of the research of the 1950s and 1960s was based on attempts of a persuader attempting to change attitudes in an audience, but William J. McGuire (1964) investigated factors that induced resistance to persuasion, producing a work that changed the focus of persuasion research. Using some novel techniques to involve people in creating their own defenses against persuasion, McGuire developed "inoculation theory," which focused on a strategy analogous to physical immunization against disease. He used what he called "cultural truisms"; that is, beliefs one holds that are so ingrained within the cultural milieu that they had never been attacked. First, a cultural truism would be mildly attacked. Because the subject had never dealt with such an attack, he or she needed help in developing a defense against it. Pretreatment in the form of supportive statements and refutational arguments was given by an instructor. If the pretreatment was assimilated, the subject could then provide counterarguments and defenses against subsequent attacks.

McGuire's Model of Persuasion

McGuire (1968) also developed a model for persuasion that emphasized its processes: attention, comprehension, yielding, retention, and action. The model was based on Hovland's work, which took a learning theory approach to persuasion; that is, a message is more likely to change an attitude if by adopting the position advocated in the message the person receives positive reinforcement. Attention and comprehension were considered to be receptivity and learning factors, and yielding equaled acceptance of the message purpose or attitude change. Most laboratory studies up to this point stopped there. McGuire extended the idea that persuasion stopped with attitude change by recognizing that to achieve persuadee action at a later time, retention of the message was necessary. Also, in testing receptivity, McGuire found that receivers with high self-esteem were receptive to persuasive messages because they have confidence in their initial positions. Yet they were resistant to yielding because they were satisfied with their existing attitudes. He also found that receivers with high intelligence were receptive to a message because they have longer attention spans and are better able to comprehend arguments. Yet they, too, resisted change due to confidence in existing attitudes. This demonstrated opposite effects on receptivity and yielding in a curvilinear relationship between the variables. This also led him to conclude that receivers with moderate levels of self-esteem and intelligence will be more affected by persuasive messages.

Zimbardo and Leippe (1991) added additional steps to the model—exposure at the beginning and, replacing action, translation of attitude to behavior at the end. Exposure precedes attention because people cannot attend a message until they are exposed to it. This is particularly appropriate with advertising on multichannel television. Although advertisers put their messages on television, there is no guarantee that the right consumers will be exposed to them. Television ratings are important because the more people who watch a program means more people are exposed to the commercials. Zimbardo and Leippe changed McGuire's "action" to "translation of attitude to behavior" because it recognizes the strength of attitude-consistent behavior. In other words, if a message influences behavior, the new attitude formed by the message must guide behavior in a relevant situation (p. 137).

Diffusion of Innovations

Another development in the late 1960s was the *diffusion of innovations* developed by James Coleman who investigated how doctors decided to adopt new antibiotic drugs (Rogers, 1982). Peer networks influenced doctors more than scientific evaluations by university medical schools and pharmaceutical firms. The diffusion process occurred through a combination of mass and interpersonal communication, and often took years until an idea had spread. It is a complex process that begins with the people involved who exist within a system. Their variables, including personality, social characteristics, and needs, are examined. Next, the social system itself has to be looked at in terms of its variables. Third, the characteristics of the innovation are analyzed. The adoption of the innovation itself may vary from optional decision, collective decision, or authority decision. All of this occurs in networks in which change takes place. Mass communication channels may stimulate change, but interpersonal networks are crucial to the process. Innovation occurs as the result of interaction along the links of a network. Individuals can modify innovations as part of the adoption of them. This theory is of particular importance to those who are interested in attitudinal and behavioral change in a natural setting such as in a developing nation or an organization.

Recent Research on Attitudes

Recent research on attitudes has focused on the content and formation of attitudinal responses apart from their correlation to behavior change. McGuire (1985) has predicted that the 1990s would bring renewed interest in attitudes and attitude systems in general and in the structure of attitudes in particular. What this new research recognizes is that people have different and even contradictory needs that determine their attitudinal responses.

The *elaboration likelihood model* (Petty & Cacioppo, 1986) examines centralized processing of information for attitude formation on the basis of a person's motivation to do so as well as the person's abilities to engage in message and issue-related thinking. Motivation to engage in persuasive transactions is related to attention factors, message quality, a person's involvement in the issue, and a person's ability to process persuasive argument. What this means is that if a person does not care about a topic, she/he is not likely to expend much energy to process the information in the message. Such a person can be expected to rely on extra-message peripheral cues such as the attractiveness of the persuader or the persuader's credibility. Conversely, if the persuadee cares about the topic at hand in a personal way, he/she is likely to devote great energy to process the message content. In the latter case, evidence becomes important because, if it is sound, the person will be influenced by it (Reinard, 1988).

Research on Persuasion and Behavior

In the 1970s, experimental research on attitudes waned, and more emphasis was placed on behavior and media influence. Studies that attempted to link attitude to behavior changes have not been able to demonstrate a direct correlation between attitude change and some desired behavior change. A new development has been to measure attitudes toward behavior and intentions to carry out a behavior. Researchers are attempting to determine what can enable them to predict behavior. Fishbein and Ajzen's *model of reasoned action* (Ajzen & Fishbein, 1980) measures the strength of intentions to perform behaviors with strong predictive results. There are two important determinants of intentions, however, that are related to attitudes. First, there is the attitude toward the relevant behavior, based on beliefs regarding the behavior and its likely outcomes. Second, the approval or disapproval of significant people, which are attitudes or subjective norms, toward the desired behavior will also be taken into consideration.

Attitudes may predict behavior when an attitude is strong and clear, when the attitude is relevant to the behavior called for by the situation at hand, when the attitude and behavior have strong links to the same components of the attitude system, and when the attitude is important to the individual (Zimbardo & Leippe, 1991). Advertising research, however, reveals that people will have a strong positive attitude toward an advertised product and yet will not buy it. Zimbardo and Leippe explain that this occurs because the attitude and the buying behavior are connected to different components of the attitude system relative to the product. People may think an advertisement has a cute or loveable image, but they may not take the product seriously enough to purchase it.

When people are truly committed to an attitude, it is more likely that behavior consistency will occur. Citing the remarkable attitude-behavior consistency of the Chinese student demonstrators in Tiananmen Square in Beijing in 1989, Zimbardo and Leippe conclude that "people act in accord with their attitudes on matters that matter, sometimes no matter what" (p. 196). Another predictor of behavior is the goal of the person who enacts the behavior. Bandura (1979) found that explicitly defined goals create incentive to carry them out.

Bandura's (1986) *theory of observational learning* links behavior and behavior change to modeling that people observe in their homes, among their peers, and in the mass media. According to this theory, modeling influences produce new behaviors because they give people new information about how to behave. Through observation, people acquire symbolic representation of modeled activities that serve as guidelines for their own behavior. Observational learning results when models exhibit novel patterns of thought or behavior that observers did not already possess but which, following observation, they can produce in similar form. Modeling also strengthens or weakens inhibitions over behaviors that have been previously learned. Modeling can also encourage people to engage in behavior that they had once perceived as threatening. Modeling influences, thus, can serve as instructors, inhibitors, disinhibitors, facilitators, stimulus enhancers, and emotion arousers. When people see models express emotional reactions, they are likely to experience emotional arousal. Of course, heightened arousal depends upon how the modeled emotional reactions are perceived by the observer. It is obvious that modeling can be an important propaganda strategy, especially when members of an organization wear uniforms, participate in rituals, and reap positive rewards.

There are four processes necessary to acquire new behavior: (a) attentional processes, (b) retention processes, (c) motor-production processes, and (d) motivational processes. The first process is that of attending to a modeled behavior, then subsequently relating to it. How people relate to other's behavior is determined by perception, motivation, needs, and goals. People are inclined to pay attention to behaviors that have functional value to them. Successful modes of behavior tend to gain more attention than unsuccessful ones. Also, if the person doing the modeling is considered attractive or a friend, more attention will be given to observing that person. This is why children in communities with aggressive models for friends may join gangs and engage in aggressive behaviors. They have less opportunity to befriend other types or to observe prosocial behaviors than children who live in more pacific communities.

Second, what has been observed has to be retained in the memory. Bandura says the modeled behavior has to be stored in some symbolic form. His studies found that subjects who expressed modeled behaviors in concise terms or vivid imagery remembered them better.

Third, production processes have to be activated, for they convert symbolic forms into appropriate action. This requires initiation of responses, monitoring, and refinement on the basis of feedback. When a behavior is performed, feedback, coaching, and reinforcement assist its adoption.

Fourth and most important, the actual performance of the modeled behavior requires motivation to do so. The primary motivation is the observation of positive consequences associated with the new

behavior. Repeated observation of desirable consequences associated with a behavior provides a strong motivation to perform a
behavior. Reinforcement is important to modeling behavior when it
is used as an antecedent to the behavior. According to Bandura, the
anticipation of positive reinforcement can effectively influence what
is observed and the degree of attention paid to the observation of a
given behavior. In other words, learning new behaviors through
observation can be more successful if those observing the behavior
are told ahead of time that they will benefit from performing the
behavior.

The whole notion of consequences of behavior is still under consideration. Ward Edwards (1954) developed a model know as *SEU:
subjective expected utility model,* based on an economic theory known
as utility maximization theory or "riskless choice." This model suggests that when faced with behavioral choices, people tend to choose
the alternative that has the highest expected utility, thus acting in
their own interests. Gerald Miller, in the afterword to Cushman and
McPhee's work on message-attitude behavior relationships (1980),
suggests that people have expectations related to their behaviors and
that they may influence reception of related messages. Further, Miller
indicates that people may behave according to perceived rewards
and punishment for carrying out the behavior. People may not have
supportive attitudes but will behave according to consequences.

Marwell and Schmitt (1967) developed a list of strategies for persuasion that focus on persuadee outcome rather than on the content
of the messages used in their study. They developed sixteen "compliance-gaining" strategies with both positive and negative consequences, including reward, punishment, debts, altruism, and conformity. L. R. Wheelis, R. Barraclough, and R. Stewart (1983) concluded
in their review of compliance-gaining literature that inherent in a
successful compliance-gaining attempt is the persuader's power.
Their definition of power is "the perceived bases of control that a
person has over another person's behavior that would not have
otherwise occurred" (p. 120). Perceptions of power vary with an
individual's sense of whether external forces are more controlling
than internal strength.

A well-known compliance-gaining tactic is known as low-balling.
This refers to getting someone to agree to a very attractive transaction—a business deal or a sale—and then, on the basis of some
excuse, changing the deal so that it costs more. For example, a new
car may be advertised at $400 below blue book price. The salesperson
lets the customer drive the car for a day before sealing the transac-

tion. Then the salesperson tells the customer that the price has to be higher because of the accessories on the car. By then the customer has become committed to the purchase and rationalizes, "Well, what is $600 more when this is the car I like."

Another aspect of research into behavior has been self-attribution research. When subjects believe that the cause of a given behavior is derived from an attitude, they will consequently adopt that attitude. Valins (1966) conducted an experiment in which he showed male subjects slides of scantily clothed women. He told them that their physical reactions to the pictures were being measured. The men would hear a heartbeat each time they saw a slide, and each man was told that it was his own heartbeat. The supposed heartbeat was manipulated by increasing or decreasing the rapidity of the beats. The men were asked to rate the slides. Predictably, they chose as the best pictures those that were accompanied by rapid heartbeats. People often use their perceived behavior to discover their attitudes.

Recruitment into the religious cult of the Unification Church of Korean Reverend Sun Myung Moon, otherwise known as "Moonies," includes an invitation to a free or inexpensive dinner or weekend retreat. Once there, the recruits find themselves in the company of twenty or thirty pleasant people, eating a delicious meal, and enjoying festive dancing and singing. People are very affectionate and attentive. Zimbardo and Leippe (1991) point out that once recruits find themselves acting like Moonies and enjoying it, they may infer from their behavior that they also like and endorse Moonie ideas. This self-attribution is reinforced by commitment behaviors, such as giving a small donation or contributing some labor. Recruits may then think because they are making a commitment, they have a positive attitude toward the cult and its beliefs.

The Influence of the Media

Violence and the Media

After the turbulent 1960s, researchers turned their attention to investigations of media influence, especially in relation to violent behavior and other public concerns. In 1968, President Lyndon B. Johnson created the National Commission on the Causes and Prevention of Violence. There were seven task forces and five investigative teams who produced fifteen volumes of reports. One of these reports, *Violence and the Media*, has become a landmark study in the question of media influence. Through content analysis of television entertainment programming and survey research on actual violence in America, the researchers concluded that violence was not only a predominant characteristic on television but that it was way out of proportion in comparison to actual violence in the real world. Although they acknowledged that the majority of adults who watch television and film are not likely to behave violently as a result, the editors of *Violence and the Media* recognized that long-term and indirect effects of exposure to violence were possible (Lowery & DeFleur, 1988).

Television and Social Behavior, 1969

This was followed in 1969 by the Surgeon General's Advisory Committee on Television and Social Behavior, which produced several volumes of studies conducted prior to and during the committee's duration. The general conclusion of the studies was that viewing of violent entertainment increases the likelihood of subsequent aggressive behavior, but it should be noted that the evidence was derived from laboratory settings and from surveys, thus generalizability is uncertain.

Some of the studies cited were conducted by Bandura, others by Leonard Berkowitz, both of whom had been testing children, adolescents, and young adults in laboratory settings for more than a decade. Their conclusions were somewhat more tempered. Both Berkowitz and Bandura and their colleagues were very careful to state that they made no claim to any situation outside of the laboratory. They did find, however, that television violence could incite violent behavior in viewers.

Berkowitz said it was possible for subjects to behave aggressively in later situations if the fantasy situation on film or television seemed justified. He also indicated that repeated exposure to violence increased the probability of subsequent aggressive acts for some members of an audience, but other factors also determine what may happen—how aggressive the subject is, how hostile the media make him or her, how much the subject associates the story in film or television with situations in which he or she learned hostile behavior, and the intensity of the guilt and/or aggression anxiety aroused by exposure to the film. Bandura also found that children under certain conditions were apt to reproduce aggressive action after observing adults exhibit novel and aggressive action on the screen. A review (O'Donnell & Kable, 1982) of their extensive research concludes that sometimes media violence may be persuasively effective with the attitude changes consisting more often of modifications than of conversions. With respect to behavior changes, it can be generalized that some types of depicted violence will be found to have some types of effects on the aggression levels of some types of children, adolescents, and young adults under some types of conditions.

One of the most interesting aspects of the experimental evidence concerning the relationship between the media and behavior change is that subjects tend to be influenced by film and television characters that they perceive to be similar to themselves. Berkowitz, McGuire, and others have found that viewer identification is the central concept in the interpretation of film and television effects. The extent to which viewers rated themselves as similar to particular characters influenced their reactions to aggressors in the media.

Television and Behavior, 1982

In 1982, a second surgeon general's advisory committee recommended that other areas of television be investigated. The research that followed was extensive. Already begun in 1972 after the first surgeon general's report, the research consists of more than 3000 studies, three-fourths of which appeared after 1975 (Lowery & DeFleur, 1988). Because there was so much information available, the surgeon general, Julius B. Richard, recommended that a synthesis and evaluation of the research be undertaken by the National Institute of Mental Health (NIMH). The resulting report entitled *Television and Behavior: Ten Years of Scientific Progress and Implications for the Eighties* covered many themes, but the most publicized finding concerned the link between televised violence and later aggressive behavior in children. This link was found in both field and laboratory studies, but much work remains to be done in this area. One study in a related area suggested that aggression can be stimulated by high levels of action, even without high violence content. Furthermore, the report emphasized that emotional arousal created by television stimuli that was not necessarily violent had a relationship to aggressive behavior. Increased levels of arousal can lead to excitement that may be channeled into aggression, thus television content that is exciting could also possibly induce aggressive behavior. In many respects, the report asked more questions than it answered.

Cultivation Studies

Watching violence on television seems to have caused large numbers of Americans to be fearful, insecure, and dependent upon authority, according to cultivation studies by Gerbner, Gross, Signorelli,

Morgan, and Jackson-Beck (1979). The most significant and recurring conclusion of their long-range study was that "one correlate of television viewing is a heightened and unequal sense of danger and risk in a mean and selfish world" (p. 194). The researchers felt that this would lead people to demand protection and even welcome repression in the name of security. A study of students in junior and senior high schools revealed that those who were heavy viewers of crime shows were more likely to have anti-civil libertarian attitudes (Carlson, 1983). These studies indicate that television influences political learning and in the case of televised violence, may produce an increasing dependence on the exercise of authoritarian power in society. Comstock (1980) views television as a reinforcer of the status quo in society. He believes that television portrayals, particularly violent ones, assign roles of authority, power, success, failure, dependence, and vulnerability in a manner that matches the real-life social hierarchy.

Prosocial Behaviors and Television

Other researchers have found that some television programming creates the learning of prosocial behaviors. Liebert, Neale, and Davidson (1973) found that children learned altruism, self-control, and generosity from television viewing. Stein and Friedrich (1972) demonstrated that children learned prosocial behaviors such as cooperation, nurturing, and expressing feelings after watching television programs such as *Mr. Rogers*. Laboratory and field studies reviewed in *Television and Behavior* (Pearl, Bouthilet, & Lazar, 1982) indicate that behavior such as friendliness, cooperation, delay of gratification, and generosity could be enhanced by exposure to relevant television content. Lowery and DeFleur (1988) state that people learn from television, and it can no longer be regarded as mere entertainment. "It is a major source of observational learning for millions of people. In that role it may be one of the most important agencies of socialization in our society" (p. 384).

Pornography

As public standards regarding film and television content related to sex and nudity became less rigid, the public began to be concerned about pornography, especially where women were represented as victims of violence. Research on the effects of filmed pornography (Donnerstein & Malamuth, 1984) has suggested a possible link between pornography and violence against women. It was found in laboratory settings that after exposure to aggressive pornography, some men showed less sensitivity toward rape victims, an increase in the willingness to say they would commit rape if not caught, an increase in the acceptance of certain myths about rape, and an increased aggressive behavior against women in a laboratory experiment. The overall link between media violence against women and real violence against women is as yet inconclusive, but researchers are actively exploring it in both laboratory and field studies.

Health, Families, and Politics

Other topics reflecting public concerns that have been subjects of television research are health, families, and politics. An increasingly health-conscious public may view physically fit men and women in entertainment programs, but they will not necessarily see them behaving in healthy ways. Dramatic characters on television ate or drank or talked about doing so 75% of the time they were on screen. Instead of eating nutritious meals, television adults snacked 39% of the time, and television children snacked 45% of the time. Alcohol is the beverage most frequently consumed on television, twice as much as coffee or tea and fourteen times as often as soft drinks. Alcohol is shown or discussed in 80% of prime-time programs, not counting commercials. Although few television characters are seen smoking, there were no instances of antismoking sentiments expressed. Although many cars and trucks are shown on television, seldom do their drivers use seat belts (Lowery & DeFleur, 1988).

Concerns voiced about family by politicians, counselors, and clergy has prompted research regarding both the portrayal of families on television as well as the effect of television on family and social interactions. Lynda Glennon and Richard Butsch (Lowery & DeFleur, 1988) content analyzed 218 family series, finding that the middle class was overrepresented; whereas, the working-class family was underrepresented. Working-class fathers were often depicted as inept, dumb, or bumbling, leading the researchers to speculate that working-class children might perceive their fathers as inadequate and inferior. Middle-class families appeared to be economically successful and often able to solve problems easily. The researchers felt that the idealized portrayals of these families might lead viewers to question the adequacy of their own families.

Another of Glennon and Butsch's findings was that heavy television viewing is linked to poor family communication and tension (see also Stoneman & Brody, 1983). However, Robert Kubey and

Mihaly Csikszentmihalyi (1990) found by having subjects report through electronic pagers that heavy television viewing with the family is a more positive experience than viewing alone and possibly increases the time a family spends together. They found that families talked during programs thus making television viewing more cheerful and sociable. Their major finding, however, was that television viewing makes people passive and less alert; whereas, families who engaged in nontelevision activities felt more alert and active. Although family life, daily schedules, and social interaction have been profoundly affected by television, no area has been more reshaped by television than politics.

Politicians have to voice "sound bites" to ensure fifteen second coverage on the evening television news, and television commercials account for a major portion of campaign budgets. The television image of the candidate has become crucial to voter decisions. More and more voters are abandoning party lines to split their votes among candidates of different parties. There is evidence that there is a growing reliance on issues to make voting choices. Lowery and DeFleur (1988) predict that mediated information may play a greater role in elections; whereas, "reinforcement and crystallization, in the sense of cultivating prior loyalties, presumably will have a reduced role" (p.418).

The Agenda-Setting Function of the Media

One powerful feature of mass communication is its agenda-setting function. Early research on this concept began when Maxwell McCombs and Donald Shaw investigated what voters in North Carolina said were the key issues in the 1968 presidential campaign. They compared this data with the key issues presented in television news, newspapers, and news magazines and found a startlingly high relationship. The news media had not told the voters what to think, but they had told them what to think about. Agenda-setting emphasized the gatekeeping aspect of the news. Numerous studies have been done in this area yielding sufficient evidence to conclude that media gatekeepers formulate meaning—selecting, screening, interpreting, emphasizing, and distorting information.

Spiral of Silence

Another concept, less widely accepted than agenda-setting, is known as the *spiral of silence* (Noelle-Neumann, 1991). This theory describes people supporting popular opinions and suppressing unpopular ones in order to avoid social isolation. Assumptions made by this theory are that society threatens deviant individuals with isolation, individuals fear isolation continuously, this fear of isolation causes people to assess the climate of opinion at all times, and the results of this assessment affect behavior in public, especially the open expression or concealment of opinions. Although perceptions of dominant opinions are shaped by the media, critics of the spiral of silence point out that tolerance of deviant opinions differs from society to society. Indeed, dissent, if valued in a free society, makes social isolation unlikely. When new issues penetrate public discussion, the spiral of silence is broken.

Dependency Theory

Both the agenda-setting and the spiral of silence theories focus on the media as instruments for the distribution or withholding of information, giving issues legitimacy and shaping public opinion.

Sandra Ball-Rokeach's *dependency model* (1976) explains why people are reliant on the media to set the agenda for public discussion. In a complex society where there is a proliferation of information, people rely on the media for information about that which they do not have immediate knowledge. An important premise of dependency theory, however, is that people do not use the media separately from other social influences in which they and the media exist. How people use and react to the media is influenced from what they have learned about society in the past, including what they learned from the media in the past, as well as what is happening in the present. Thus, a certain piece of media information and subsequent conversations about it will have quite different conseqences upon different people, depending upon their previous experiences and social conditions at the moment. Because dependency theory encompasses the interactive nature of media, audience, and society, it is a more comprehensive theory than others that emphasize simple cause and effect. Dependency theory also recognizes that more urban and industrialized societies have more dependency on the media, and as social change and conflict increases, so does public dependency on the media.

Dependency theory also accounts for effects of the media, which can, in turn, affect society as well as the media. Ball-Rokeach delineates three types of effects: cognitive, affective, and behavioral. The cognitive effects are (a) ambiguity resolution, (b) attitude formation, (c) agenda-setting, (d) expansion of the belief system, and (e) value clarification. Affective effects are emotional responses to mediated information which can create strong feelings about parts of society and/or desensitize people to violence because of excessive exposure. Behavioral effects may be initiating new behaviors or ceasing old ones. Any or all of these effects are likely to be felt only by people who depend upon media information.

Look at a recent example of the effects of media coverage of a controversial event to see how this may work. When Anita Hill, professor of Law at Oklahoma University, testified during the Senate hearings on the nomination of Clarence Thomas to the Supreme Court, sexual harassment became a news agenda item. People who watched the hearings on television or followed them in the newspapers may have experienced all three types of effects.

The term *sexual harassment* was clarified for some, made ambiguous for others. Whether people believed Hill, attitudes about sexual harassment were formed and sexual harassment became more of an agenda item than it had previously been. Public discussion regarding appropriate behavior at work and in school intensified, and in the process, belief systems no doubt expanded, and some values were clarified. Strong emotions were felt, especially by those who had experienced sexual harassment in the past, and many women came forth to talk about their experiences. There must also have been behavior changes, especially the cessation of practices that were suspect. The agenda regarding sexual harassment was prominent in October 1991 until it no longer was a media story, but the effects of it over a long-term are yet undetermined.

Uses and Gratifications Theory

Most mass communication theories focus on what the media does to the receiver, but *uses and gratifications theory* focuses on what the receiver does with the media. The consumer of media is viewed as an active selector and goal-directed user of it. The assumption is made that the user of media is responsible for choosing media to meet psychological and sociological needs. Elihu Katz has found in his research "overall patterns that suggest that individuals specify different media for fulfilling different kinds of needs" (in Williams, 1989, p. 71). Human needs are the primary consideration of uses and gratifications studies and include the need to be diverted as well as informed. Katz views mass communications as "an elaborate system of cultural, social, and psychological 'services.'" After three decades of research on this theory, it has been codified with an understanding of attitude formation based on a consumer's expectancy of media and evaluation of it. One would, therefore, seek gratification of needs based on one's expectancies of the media content. As one's needs get satisfied, expectations are intensified, thus the effect is cyclical. One criticism of this type of research is the ambiguity surrounding the concept of need. A survey of cross-national studies found that four basic clusters of needs emerged: self and personal identity, social contact, diversion and entertainment, and information and knowledge about the world (Roberts & Maccoby, 1985). Most needs can be fit into one of the reduced categories.

There may be links between uses and gratifications and effects. Most research in this area centers on political campaigns, news, and wars. People tend to turn to media for information and issue salience in these areas. With regard to the political campaign, they will receive more than information because the objective of a campaign is to influence prospective voters.

Uses and Dependency Theory

Some researchers argue that dependency theory and uses and gratifications theory are not mutually exclusive, for although individuals make choices about using the media, the media influences individuals as well. Alan Rubin and Sven Windahl (1986) have combined both approaches into what they call the *uses and dependency model*. This model shows societal systems and media systems interacting with audiences to create needs in individuals. The needs influence the individual to choose both media and nonmedia sources of gratification, which subsequently lead to dependencies on the sources. Effects are cognitive, affective, and behavioral, as in dependency theory, and the results are then fed back into the societal and media systems. Rubin and Windahl (1986) suggest that people will narrow the search for certain need fulfillment to few media and will therefore be more susceptible to influence. A businessperson may, for example, rely on one newspaper for business information, thus becoming dependent upon it and more likely to adopt its views.

The multitude of studies on the effects of television on human behavior has underscored society's concerns with effects. It is generally accepted that media does influence individuals but does so among and through a nexus of mediating factors and influences. Mass media is viewed as a powerful contributory agent but not the sole cause in the process of reinforcing existing conditions or in bringing about change.

The Limitations of Effects Research

Research on the effects of mass media continues to thrive, but it has not become the united behavioral science envisioned by its pioneers. Lazarsfeld regarded mass communication research as "administrative research" in 1941, suggesting that research be carried on in the service of some kind of administrative agency and defining it as social science research primarily concerned with effects. Although government-sponsored research yielded important findings about the effects of various media, it has not been as prevalent as marketing and advertising research. The broadcasting industry regards research as vital to decision making. Meanwhile, other forms of research are taking hold. There is criticism of empirical and experimental research because research questions are often limited by laboratory methods and laboratory settings.

Roberts and Maccoby (1985) point out three major criticisms of experimental research on media:

1. An effect that is attributed to a larger unit may derive from one or more of its components, but it may be totally unrelated to other components. For example, stimuli for experiments related to violence in media range from single scenes to specifically prepared sequences, thus subjects view a specific violent act, which is something quite different from an entire program or film.

2. Researchers tend to be more concerned with media content as opposed to media techniques. Furthermore, they categorize media content subjectively, for example, by genre or by topic.

3. What is used as a stimulus to determine effects may not be representative of media content. For example, what may be used as a prosocial stimulus for children as subjects in an experiment may be totally unrepresentative of a child's typical television diet. Also, what is regarded by the researchers as a type of stimulus may not be perceived that way by the subjects. A researcher's "violence" may be a subject's "playful competition."

Roberts and Maccoby stress an important adage, well-known in communication studies: "Meanings are not in messages, but in people" (pp. 543-44).

Finally, as Jesse Delia (1987) has pointed out in his comprehensive history of communication research,

the received view constructed the history of communication research . . . [and] privileged a particular model of scientific practice . . . [which] has profoundly affected the assumptions defining the parameters of the field . . . [and] marginated explorations of the relationship between culture and communication. . . . A deep tension was thus built into the mass communication field from its inception. It aimed to organize the whole scope of concern with the mass media under a single, encompassing umbrella, while its focus on scientific research placed historical and critical studies on the margin. (pp. 21, 71)

The dominant paradigm of effects resulting from the transfer of a message from a source to a receiver has been challenged, and questions related to the functions of cultural communication within the total process of society are now being asked.

Cultural Studies

The most prominent ideas for the cultural study of communication came from Great Britain. Raymond Williams, who was a fellow of Jesus College, Cambridge, opposed the study of mass communications because he felt it limited studies to broadcasting and film exclusively and because it conceived the audience as a mass. Rather he proposed that communication be studied as a set of practices, conventions, and forms through which a shared culture is created, modified, and transformed. In his works (1958, 1961, 1966, 1973), he examined how culture reproduces and articulates existing social structures and how media maintains industrial economic societies. The other prominent British researcher is Stuart Hall who began his work at the Centre for Contemporary Cultural Studies at the University of Birmingham. Hall sees communication as encompassing a wide variety of cultural expression and ritual forms of everyday life. Fundamental to Hall's work (1977, 1980, 1984) is the encoding process or message formulation in the media together with social and economic conditions that explain why and how viewers decode messages in a variety of ways. Hall says that a message "hails" a person as if it were hailing a taxi. To answer, the people must recognize that it is them, and not someone else, being hailed. To respond to the hail, the people recognize the social position that has been constructed by the message, and if their response is cooperative, the position has been adopted. Thus, television viewers may be hailed as conformists or sexists or patriots. If the viewers accept the position of the program, then they constitute themselves as subjects in an ideological definition that the program proposes.

There are essentially three social positions: dominant, oppositional, and negotiated, although Hall speculates there could be multiple positions. The dominant position is produced by a viewer who accepts dominant ideology in the media. Oppositional is in direct opposition to the dominant ideology in the media or acceptance of an oppositional point of view. Negotiated positions are produced by viewers who fit into the dominant ideology but who need to resist certain elements of it. Negotiated positions are popular with various social groups who question their relationship to the dominant ideology.

Cultural analysts may examine audience decoding through ethnographic methods, using in-depth interviews, often over time, to determine how people actively use television to make sense of social experience and of themselves. Cultural critics also work in a manner similar to literary critics, but the texts are the mediated messages of television, newspapers, and film as well as the behavior of people as it has been shaped by the media. They "read" the "text" to construct its meaning.

Essentially, cultural studies are concerned with the generation and circulation of meanings in industrial societies. James W. Carey (1988) says the sources of cultural meanings are in "construable signs and symbols, . . . embedded in things; some relatively durable such as artifacts and practices, some relatively transitory like fashions and follies" (p. 11). In a later work (1989), Carey stresses that human needs and motives must be studied within the context of history and culture. John Fiske (1987) sees television as "a bearer/provoker of meanings and pleasures" (p. 1) and thus as a cultural agent. The view of media as cultural agent and the construction of meaning by the users of the media is a view that tries to understand human behavior rather than explain it. Rather than attempt to predict human behavior as social scientists do, cultural analysts attempt to diagnose human meanings.

In addition to the works cited on cultural studies, the journal *Critical Studies in Mass Communication* is a major source for cultural studies of the media. We believe that the student of propaganda needs to be conversant with both social science and cultural studies. Our model of the process of propaganda in Chapter 8 represents a broad conceptualization based on both approaches. The nature of research in propaganda and persuasion is and always has been interdisciplinary.

Conclusion

Research on the nature and effects of propaganda flourished during the World War II years. After the war, research generated into persuasion and communication studies of effects. Research questions were concerned with the variables of communication interaction, especially with regard to attitudes and attitude change. Later, attempts were made to predict behavior and behavior change. With regard to the focus of the book, it would be useful to have a catalogue of practices relevant to propaganda that produce effects, but it is not possible to develop such a catalogue. The most pertinent conclusion that one can draw after such a review of more than seventy years of research is that individual differences and contexts determine the nature of effects. It is also important to pay attention to the historical and cultural contexts in which propaganda and persuasion occur, and especially to recognize that people construct different meanings according to their social experiences.

Generalizations About Propaganda and Persuasion Effects

When we attempt to make generalizations, we are confronted by the everchanging nature of what is under study. The media undergo continuous changes, and those changes are primarily related to technology. Social, political, and cultural changes in society are not only continuous, but dramatic, as we have witnessed in Europe and the former Soviet Union from 1989 to 1991. What may be a valid generalization today may become obsolete a short time later. Nevertheless, there are a few generalizations that can be made regarding propaganda and persuasion.

First, it seems safe to say that communication effects are the greatest where the message is in line with the existing opinions, beliefs, and dispositions of the receivers. Selectivity in the perception of messages is generally guided by preexisting interests and behavior patterns of the receivers. The result is that most messages are more likely to be supportive of, than discrepant from, existing views. Furthermore, mass communication effects tend to take the form of reinforcement rather than change.

Second, when change does occur, it does so as the result of a multitude of factors including mass media, socially contextual conditions, group interaction, the presence and influence of opinion leaders, and the perceived credibility of the source or sources of the message. Topics that are most likely to be influential are on unfamiliar, lightly felt, peripheral issues that do not matter much or are not tied to audience predispositions. Issues that are deeply rooted and based on values and past behavior patterns are not as likely to change. Ideas related to political loyalty, race, and religion tend to remain stable over time and resistant to influence. It is as John Naisbitt (1982) said in *Megatrends*: "When people really care about an issue, it doesn't matter how much is spent to influence their vote; they will go with their beliefs. When an issue is inconsequential to the voters, buying their vote is a snap" (p. 91).

Third, there is an economical aspect in the way we maintain consistency of attitudes and behaviors that gives a propagandist the advantage. As Karlins and Abelson point out, a propagandist does not have to win people over on every issue in order to get their support. If the propagandist can get people to agree with him or her on one or two issues, then their opinion toward him or her may become favorable. Once that has happened, and the mention of the person's name evokes a favorable response in the people, they may find themselves inventing reasons for agreeing with other issues advocated by him or her (1970).

Fourth, people can appear to accept an idea publically without private acceptance. Behavior can be guided by a system of rewards and punishments that do not require attitude change. Furthermore, public compliance will continue under conditions of surveillance by authority but not necessarily under conditions of nonsurveillance.

Finally, the greater the monopoly of the communication source over the receivers, the greater is the effect in the direction favored by the source. Wherever there is a dominant definition of the situation accompanied by a consistent, repetitious, and unchallenged message, the greater the influence of the message.

5 Propaganda and Psychological Warfare

Propaganda is an essential element in warfare, going back to the pre-Biblical period. It was, however, during World War I that sophisticated techniques of propaganda were utilized that eventually created negative attitudes in the twentieth century toward both propaganda and the potential dangers of mass media influence. In the interwar period radio broadcasting became important and was increasingly used by the European nations in the political conflicts leading up to World War II. Propaganda played a significant role in the rise of both Communism and Fascism, and reached a new level of scientific sophistication during the war. In the period after 1945, propaganda became a major weapon in the ideological struggle between East and West.

The use of propaganda as an integral part of waging war has been a basic part of human history. War itself can be considered to be a violent means of attaining a specific objective, but there has always been a continuous flow of carefully directed propaganda messages that seek to bring about much the same result, but in a nonviolent manner. In a book devoted to the subject, Paul M. A. Linebarger (1954) defined psychological warfare as "comprising the use of propaganda against an enemy, together with such other operational measures of a military, economic, or political nature as may be required to supplement propaganda" (p. 40). Harold D. Lasswell, one of the pioneers in propaganda studies, pointed out that psychological warfare is a recent name for an old idea about how to wage successful war. "The basic idea is that the best success in war is achieved by the destruction of the enemy's will to resist, and with a minimum annihilation of fighting capacity" (1951, p. 261).

By its very nature, the use of propaganda for such directed purposes commences long before actual hostilities break out or war is declared. It also continues long after peace treaties have been signed, and soldiers have gone back to their homes. It is a continuous process, shifting in emphasis as required. It is not hindered by the usual constraints of war such as terrain, arms, or specific battles, but is free to float as only human minds can. The success or failure of these campaigns cannot always be immediately measured, and the results are often known only years later.

Throughout history there were recorded instances of psychological warfare. One of the best known is the biblical story of Gideon, who created panic in the numerically superior Midianite camp by equipping 300 of his men with a torch and trumpet each. Conventional warfare of the period called for one such equipped soldier for every 100 men, and Gideon was therefore able to create the illusion of an army of more than 30,000. These three hundred were strategically placed around the Midianite camp in the dead of night, and upon command they each revealed their torches while blowing on their trumpets. Thinking themselves under attack by a superior force, the enemy became confused, and even attacked each other. Eventually the Midianites gave up and fled the battlefield with the Israelites in hot pursuit (Book of Judges, Chapter 7).

There are many other examples of successful employment of psychological techniques used in warfare, such as Cortez's use of horses as instruments of terror, as well as the exploitation of the indian legends concerning the "Fair God" in his conquest of Mexico; the ancient Chinese use of rockets, not as weapons but to intimidate their enemies; the Boers' use of commando units to attack the British far behind their own lines in South Africa during the Boer War and their anti-British appeal for sympathy on a worldwide scale; and the widespread use of a variety of propaganda appeals from both sides during the American Revolution. The American colonists particularly delighted in pointing out the class distinctions between the British officers and their enlisted men. Even in so-called primitive cultures, the use of drums before battle, or the conjuring up of magic spells all serve to unnerve the enemy. Thus the use of psychological techniques of persuasion for war propaganda purposes is not really new, but the emergence of new forms of information dissemination and the increased sophistication in the understanding of human behavior greatly increased its application and intensity in the twentieth century.

It is interesting to note that the term *psychological warfare* is distinctively an American one; the British, with greater candor refer to these activities as *political warfare*. Daniel Lerner (1951) has noted that what we are talking about when we speak of psychological warfare is the use of symbols to promote policies, that is, politics. Propaganda is, after all, a manipulation of the symbolic environment, and although it can be carried out independently of the physical environment, it can also under certain circumstances be shaped by that environment. Thus the development of new technologies of communication has altered the way in which propaganda is disseminated, but it would be wrong to suggest that old methods are automatically discarded in favor of the new. There continues to be a considerable overlap of media usage, and total propaganda campaigns will encompass all available forms of communication, from the very effective oral tradition still widely used to the most sophisticated modern electronic systems.

It is true to say that where there is a communication channel, there also exists a potential propaganda medium. An excellent example would be the increased use in the last twenty years of the technology of Xerography to photocopy large quantities of information for easy distribution. In the United States photocopy machines are widely available to all who would wish to use them; in the Soviet Union, however, until very recently, all (official) photocopy machines were under the control of the state, and their use was thus limited. This did not stop Soviet dissidents from producing their material on such machines, but the policies of information control made the (for us) common photocopy machine an exotic and much valued propaganda tool in the Soviet Union. Even in the age of glasnost, there are still few very such machines available for use by the average Soviet citizen, but in the wake of the collapse of the Communist party, communications, in what is now a commonwealth of independent nations, are now almost totally open.

The public seems most familiar (and comfortable) with the use of propaganda as a wartime activity, a notion that has contributed to the generally negative connotations associated with the term. It is true that it is in times of political conflict that propaganda becomes most visible, as groups use directed persuasion to achieve their goals. Propaganda of this sort must be viewed in its specific historical context, for without this context such symbolic manipulation can later appear to be gross distortions of reality, racist, naive, and essentially silly. "Who would have believed that?" we exclaim looking at wartime posters showing the Japanese soldier as a barbaric, apelike subhuman. The fact is that within its historical context, such impressions were readily accepted as part of the mythology created by the reality of the conflict (for example, the sneak attack on Pearl Harbor), and the collective public mentality that develops is eager to believe such stereotypes.

Figure 5.1. The availability of propaganda images such as this taken out of their wartime context continues to be a problem. This cartoon by Sy Mover, portrays the Japanese enemy as an apelike barbarian, a familiar device used by both sides. After the Japanese executed captured American airmen who had bombed Tokyo on April 18, 1942, President Roosevelt referred to the "barbarous execution by the Japanese government," inspiring this caricature.

Figure 5.2. This is a still from the film *Hitler's Children* (1943) showing Tim Holt being indoctrinated into the Hitler Youth movement. The films of World War II are still shown regularly on American television, and are widely available in video stores. The question is how does the continued showing of these wartime stereotypes reinforce current attitudes?

It is often strange to look back with nostalgia on historical artifacts of propaganda, such as wartime posters, leaflets, and especially motion pictures made during the conflict, for they dramatically reveal how context-bound certain types of propaganda can be. We no longer think of the Germans or the Japanese as brutal, rapacious enemies, but these anachronistic artifacts remain. The West German government has been particularly concerned with the showing of old war movies on American television, claiming that this practice continues to provide new generations of Americans with a distorted view of the present German character. There is a certain justification to this claim.

Countering the residual power of psychological warfare has proven to be a difficult problem. The German government has debated for decades the question of how much Nazi history to present to German schoolchildren, and even to the general public. Recent exhibitions of Nazi art and cultural artifacts have attracted large crowds in Germany because this has been a "hidden" part of official German history since 1945. The Japanese have carefully rewritten their high school history textbooks to downplay their wartime activities, or to cast them in a less horrific light. This act has precipitated angry official reactions from other Asian nations, such as China and Korea, who want to have the youth of Japan constantly reminded of the "true" history of Japan's Asian conquests. The reason for the unwillingness to let go of these potent propaganda images is that they have become part of the official history of nations. If one nation decides to change its image, then this causes an imbalance in the other nations. Thus for the foreseeable future, Japan and Germany must always be reminded that they were the enemy in World War II. A series of events commemorating the 50th anniversary of the attack on Pearl Harbor in December 1991 made this painfully obvious. President George Bush stated that the United States did not need to apologize for the dropping of the two atomic bombs on Japan, and the Japanese Parliament in turn reacted by refusing to ratify a resolution calling for an apology for Japanese aggression during the Second World War. The use of atomic weapons on Japan in 1945 has increasingly been used in Japan to justify an image of Japan as the victim of atrocities far outweighing the attack on Pearl Harbor (Weisman, 1991).

World War I and the Fear of Propaganda

In the foreword to a book on the history of propaganda in World War I, Harold Lasswell (1938) noted the following.

There is little exaggeration in saying that the World War led to the discovery of propaganda by both the man in the street and the man in the study. The discovery was far more startling to the former than to the latter, because the man in the study had predecessors who had laid firm foundations for his efforts to understand propaganda. The layman had previously lived in a world where there was no common name for the deliberate forming of attitudes by the manipulation of words (and word substitutes). The scholar had a scientific inheritance which included the recognition of the place of propaganda in society. (p. v)

At the end of World War I even the scholars were surprised by the apparent power that propaganda had exhibited as the conflict raged over almost the entire globe, for nothing in previous historical experience had prepared them for the potent combination of the perfect social, political, and economic conditions with the newly established power of the mass media. By 1914, the nations involved in the war had made the mass media an important part of their social infrastructure and this allowed propaganda activities to assume a role of greater significance than ever before.

Each nation, with the exception of the Soviet Union (which is a special case that will be examined later), was able to call upon established systems of communication, such as the press or motion pictures, as well as skills developed during peacetime, to aid in the propaganda effort. By 1914 advertising had developed into a highly sophisticated form of persuasion, as was the skill of press agentry, and both were put to good use in creating propaganda messages or obtaining press coverage of specific events such as warbond rallies. Linebarger (1954) pointed out that the character of the indigenous communication systems dictated the way in which each nation approached the use of propaganda. Thus the British, who had one of the world's finest international newsgathering and distribution systems in 1914, backed by a sophisticated domestic "free" press and extensive experience in international communication for technical and commercial purposes through their ownership of undersea cables, turned this background to excellent advantage. The Germans, on the other hand, had a more regimented press system and a much more limited network of international telecommunications connections. The Americans, who only entered the war in late 1917, nevertheless used every available form of communication at hand. This included not only the enormous power of the most extensive mass media system in the world but also the churches, the YMCA and Chatauqua groups, and the large number of private clubs and organizations found in such a polyglot society. The French, on whose ground the battles were being fought, used their professional skills at diplomacy to ensure that messages emanating from Paris received a very sympathetic hearing. The result of all of this utilization of existing skills was a barrage of propaganda messages that assaulted the ears of civilians and soldiers at every turn. In no previous conflict had "words" been so important, reflecting as it did the fundamental change in the nature of war in an age of mass communication and mass production—the first global conflict of the emerging mass society. For no longer did single battles decide wars; now whole nations were pitted against other nations, requiring the cooperation of entire populations, both militarily and psychologically. (One reason that the Russian army did not play a decisive role in World War I was the confusion and subsequent low morale of the population, which eventually became one of the direct causes of the Russian Revolution in 1917.)

British Propaganda

The British took the lead in propaganda activities because they were forced to think seriously about it earlier than any of the other belligerent powers. This was because at the outbreak of war in August 1914, only in Britain was there an internal disagreement about entering the conflict. Unlike the other major powers on the continent, Britain did not have universal conscription into the army, and thus the decision to mobilize its armed forces was more of a political one than in France or Germany. In Britain, the Liberal party that had been in power since 1905 was predominantly antiwar, as was the opposition Labour party, and there was a widespread pressure to remain neutral in what was seen as primarily an Austro-Hungarian dispute in southeastern Europe. The Germans unwittingly settled this internal dissension when they decided to invade Belgium while marching to attack France, for Belgium's neutrality had been specifically guaranteed by the Great Powers, including Germany. The Germans miscalculated that the British would not go to war over a "mere scrap of paper," but when Belgium actually resisted the "dreaded Huns," the British became united in their resolve to defend "brave little Belgium!" By September 1915, more than 2,250,000 volunteers had enlisted in the British army (Roetter, 1974). The circulation of atrocity stories coming out of Belgium signaled the first major propaganda salvo, and had an immediate impact on British public sympathies.

The chief agency for developing this successful patriotic campaign in England was a private organization, the Central Committee for National Patriotic Associations, which was formed in late August 1914, immediately after the war started, with Prime Minister Asquith as the honorary president. This group organized lectures, patriotic clubs, and rallies in cities and counties, and also extended its influence into the far reaches of the British Empire to ensure that there was no opposition to the war among the subjects of the king. (In Canada, as an example, many French Canadians had long opposed the British Crown, and they saw no reason to fight what was essentially a British war.) Of special interest was the Neutral Countries Subcommittee, which used the direct personal approach to enlist sympathy and support from countries not in the war. Distinguished Britons lent their names to this enterprise, and as a result acquaintances, colleagues, fellow workers, or business associates in neutral countries received a flood of propaganda materials. More than 250,000 pamphlets, booklets, and other publications were distributed in this manner between August 1914 and September 1918 (Bruntz, 1938). Another important organization that was eventually appointed to coordinate all British propaganda activities after March 1918 was the War Aims Committee, founded in June 1917 and initially formed to combat pacifism in Britain. (There were still enough Britons against all forms of armed conflict to warrant such an organization.)

The first official propaganda organization in Britain was the War Propaganda Bureau, which concerned itself initially with the distribution of printed materials inside neutral countries, and eventually inside Germany itself, which it did through sympathizers using the mails from Holland and Switzerland. When Lloyd George became prime minister in 1916, dissatisfied with British propaganda efforts and in an attempt to avoid what had become a very confused and decentralized situation, he reorganized the War Propaganda Bureau and created the Department of Information. This agency concentrated on enemy civilian psychological warfare outside of Britain whereas the National War Aims Committee dealt with internal propaganda efforts.

The concept of mobilizing such a massive propaganda effort was so new that it had taken the relatively experienced British nearly five years to devise a workable system of propaganda management suitable for a great power at war. In the end the British became quite adept at coordinating their efforts at external political warfare aimed at the enemy with the internal, morale-building efforts of news-propaganda. By the time of World War II in 1939, these lessons had been thoroughly learned.

German Propaganda

The Germans, on the other hand, were never able to gain the same degree of control over their propaganda activities, and in the end they had only limited success in making their political ambitions clear to important neutral countries such as the United States. Long after the war there were many in Germany who attributed their loss to the superiority of British propaganda; foremost among these was Adolf Hitler, who in *Mein Kampf* praised the British efforts and noted that the British had understood that propaganda was so important that it had to be handled by professionals. This belief that Allied (American efforts were also lauded) propaganda had been a major contributor to Germany's defeat became a part of the mythology of the Nazis, which held that the German army could not be defeated on the field, and that only a "stab in the back" had betrayed the German people in 1918. Thus the enemy's successful use of propaganda itself was used as a form of propaganda to make the German people wary of becoming complacent and, therefore, susceptible to information from outside sources. The importance of propaganda as an extension of modern warfare was not lost on the fascist German leaders during the interwar period, as we shall examine later in this chapter.

Initial German international propaganda efforts were amateurish, consisting mainly of using enlisted writers and scholars to explain why the Allies were responsible for starting the war. Unfortunately, all they succeeded in doing was to create antagonism in the targeted countries with their arrogance in the face of the atrocity stories coming out of Belgium and France. The stodginess of the German military communiques also failed to garner any worldwide sympathy. Essentially German propaganda lacked both organization and moral drive, and they did not receive the cooperation from the international press for which they had hoped. The British Royal Navy dealt the German efforts a serious blow when on August 15, 1914, they cut the undersea cable linking Germany and the United States. This deprived the Germans of the means to communicate and effectively shut off attempts to make their position on the war clear to the neutral American population. Before transatlantic radio service could be established, the European Allies had already created the propaganda agenda for the American public, and stories of German atrocities in Belgium and elsewhere were being widely circulated.

For once the vaunted German efficiency failed to operate, and there was never any real coordination of the various German propaganda efforts throughout the war. Even the German Foreign Office seemed to be unaware of the importance of trying to establish goodwill and support for the German cause. Roetter suggests that most of the German diplomats were so convinced of the "rightness" of Germany's cause that they felt no need to justify it, and in any case, it was always arrogantly stated that "the War would be over by Christmas" (1974, pp. 38-39). Eventually the Foreign Office did establish a special department to deal with overseas propaganda, but there was virtually no cooperation from the armed services. (At the outbreak of the war, the army had only one officer who was in contact with the press.) One of the most serious problems was the enormous amount of conflicting information that was sent out by the various civilian and military authorities, and this conflict became a major source of the internal struggle for political control of Germany as the war continued on. As the military invariably won these arguments, it tended to underscore for both the German people and those overseas that Germany was essentially a military state. It was very difficult for most of the neutral countries to understand the German military argument that it had been forced to defend the decaying Hapsburg Empire by invading poor Belgium.

The biggest philosophical difference was that whereas German propaganda efforts were only able to convey the fact that the war was being fought to avenge the country's honor, the British were able to make the war appear to be, as H. G. Wells put, "the war to end all wars"—that is, the war that would defend humanity everywhere. Germany was never able to claim a moral position to compete with this platitude. What the Germans failed to learn in World War I, they studied and applied with a vengeance in World War II. Hitler did not really care what the rest of the world thought about his policies; he was mainly concerned with domestic propaganda success.

American Propaganda

American propaganda, which the Germans admired so much, was the work of two agencies. The civilian agency was the Committee on Public Information (CPI), which became known as the "Creel Committee" because of its chairman, George Creel, who had been a newspaper editor. The committee also had as members the secretary of state, and the secretaries for the army and the navy. (An excellent history of the CPI is Vaughn, 1980.) The military agency was the Propaganda Section (or Psychologic Section) of the American Expeditionary Forces, under Captain Heber Blakenhorn, also known as G-2D. The CPI had the advantage in George Creel of a leader who had the confidence of President Wilson, and he was therefore able to force a coordination of propaganda efforts with other civilian and military agencies. Creel (1920), in his fascinating book about his wartime work, *How We Advertised America*, saw the conflict as "the fight for the minds of men, for the 'conquest of their convictions,' and the battle-line ran through every home in every country" (p. 3). His approach to the problem was to use a technique that he thought Americans knew best—sales. He noted, "In all things, from first to last, without halt or change, it was a plain publicity proposition, a vast enterprise in salesmanship, the world's greatest adventure in advertising" (p. 4). Operating with a wide mandate, and with a relatively loose organizational structure, the CPI used every available means of communicating with the American public with an intensity never before devoted to a single issue in the United States. Creel (1920) congratulated himself on the fact that

> there was no part of the great war machinery that we did not touch, no medium of appeal that we did not employ. The printed word, the spoken word, the motion picture, the telegraph, the cable, the wireless, the poster, the signboard—all these were used in our campaign to make our own people and other peoples understand the causes that compelled America to take arms. All that was fine and ardent in the civilian population came at our call until more than one hundred and fifty thousand men and women were devoting highly specialized abilities to the work of the Committee, as faithful and devoted in their service as though they wore the khaki. (p. 5)

The output of the CPI was intended mainly for domestic consumption, and as Creel stated above, the American public was subjected to an intense barrage of propaganda messages. Of particular interest was the use of the oral tradition in the form of the "Four-Minute Men," who were volunteer speakers in local communities who would lecture on the war at a moment's notice to any interested group wishing to acquaint itself with the facts. The growing American film industry was enlisted to make propaganda movies, and the CPI encouraged the showing of these in neutral countries, while the fledgling radio medium was used to broadcast messages from the United States to the Eiffel Tower in Paris, and from there to most of the neutral European countries. The CPI also had commissioners in every foreign neutral and Allied nation whose job it was to disseminate daily news to the local press.

In the final assessment of the success of the CPI we must be careful to distinguish between the immediate results and the long-term

Figure 5.3. "We Can, We Must, and We Will!" A cartoon created by Charles H. Sykes, which first appeared in the Philadelphia *Evening Public Ledger*, in June 1918. This cartoon, aimed at mobilizing the American labor force, was circulated by the National Committee of Patriotic Societies as part of its work to enlist cartoonists for the war effort.

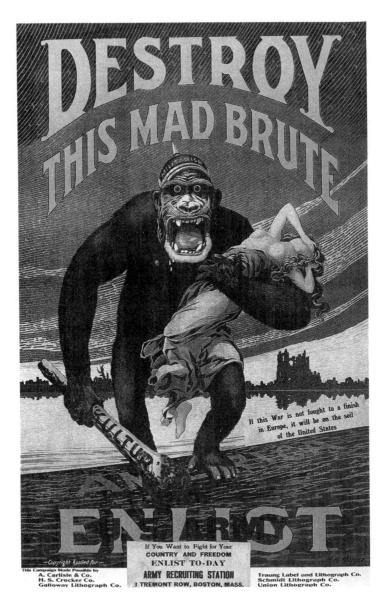

Figure 5.4. "Destroy This Mad Brute." A cartoon by H. R. Hopps c.1916, which shows the German soldier as a rapacious brute. Note the bloody club of *kultur* and the destruction of Europe in the background, as the brute now stands on American soil. The imagery of "defiled womanhood" was widely used in both world wars as strong appeal to the most basic emotions.

effects on American society. As an agency of psychological warfare the CPI was extremely successful and it created a war psychosis in the United States that went a long way in providing the moral and material support required by the armed services. However, when the war finally ended, and the Wilsonian concept of a war to "make the world safe for democracy" proved to be largely unfounded, the American public and especially the politicians began to question seriously both the tactics and the intensity of the CPI's propaganda activities. The boosterism mentality that accompanied so much of the domestic activities of the CPI when contrasted with the loss of so many American lives, especially in the face of the disillusionment with the settlement of the war, left a bad taste in the mouths of Americans. In turn this lead to a justified suspicion of the power of organized propaganda, and ultimately encouraged the pacifist and isolationist tendencies that existed in the United States for the next twenty years. As Linebarger (1954) noted, "A more modest, more calculated national propaganda effort would have helped forestall those attitudes which, in turn, made World War II possible" (p. 68).

American military propaganda activities concentrated on morale and surrender leaflets because radio loudspeaker technology did not exceed the power of the megaphone by much at that time. Therefore, most communication with the enemy had to be in one of the most basic forms of all—the printed leaflet. The British and French had pioneered in this form of propaganda, but the Americans developed some of their own inventions, and balloons and airplanes were the chief methods of dispersement, but later special leaflet bombs and mortars were also used very effectively. The messages in these leaflets were essentially antimilitaristic and prodemocratic, stressing the class differences between the German leaders and the enlisted men (the same tactic as used in the Revolutionary War!), and also reminding German soldiers that American industrial might had now entered the war. The primary mission was to induce an attitude of surrender, and here the Americans really excelled for they were able to promise the half-starved German infantry first-class American food and care, and return to loved ones, all under the rule of international law. It soon became obvious that food was the most popular subject of appeal, for this had become an obsession with the starving German soldiers and civilian population.

Instead of attacking these issues directly by countering the information in the leaflets, the German high command attacked the whole concept of such demoralizing propaganda as being unethical, and stressed that German soldiers were expected to do their duty and would not be influenced by such messages. Of course this tactic failed and German soldiers surrendered in large numbers to the American and Allied forces in the last months of the war. Once again, the German army's reluctance to get their hands dirty in psychological warfare cost them dearly, but one must also point out that they had very few propaganda issues with which to counter, for unlike the domestic conditions in Germany, there was very little deprivation and starvation in the Allied countries, especially after America entered the war in 1917. Propaganda is most successful when it has a firm footing in observable reality.

Atrocity Propaganda

Perhaps the most significant single feature of World War I propaganda was the wide dissemination of atrocity stories as a means of discrediting the enemy. Often called "hate propaganda," most of the atrocity stories concentrated on three types of alleged cruelties: (a) massacre, such as the slaughter of the Armenians by the Ottoman Empire, supposedly under the encouragement of the Germans; (b) mutilation, such as the gouging out of the eyes of German soldiers; and (c) the mistreatment of both soldiers and civilian populations by starvation or actual torture. Such forms of propaganda are designed to stiffen the fighting spirit of entire nations, to create fear of defeat, and also as a more practical means to raise funds and encourage enlistment to halt these inhuman acts. Ultimately, it also served the purpose of prolonging the fighting and creating more severe conditions for surrender.

There were literally hundreds of books and pamphlets devoted to the most graphic details of supposed atrocities committed by both sides. Stories emanating from Belgium had a particularly strong influence in the Allied countries because of the large number of Belgium refugees who fled to neutral nations in 1914. The popular notion comparing the German soldier to the "Hun" of old (the Huns were actually Mongols from Central Asia), inspired by a careless remark made by the Kaiser in 1899 when he admonished the German contingent off to fight the Boxer Rebellion in China to "behave like Huns," became a central theme of propaganda attacks against the Germans. These atrocity stories, a few based upon real incidents but most without foundation, formed the core of the anti-German propaganda aimed at the United States in the years before America entered the war.

There were many atrocity stories that were widely circulated in the United States and other neutral countries; two have special significance. (Other atrocity propaganda stories have already been discussed in Chapter 4.) On October 9, 1915, Edith Cavell, a Red Cross nurse working in Brussels, was found guilty by a German court martial of helping British and French soldiers to escape into neutral Holland. She was sentenced to death and executed by a firing squad on October 12. She could have saved herself by professing ignorance of the law, but instead she openly admitted that many of the escapees had gone back to join their units; thus she was manifestly guilty of having committed a capital offense according to the German military code. This daughter of an English clergyman stated at her execution, "Standing before God and eternity, I realize this—patriotism is not enough. I must be free from hate and bitterness!" These words were carved on the monument to Edith Cavell in central London (Read, 1941). Edith Cavell became an instant martyr to the cause of propaganda and her "cold-blooded murder" was used to give credibility to the other atrocity stories coming out of Belgium. Even the supposedly neutral American press printed full accounts of the fifty-year-old nurse's courage in the face of her executioners. In Britain even to this day Edith Cavell remains a symbol of courage and loyalty.

There is an interesting sidelight to this story that demonstrates the failure of the Germans to understand the value of propaganda. The French had shot several women spies, one of them as early as August 1914, and at least two after Edith Cavell's execution, but the Germans failed to use these events to their advantage, and they were not even reported in the American press. A later attempt by the Germans to make a propaganda event of the execution by the French of the Dutch-Javanese entertainer and professional spy Mata Hari seemed to lack appeal when compared to the death of the English nurse. (Of course, the Mata Hari story later achieved immortality through the efforts of Hollywood, which, in 1931, produced a movie about her exploits featuring the extremely popular actress, Greta Garbo.) In the United States and other neutral nations, the Germans were hard-pressed to counter their constant portrayal as a barbaric nation that readily executed women.

The other propaganda event of significance was the furor that surrounded the sinking of the luxury liner *Lusitania* on May 7, 1915, by a German U-boat—without any prior warning and with a loss of 1,198 lives, 128 of them American. Whether the sinking of the ship was justified by the fact that the ship was carrying arms did not seem to matter at the time, for both the British and American press used the incident to reinforce increasingly hostile attitudes toward German acts of atrocity. In one of those curious acts of history, just five days after the sinking to the *Lusitania*, the British government issued

its long awaited *Bryce Commission Report* on the accuracy of the
stories of German atrocities. This commissiom, headed by a prominent British legal expert, had been formed in early 1915 as a result of
a public demand to know the truth about the German outrages.

The final report, which found "a compelling mass of evidence" to
substantiate the atrocities, was translated into thirty languages and
was widely circulated and reported in the United States (Read, 1941,
pp. 201-204). The findings of the Bryce Commission only served to
accentuate the "barbarity" of the ship's sinking, despite the fact that
the Germans may have had some justification for their actions during
a state of war. Today there is still considerable doubt about the
depositions taken by the Bryce Commission from Belgium refugees,
and there is the suggestion that the commissioners were themselves
caught up in the hysteria of war (Roetter, 1974).

Reaction to World War I Propaganda

There is little doubt that propaganda was effective as a weapon of
psychological warfare in World War I, but as indicated in Chapter 4, this
must be viewed in its historical context. For the first time in history nations
were forced to draw on the collective power of their entire populations
by linking the individual to a larger societal need. As DeFleur and
Ball-Rokeach (1982) have pointed out, "It became essential to mobilize
sentiments and loyalties, to instill in citizens a hatred and fear of the
enemy, to maintain their morale in the face of privation, and to capture
their energies into an effective contribution to their nation" (p. 159).

As a result, the general public indicated a response to mass media
messages as never before, and this reaction reinforced already existing fears about the potentially dangerous role of the mass media in
a mass society. It was at this time that social scientists were beginning to conduct the first research that suggested that the acquisition
of information from the mass media was a complex process, largely
involving individual predispositions, and questioning the myth of
the "mass audience." Nevertheless, the prevailing theories of psychology and the instinctual understanding of the way in which the
mass media worked were still influential, and reinforced by the
visible success of wartime propaganda efforts, this lead to a misinterpretation of how powerful the media really were. There was little
appreciation of the specific social and political conditions that had
made World War I propaganda so effective, and these incomplete
perceptions colored much of the thinking about the mass media in
general and propaganda in particular for the next twenty years.

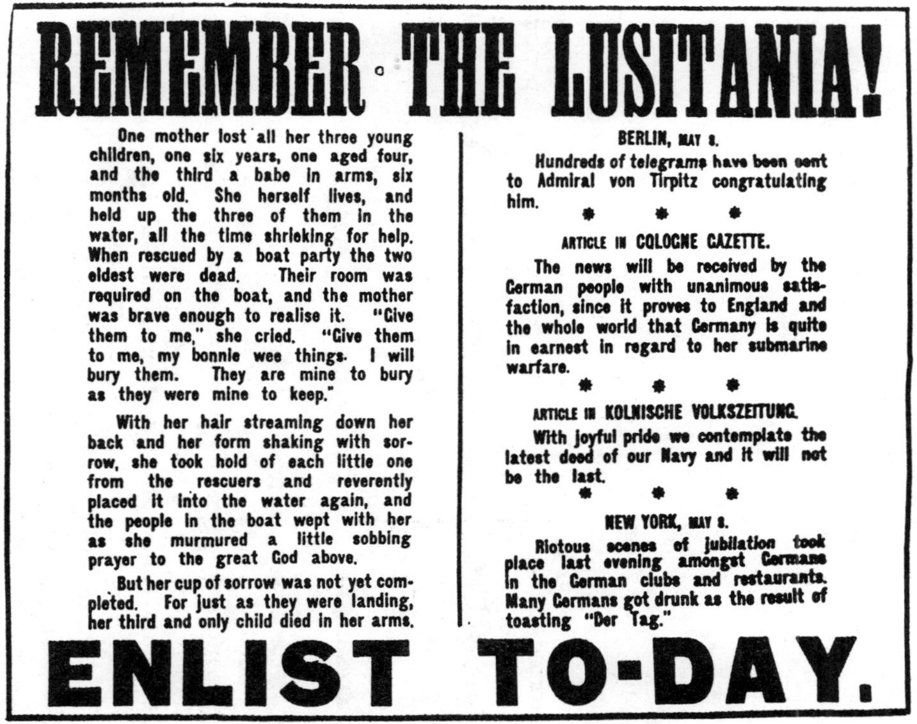

Figure 5.5. A poster that appeared a week after the passenger liner *Lusitania* was sunk by a German U-boat on May 7, 1915 with a loss of 1,198 lives, 128 of whom were American.

Figure 5.6. An anti-German poster showing a supposed atrocity. Note that the kaiser is depicted as approving of the nurse's actions, thus linking him directly with such German atrocities.

The Interwar Years, 1920-1939

The role of propaganda in the period between the two world wars can be characterized by three political developments: the Russian Revolution and the rise of the Communist Soviet Union; the strong isolationist impulse in the United States as a direct result of disillusionment with the outcome of World War I; and the rise of the fascist states, especially Nazi Germany. All three of these historical developments played a direct role in the outbreak of hostilities again in 1939, only this time all of the belligerent nations were aware of the necessity of both offering and countering propaganda in the strongest way possible.

The Emergence of Communist Propaganda

The philosophical underpinnings of the Russian Revolution lay in the adoption of an interpretation of the works of Karl Marx by a group of dissident Russian intellectuals, particularly Nikolai Lenin and Leon Trotsky. Ironically, it was the German, General Erich von Ludendorff who arranged to have Lenin return to Russia from exile in Switzerland in 1917, specifically to sow the seeds of revolution that would end the war on the eastern front, thus making more German troops available to confront the Allies in the West. Lenin finally succeeded in his Bolshevik Revolution in November 1917 when he overthrew the provisional government of Alexander Kerensky, which had earlier deposed Czar Nicholas II in March. The Bolsheviks came to power determined to create a new social order, but faced the immense task of transforming the thinking of a largely rural population of more than 170 million, many of whom were illiterate and most of whom were hungry.

To achieve their ends, the Soviet rulers erected an immense network of propaganda that included massive programs of political as well as practical education. Lenin mobilized every available form of communication (and entertainment) to meet this goal: the press, educational institutions, the arts, and even science all became part of the intensive internal propaganda system designed to play the central role in the creation of a Communist state. Controlled from the top, the arms of the Soviet propaganda machine reached into every aspect of Russian life, down to the local level where clubs and other quasi-social organizations received political education from trained propagandists. The establishment of reading rooms in even the smallest villages encouraged guided discussions, while films were accompanied by question and answer sessions. All of this was under the control and tight supervision of the Agitational-Propaganda Section of the Central Committee of the Communist party, known as Agitprop, which was attached to every division of the Communist party down to the smallest local cell (Maxwell, 1936). While the internal political convulsions continued in Russia until the late 1950s, this intensive propaganda infrastructure was absolutely crucial to the establishment of the new Communist state. It was the most extensive and long-lasting propaganda campaign in modern history, finally coming to an end with the momentous events in the Soviet Union in 1990-1991, which witnessed the end of the Communist party's hold on that country.

The Communists used a variety of symbolic and political devices to enhance their propaganda program. Foremost among the political devices was the concept of the imminent threat or plot, much as had been used in the French Revolution, which allowed the threat of brutality or retaliation to be used against political enemies or merely those who questioned party actions. The Hammer and Sickle was a strong visual symbol, and it received wide international recognition, but for many years the Soviet Union was restricted from lavish spectacle because of the spartan internal conditions. Even the *Internationale* was not played in the October uprising because the band did not know it; the Marseillaise was played instead! For many years, until the recent events which have destroyed the power of the Communist party, the Soviet Union engaged in massive spectacles of military might and of civilian solidarity. These symbolic displays became a staple of worldwide Communist propaganda, symbolizing the importance of the collectivity over the individual. Until very recently the Soviets still held massive May Day parades of military equipment, but the dire economic position of the USSR and the widespread dissatisfaction of the public gave a hollow ring to such events. The Soviet people are now quite capable of seeing the difference between the propaganda inherent in such displays of military might, and reality of a failed consumer economy. Such ostentatious displays have also lost their international propaganda power for all but the generals in the Pentagon, who continue to monitor the potential of Soviet militarism. The breakup of the Soviet Union into a series of smaller states is now a reality. However, events have moved so fast in such a short period of time, that it would be foolish to predict the exact shape and political affiliations which will emerge from the ruins of the massive Communist state. It is highly unlikely that these parades and other displays of collective solidarity will continue and it may well be that they have already reached a point where they have a negative propaganda value for the average Soviet citizen!

Because an articulated part of the Bolshevik program was to export Communism to all parts of the world—"the world Revolution"—Russian propaganda activities took on a worldwide dimension in the interwar period. In every country there sprang up national Communist parties, which in the period before the Stalinist purges of the mid-1930s were directly under the control of the Soviet Union, all aimed at establishing the international solidarity of the working class. Such sentiments had enormous appeal during the Depression, when unemployment, hunger, and general disillusionment with capitalism all contributed to a rise in the interest in Communism in the Western democracies, especially inflation-wrought and war-weary Germany. Even in the United States the Communist party and the "Popular Front" of pro-Soviet organizations attracted millions of members in the period 1935 to 1939, before the ill-fated Stalin-Hitler pact of August 1939 shattered their unity and created a schism with Moscow (O'Neill, 1982).

American Isolationism

As a direct result of their unsatisfactory experiences with the outcome of World War I, and led by their politicians, the American people turned inward during the period 1920 to 1941. The "America First" movement gained in popularity as people seemed to want to turn away from the turmoil in Europe, and the severe effects of the Depression created a further impetus to concentrate on domestic issues. The reaction against government propaganda was particularly virulent, as those responsible for creating the successful campaigns during the war seemed to be only too eager to explain how it was all done. George Creel had published his book *How We Advertised America* in 1920, and this precipitated a lengthy (and somewhat justified) suspicion of propaganda. This fear was enhanced by obvious role played by propaganda in the rise to power of Hitler, and the increased use of propaganda by the Nazi Reich and the other fascist states such as Italy. Despite the lingering suspicion of propaganda, the social and political conditions of the Depression made the American public highly susceptible to the messages of those who promised them salvation from their economic problems. Many such saviors appeared during this period, but the two most prominent and successful demagogues were the populist governor of Louisiana, Huey Long, and the ultraconservative Roman Catholic priest from the suburbs of Detroit, Fr. Charles E. Coughlin.

Huey Long, who went on to become a U.S. senator, ran the state of Louisiana like a dictatorship between 1928 and the time of his assassination in 1935. Known as "the Kingfish," (after a character on the "Amos 'n Andy" radio show), he had serious aspirations to become president. Long had courted the press outrageously by playing the country bumpkin (he once received a German naval commander on an official visit to the State House in his green silk pajamas), and he was able to use this publicity to further his "share the wealth" philosophy. In April, 1932 he rose on the Senate floor to make a major speech, in which he said: "Unless we provide for redistribution of wealth in this country, the country is doomed . . . I tell you that if in any country I live in . . . I should see my children starving and my wife starving, its laws against robbing and against stealing and against bootlegging would not amount to any more to me than they would to any other man when it came to a matter of facing the time of starvation." What Long was saying, as Brinkley (1982) notes, was that "the nation faced a choice. It could act to limit large fortunes and guarantee a decent life to its citizens, or it could wait for the otherwise inevitable revolution" (p. 44). This rhetoric won for Long an immediate reputation as a radical and the champion of the "little people." After Franklin Roosevelt was elected in 1932, Long tried to force his share the wealth philosophies on the Democratic president through a series of radio speeches. Roosevelt rejected his views, and privately thought of Long as a dangerous nuisance. Rejected by the bulk of the Democratic party, Long then formed a Share Our Wealth Society in February 1934, which he hoped would encompass a nationwide system of local clubs of people who shared this philosophy.

To get his message across to the public, Long developed a strong propaganda strategy that allowed him to bypass the normal media channels. His publication *American Progress* (1933) had only a small paid subscription list, but was mailed free to 300,000 people, which on occasion grew to 1.5 million. His autobiography, *Every Man a King* (published in October 1933), while not a best seller, was given away free to anyone who wanted it. He also had a staff of sixty stenographers (this was in the days before photocopying) that sent out letters, circulars and pamphlets proclaiming his activities and programs to this enormous mailing list. Radio was most important to Long, and by 1935 he was a regular and by all accounts, very popular speaker on the NBC radio network. He used a highly effective, personal and folksy style in his broadcasts. He usually began:

> Hello friends, this is Huey Long speaking. And I have some important things to tell you. Before I begin I want you to do me a favor. I am going

to talk along for four or five minutes, just to keep things going. While I'm doing it I want you to go to the telephone and call up five of your friends, and tell them that Huey is on the air. (Barnouw, 1968, p. 49)

According to Barnouw, this device produced steadily mounting audiences. Brinkley (1982) notes that "Long's national reputation grew at an astounding rate through the spring and summer of 1935, and the size and distribution of his Share the Wealth Clubs grew with it. . . . Long seemed to many to be on the verge of creating a genuine new force in American politics, one whose ultimate power nobody could yet predict" (p. 80). There were genuine fears that Long, if elected, would create a political structure that was similar to the European fascist states, although he had never identified himself with the fascist cause. All that became moot, however, when he was shot and killed in the Louisiana capitol building on September 10, 1935. It is one of history's little ironies that President Roosevelt heard the news of Long's death while entertaining two guests at his home in Hyde Park; Joseph P. Kennedy had brought Father Coughlin along to try and heal the breach between the president and the priest (Barnouw, 1968).

Father Charles Coughlin was born in Hamilton, Ontario, in 1891 and rose from relative obscurity to become one of the major public figures during the years of the Depression, almost solely through his extraordinary command of the new medium of radio. He had begun to use radio in 1926 when he was a priest at the Shrine of the Little Flower in Royal Oak, Michigan. By the late 1920s he discovered that the listeners to his modest weekly Sunday radio broadcast were interested in more than just his religious sermons, and after 1930 he switched almost exclusively to political topics. He addressed himself to the issues of the day—the hopes and fears of his largely working-class audience, and found that this created a strong response during this time of great uncertainty. Barnouw (1968, p. 45) notes that "his subject matter involved a diversity of political strands, stemming from varied sources. Sometimes he spoke of the perils of Communism, the 'red serpent.' Sometimes he pleaded for the remonetization of silver, and sounded like a Populist leader of the turn of the century. More often he castigated those of wealth and power, 'dulled by the opiate of their own contentedness.'" Brinkley, who has made a study of Coughlin's technique as a radio performer, notes that

Most important was the warm, inviting sound of his voice, a sound that could make even the tritest statements sound richer and more meaningful than they actually were. And there was, too, the ability to make the sermons accessible, interesting, and provocative to his audience. . . .

Coughlin used a wide variety of rhetorical techniques: maudlin sentimentality, anger and invective, sober reasonableness, religious or patriotic fervor. Rarely did successive broadcasts strike precisely the same tone, and in this unpredictability lay much of Coughlin's appeal. (p. 97)

Coughlin was able to exploit radio at a time when the medium was just beginning to become an important and integral part of American culture. While it was difficult to estimate the exact size and demographic composition of his audience, it was extremely large, and seemed to consist of people from all strata of society, but with one common denominator—they were all disaffected in some way with American society. Financial contributions poured in from across the country allowing him to purchase radio time. At the height of his popularity he received more mail than anyone else in America. His Sunday sermons were widely reported in the Monday newspapers, and "national magazines carried feature articles about the phenomenal success of the 'Radio Priest'" (Brinkley, 1982, p. 101).

Coughlin became more politicized as the Depression wore on, aiming his wrath at Wall Street and the international bankers who he felt controlled the world's economy and precipitated the Depression. Coughlin started his own quasi-political party, the National Union for Social Justice in 1934 and set out on a speaking tour across the country to attract voters. Everywhere he went he attracted large audiences, and it was estimated that the National Union had 8.5 million members in 1936. The problem was that the organization had no real structure beyond being a member of Coughlin's radio audience—really nothing more than names on a mailing list.

At a time when the economic uncertainties had created a potentially volatile public open to suggestions as to how American society should respond to the crisis, there was some concern about the growing power of the protesting voices of both Long and Coughlin. Things came to a head on March 4th, 1935, when Roosevelt's friend and former director of the National Recovery Administration, General Hugh S. Johnson made a famous speech at the Waldorf Astoria attacking both Long and Coughlin. In the speech, broadcast by the NBC radio network, he said,

You can laugh at Huey Long—you can snort at Father Coughlin—but this country was never under greater menace . . . Added to the fol-de-rol of Senator Long, there comes burring over the air the dripping brogue of the Irish-Canadian priest . . . musical, blatant bunk from the very nostrum of religion, it goes straight home to simple souls weary in distress. . . . Between the team of Huey Long and the priest we have the whole bag of crazy and crafty tricks . . . possessed by Peter the Hermit, Napoleon Bonaparte, Sitting Bull, William Hohenzollern [the Kaiser], Hitler, Lenin . . . boiled down to two with the radio and the newsreel to make them effective. If you don't think Long and Coughlin are dangerous, you don't know the temper of the country in this distress! (Barnouw, 1968, p. 48)

Johnson's hour-long speech was enthusiastically applauded at the Waldorf-Astoria, but the White House remained silent because the administration was concerned that Johnson had focused unwanted media attention on the two demagogues. The newspapers were already calling this "the battle of the century," (Brinkley, 1982, p. 6) and NBC provided free time to both for replies. The biggest fear was that they would join their forces to forge a formidable challenge to Roosevelt's reelection in 1936. However, despite the size of both Huey Long's Share The Wealth Clubs, and Fr. Coughlin's National Union for Social Justice, neither was able to mount a serious threat to Roosevelt in the 1936 elections, although the evidence indicates that the president did not take either of them lightly. The death of Long seemed to have an effect on Coughlin and he went into a decline after his political party obtained less than 2% of the total vote in the 1936 election. Coughlin finally moved over the edge of attacking international bankers into a blatant anti-Semitic stance in 1938; and he also favored neutrality when war began in Europe in 1939. In 1942 his publication *Social Justice* was banned from the U.S. mails, and he was threatened with formal charges of sedition. In May 1942, Coughlin quietly announced that he was severing all political ties "on orders from Church superiors." He remained in Detroit the rest of his life, where he died in 1979.

As Brinkley (1982) notes: "Huey Long and Father Coughlin faded so quickly from public prominence that it was easy in the ensuing years to forget how powerful and ominous they once had seemed. . . . [They] seized upon vague anxieties that had afflicted their society for many decades—the animosity toward concentrated power, the concern about the erosion of community and personal autonomy" (p. 261). Both had instinctual abilities to communicate their ideas to sympathetic audiences, demonstrating that the new medium of radio, with its inherent capacity to become "personal," was a potent force for propagandizing in modern society.

The Institute for Propaganda Analysis

The Institute for Propaganda Analysis (IPA) was started in October 1937 by Columbia University professor Clyde R. Miller who became its chief executive. (The best history of the IPA is Sproule, 1983.) Miller, who as a reporter during the First World War was convinced that he had been hoodwinked by propaganda, was one of a group who were concerned that the renewed interwar propaganda battles would once again draw the United States into a futile European conflict. The opinion leaders and educators who established the institute were not only concerned with war propaganda, but also with such domestic propaganda issues as the Ku Klux Klan, the Communists, domestic fascism and the role of advertising, all as possible threats to the democratic way of life. The overarching concern was that the increasing volume of propaganda from numerous sources was inhibiting people's ability to think clearly and straight. Miller received a $10,000 grant from Edward A. Filene, a wealthy Boston merchant and liberal-minded philanthropist who was "afraid that America was becoming the victim of propaganda (the year was 1936), that Americans had lost their capacity to think things through" (Sproule, 1983, p. 488). Miller had no difficulty in recruiting a distinguished group of academicians to serve as officers and also on the advisory board of the institute.

The institute immediately started a monthly bulletin, *Propaganda Analysis*. In the second issue (November, 1937) it published the famous seven common "devices" or "abc's of propaganda analysis." These were:

- *Name Calling.* Giving an idea a bad label, and therefore rejecting and condemning it without examining the evidence.
- *Glittering Generality.* Associating something with a "virtue word" and creating acceptance and approval without examination of the evidence.
- *Transfer.* Carries the respect and authority of something respected to something else to make the later accepted. Also works with something that is disrespected to make the latter rejected.
- *Testimonial.* Consists in having some respected or hated person say that a given idea or program or product or person is good or bad.
- *Plain Folks.* The method by which a speaker attempts to convince the audience that he or she and his or her ideas are good because they are "of the people," the "plain folks."
- *Card Stacking.* Involves the selection and use of facts or falsehoods, illustrations or distractions, and logical or illogical statements in order

to give the best or the worst possible case for an idea, program, person, or product.

- *Band Wagon*. Has as its theme "everybody—at least all of us—is doing it!" and thereby tries to convince the members of a group that their peers are accepting the program, and that we should all jump on the band wagon rather than be left out. (Lee & Lee, 1979)

After discussing how these propaganda devices were used, the bulletin noted: "Observe that in all of these devices our emotion is the stuff with which propagandists work. Without it they are helpless; with it, harnessing it to their purposes, they can make us glow with pride or burn with hatred, they can make us zealots in behalf of the program they espouse" (How to Detect Propaganda, 1937, p. 7). In the 1930s these seven common devices became the cornerstone of the institute's applied studies of contemporary propaganda. In one of the best examples, in the May 1938 issue of *Propaganda Analysis* they served as the basis for an incisive analysis "Propaganda Techniques of German Fascism." Thus under the category Plain Folks the analysis pointed out that

at the same time that the Führer is canonized, an attempt is made to transform him into a "man of the people." In this, the propagandists are greatly assisted by his habits; for he affects ordinary clothes, wears no medals other than his simple Iron Cross, eats plain food and that sparingly, and leads a quiet, secluded life. He is pictured as a man of the people meeting plain folks in their ordinary walks of life, enjoying with them their simple work and pleasures. . . . Jesus, a carpenter, is the Messiah of the Christian world; Hitler, a house painter, is the savior of Germany (*Propaganda Analysis*, 1938, pp. 46-47).

This simple technique of analyzing propaganda was open to criticism, especially in that it can be very subjective in evaluation; however, this seven-point analysis remains with us today and is still widely quoted in textbooks on persuasion and propaganda.

The IPA also conducted a highly successful education program that encouraged the readers of the bulletin to gather materials to conduct their own propaganda analyses. A *Group Leader's Guide to Propaganda Analysis* was developed to promote critical thinking and informed discussion about current issues. This publication also discussed how propaganda analysis could be used to scrutinize advertising, as well as academic subjects such as English literature, music, art, social science and other fields. By September 1939 the IPA's materials were being used in more than 550 high schools and colleges, as well as numerous adult civic groups (Sproule, 1983). According to Alfred and Elizabeth Lee, among the founding members of the institute, propaganda analysis caught on so readily because "it provided a badly needed perspective for current affairs" (Lee & Lee, 1979, p. viii). The institute suspended its operations in late October 1941 when it appeared that the United States was going to enter the war. In the last issue of *Propaganda Analysis* (January, 1939) under the title "We Say Au Revoir," the editorial explained the reasons for the institute's decision.

> The Institute's Board of Directors has concluded that to attempt to continue publication during the war period would probably result in weakening the confidence which the Institute has won, and impair its usefulness later. . . . The publication of dispassionate analyses of all kinds of propaganda, "good" and "bad," is easily misunderstood during a war emergency, and more important, the analyses could be misused for undesirable purposes by persons opposing the government's efforts. . . . If it were to continue it would have to analyze all propaganda—of this country and of Britain and Russia as well as that of Germany, Italy and Japan. (4, no. 13, p. 1)

The IPA was never to return. The end of World War II was immediately followed by the tensions of the ideological Cold War between the Communist and capitalist forces, and then the Korean and Vietnam wars. In this highly politicized and militarized atmosphere the Institute for Propaganda Analysis would not have been able to function as a constructive critic of American institutions without incurring the wrath of various factions. Sproule has another view on why the IPA was never revived, and why propaganda analysis declined in the postwar years. He notes that "sharing the relatively complacent public mood of the 1940s and 1950s, and implicitly or explicitly aware of the more powerful dampers on social criticism, the academicians embraced the new terminology and technology of academic social science" (1983, p. 96). Thus, the relatively simplistic forms of propaganda analysis developed and employed by the IPA became obsolete in the face of more sophisticated forms of communications research being undertaken in universities. Despite its demise, the IPA continues to serve as an ongoing symbol of the concern for the increased and sometimes subtle role of propaganda in our lives.

American isolationism remained fairly strong even after war broke out in Europe in 1939; however, there is clear evidence through opinion polls that the American public was increasingly becoming pro-Ally, while at the same time they remained antiwar. Congress was reluctant at times to give President Roosevelt approval to supply Britain with arms, but gradually relented. The United States officially entered the war against Germany on December 11, 1941, four days after the Japanese attacked Pearl Harbor. Once committed in this fashion, the American public again became the target of massive propaganda campaigns both on the home front and in the armed services. (Some of these propaganda activities are examined in Chapter 3.) Since the end of World War II the isolationist impulse has periodically risen, but the realities of the atomic age has effectively prevented total withdrawal from the world political arena, although many Americans still wish that isolationism was possible.

Hitler and Nazi Propaganda

One of the unexpected consequences of the somewhat hysterical anti-German propaganda of World War I was that it made many people, particularly politicians, suspicious of alleged atrocity stories emanating from Germany during the 1930s. The very success of the British propaganda efforts in 1914-1918 proved to be a serious handicap in getting the world to accept the reality of what was happening in Nazi Germany, and this created a disastrous delay in the public's awareness of the horrors of the concentration camps and other Nazi atrocities.

Hitler's place in the history of propaganda is assured, for as Thomson (1977) notes, "Hitler shares with Julius Caesar and Napoleon Bonaparte, the distinction of not only making massive use of new methods of propaganda but also, of quite consciously and deliberately basing his entire career on planned propaganda" (p. 111). Goebbels, who became Hitler's propaganda minister and the mastermind behind the Nazi propaganda machine, described Hitler's propaganda principles, which he extracted from *Mein Kampf*, as

> a carefully built up erection of statements, which whether true or false can be made to undermine quite rigidly held ideas and to construct new ones that will take their place. It would not be impossible to prove with sufficient repetition and psychological understanding of the people concerned that a square is in fact a circle. What after all are a square and a circle? They are mere words and words can be molded until they clothe ideas in disguise (Thomson, 1977).

In *Mein Kampf* Hitler (1939) established several cardinal rules for successful propaganda: one should avoid abstract ideas and appeal instead to the emotions, which was the opposite of the Marxist concept; there should be constant repetition of just a few ideas, using stereotyped phrases and avoiding objectivity; put forth only one side of the argument; constantly criticize enemies of the state; and identify one special enemy for special vilification. Throughout the Nazi period Hitler and Goebbels stuck rigidly to these principles, and the world witnessed a mature, cultured people—the Germans—accepting one of the most onerous dictatorships in history, which precipitated a prolonged war and eventually instituted as policy the most heinous of all crimes, genocide.

Hitler had admired the propaganda efforts of the British in World War I, as well as the work of the poet-politician Gabriele D'Annunzio, the short-lived dictator of Fiume in Italy, and the extroverted style and anti-Semitism of Karl Lueger, the Mayor of Vienna. A key to Hitler's thinking was that he saw the masses as "malleable, corrupt and corruptible," and open to emotional appeals; but especially he realized that propaganda could become much more effective if a large dose of intimidation and terror stiffened it (Zeman, 1973). Calling his political program National Socialism, Hitler immediately established a image that appealed to a wide section of the confused and demoralized German public. He promised to restore Germany to its former glory and to rid the country of the shackles imposed by the Versailles Peace Treaty, and thus rose to power with a skillful combination of power, spectacle, and propaganda.

Together Hitler and Goebbels probably understood the propaganda potential of the mass media better than anyone else alive, and they were in a perfect position to put their theories to the test. Their greatest advantage was the psychological condition of their audience, for the German Weimar government had failed to provide the leadership that would have restored German confidence and morale after 1918, and the German people were desperately searching for the answers to their political nightmare. Many of them turned to socialism and Communism; National Socialism, with its emphasis on restoring the mythical Germany of the past and the perverse charismatic leadership provided by Adolf Hitler, offered an even more palatable alternative. Germany in the late 1920s and early 1930s supplied the perfect setting for the implementation of Hitler's schemes.

The Weimar Republic had an ineffective press that was so diffused with small partisan papers that the Nazis were easily able to gain control of the newspapers in the period after 1925. Using the simple, nondoctrinaire approach, the Nazi newspapers *Volkische Beobachter* (Racist Observer) and later *Das Reich* preached the Nazi philosophy, especially anti-Semitism and anti-Communism, as well as providing information about the Nazi party itself. But newspapers were not the main vehicle for Nazi propaganda, for the emotional appeals stressed by Hitler did not easily translate into written words. There were few journalists in Germany at this time with enough skill to compete with the fiery speeches from Nazi podiums.

It was with radio that the Nazis achieved their greatest success, and this medium was used extensively as the primary medium of official propaganda. The importance of radio was stressed when the Nazi government produced a cheap, one-channel radio set for the masses (the *Volksempfänger*), and eventually introduced compulsory installation of radios with loudspeakers in restaurants, factories, and most public places. During the war, there were even "radio wardens" who checked that people were listening to the right stations! As we have seen in Chapter 3, radio also became the primary medium for overseas propaganda activities, and Hitler used directed broadcasts to those European countries in which he was trying to establish contact with German-speaking populations. Austria, particularly, suffered from a "radio war" in 1933, as Hitler attempted to incite the Austrians to overthrow their government. Radio was also extensively used to win the Saar Plebiscite in 1936, when Goebbels smuggled large numbers of cheap radios into the disputed territory in order to gain German support and to smear the anti-Nazi leader Max Brawn. On the day before the secret vote, German radio broadcast that Brawn had fled, and it was too late to counter this move so that even as Brawn was driven through the streets, he was called an imposter. Radio was also the perfect medium for communicating the almost religious fervor of Nazi spectacles, with the rhythmic chants of "Seig Heil," the enthusiastic applause, and the power of Hitler's or Goebbels' speaking style.

As we have already noted, the Germans did not have as much propaganda success with their use of the cinema—mainly because audiences were more attuned to escapist entertainment—and film propaganda, even when skillfully done, has a tendency to look too heavy-handed. This is especially true if the audience is aware that "this is a propaganda film." There were, however, some memorable German propaganda films, such as director Leni Riefenstahl's use of the Odin myth in the making of *The Triumph of the Will* (1935); Hans Steinhoff's film about the Boer War, *Ohm Kruger* (Uncle Kruger, 1941), which allowed the Germans to attack British colonialism; and Veit Harlan's *Jud Süss* (The Jew Süss, 1940), which was a subtle anti-Semitic examination of the influence of Jews on German life. Even more violent and obvious in its anti-Semitic attack was *Der Ewige Jude* (The Wandering Jew), a documentary film made in 1940 by Fritz

Hippler, the head of Nazi film production (the Reichsfilmintendant), which depicted the worst racial stereotypes, and compared Jews to a plague of rats that needed to be exterminated.

Richard Taylor (1979) reports that

> The Wandering Jew was shown at 66 cinemas in Berlin alone but Security Service reports on its reception suggest that audiences, after Jew Süss, were already tiring of anti-Semitic propaganda: "Statements like 'We've seen Jew Süss and we've enough of Jewish filth' have been heard" (p. 204-205). Nevertheless, in August 1941 the German authorities in the occupied Netherlands decreed that every Dutch cinema should include The Wandering Jew in its programme during the following six-month period. And so the film became at the same time a prelude to the holocaust, a propagandist's excuse for it, and a perverted documentary-format record of its early stages.

It is not surprising that in the face of these films that the biggest box office attraction during this period was the purely escapist Grosse Liebe (The Great Love), the story of a soldier's love, and while the film did glorify death in battle, the emotional theme underscored the audience's rejection of blatant propaganda. Commercial Nazi propaganda films with rare exceptions failed to find strong overseas markets and therefore were limited in their influence. Some of the war documentaries, as indicated in Chapter 3, did create a fear of the German army in many neutral countries, but they also had the opposite effect of reinforcing opposition to German aggression in countries such as Britain and the United States. The ultimate irony is that extracts from captured copies of these documentaries were used by the Hollywood director Frank Capra as a central part of his powerful series of Why We Fight orientation films for the U.S. army.

Posters were also used extensively throughout the Nazi Reich; these usually featured bold colors, especially red, and used large, simplistic illustrations and heavy, dominating slogans. Hitler wanted to be an architect in his youth, and he always had an appreciation for the visual—he understood the importance of strong visual symbols. Even in the period before the Nazis were able to dominate newspapers and radio, the poster became the primary source of propaganda, displaying especially the Nazi symbol of the swastika, the square-jawed pure Aryan Nazi stormtrooper, or anti-Semitic images of large-nosed Jews. These propaganda images became commonplace after Hitler came to power in 1933 and they contributed in no small measure to Nazi success (Zeman, 1978).

Figure 5.7. "All Germany Hears Their Führer With the People's Receiver." This poster extols the popularity of the specially priced "People's Receiver" which appeared about a year after the Nazis took power in 1933 and cost about $24 at the time. By the outbreak of war, 70% of all German households owned radios, the highest percentage anywhere in the world.

Figure 5.8. A poster for *The Eternal Jew* exhibition held in the German Museum in Munich in late 1937. This is an archetypical caricature of a Jew showing off shekels in the right hand and a map of the Soviet Union and a whip in the left. It did not seem to concern the German propagandists that these were contradictory symbols. A vicious film based upon this exhibition was also released in 1940.

Figure 5.9. This is just part of the crowd of 151,000 who attended the Party Day celebrations in Nuremberg in 1933 to listen to Hitler's speech. Note the massive display of flags in the background and Hitler, thrust out on the podium by himself. Such massive displays were an essential part of Nazi propaganda, designed to demonstrate public solidarity with the policies of the Nazi party.

Figure 5.10. The exterior of the House of German Art in Munich. This type of architecture was typical of the Nazi ideal, massive and harking back to a period of ancient glory. This building was used to exhibit only art works that had been officially approved by the Nazis as meeting the ideals of Aryan Culture.

The Nazis used many propaganda devices, but one that they brought to the peak of perfection in the modern era was the spectacle. Under the supervision of Hitler's official architect, Albert Speer, these lavish public displays moved from being mere exhibitions of Nazi might to becoming propagandistic works of art, designed to evoke an outpouring of emotional fervor and support. These gigantic rallies also allowed the people of Germany to perceive Hitler in the context of a restored Germany, with strong overtones harking back to the Aryan myths of the past. The annual party rallies in the city of Nuremberg were special centerpieces for the public affirmation of Nazi mythology. The Nuremberg Rallies lasted up to eight days and featured dramatic lighting, controlled sound effects, and martial music. With a cast of hundreds of thousands, these annual events were calculated to create a strong emotional resonance of patriotic hysteria in the German people. The enormous size of the rallies, encompassing participants from all parts of Germany, was specifically orchestrated to provide a sense of a pan-German community, visibly communicating that all Germans accepted the single ideology of Nazism. Ward Rutherford (1978) points out that Goebbels regarded these rallies as important because they were an effective substitute for actual participation in policymaking by the populace. In several speeches Goebbels made the point that taking part in such a rally was regarded as superior to voting in a democracy!

Finally, Nazi propaganda made extensive use of a wide variety of carefully designed symbols to emphasize their power and authority. These included the eagle, Nazi "martyr's" blood, marching—especially the goose-step—the Heil salute, the carrying of swords and daggers, the use of fire, the swastika, and the flag (Delia, 1971). Some symbols were more blatant than others, such as the skull and crossbones insignia worn by members of the Gestapo. Nazis were particularly adept at using architecture and sculpture as propaganda media, and Albert Speer masterminded the massive restructuring of Berlin and other large-scale construction projects ordered by Hitler to reflect his "Thousand Year Reich." Hitler apparently wanted to leave a monument to himself that would have dwarfed all such monuments from the past, including a triumphal arch that would have been 550 feet wide, 392 feet deep, and 386 feet high. Recanting after the war, Speer (1970) called this "architectural megalomania."

One major advantage that the Nazis had in ensuring the success of their domestic propaganda campaigns was their total control over the country. By 1933 there were no competing propaganda messages of any consequence to distract the German public. The educational system, like the Russian, was an instrument of state policy and was geared to provide an ideological justification of anti-Semitism and Nazi values. In fact, anti-Semitism became the underpinning of the Nazi propaganda campaign, as the Jews were blamed for everything that was wrong with Germany and the West. Jews were called decadent capitalists or godless Bolsheviks at the same time; it did not matter that much of the rhetoric was clearly contradictory, for Hitler's principles of propaganda required that a scapegoat be found, and anti-Semitism served both political and social ends. Through the persistent reinforcement of these messages, Hitler was able to achieve a fiery nationalism by convincing the German people that ridding themselves of Jews would create an undefiled, uncorrupt, pure Aryan nation. Socially, anti-Semitism was evoked to provide a rationale for German failure, as well as a reason to hope for a better future—once the problem had been taken care of. This was a classic propaganda ploy; Hitler was able to both demoralize the Jews and mobilize hatred against them, thus providing a justification for his political and social policies.

In the long run Hitler's domestic propaganda campaigns were successful, and it was only defeat on the battlefield that finally ended the terror within Germany. In his study of German propaganda, *The War that Hitler Won*, Robert Herzstein (1978) makes a strong case for considering the overwhelming success of Hitler's propaganda efforts in the context of their times. Since 1945, we have concentrated on the loss of the war by the Nazis while ignoring their incredible propaganda victories in Germany and elsewhere. Even after the Allies had liberated a few concentration camps, German leaders were still advocating the extermination of Jews and Bolsheviks, and were blaming the loss of the war on these groups. Ultimately Nazism and its abhorrent racial philosophies could only be defeated on the battlefield. Unfortunately, many of Nazism's worst aspects, particularly anti-Semitism, continue to manifest themselves in modern society. It is fascinating to note the continued, some would say increased, interest that exists in all things pertaining to the Nazis. Every year hundreds of books, both fiction and nonfiction, are published on the subject; movies and television shows on Nazis, both past and present, continue to occupy our screens; Nazi paraphernalia such as badges, medals, daggers, and flags (most of them fake copies) are sold at flea markets to collectors; and so-called neo-Nazi groups like the skinheads continue to claim inspiration from the racial ideologies of Hitler. Why all of this interest after more than fifty years? Clearly the material symbology of the Nazis has left behind a powerful memory on our culture. We are perversely fascinated by a society and its culture that could have had such high aspirations and intellect on the surface, while committing such unspeakable cruelties to achieve those ends. How could a society that gave us Bach, Beethoven, and Goethe have also given us Buchenwald? We all recognize the popular culture image of the cultured Nazi officer, in his well-cut military uniform, listening to Wagner, while at the same time ordering the deaths of hundreds of Jewish prisoners! Robert Herzstein was right, the historical persistence of these images is a testament to the strength of Nazi propaganda.

World War II

In many ways the propaganda efforts of the belligerent nations in World War II were predictable, following the discovery of the potential of psychological warfare in World War I. The major difference, as we have already noted in Chapter 3, is that radio became the principal means of sending propaganda messages to foreign countries. The traditional propaganda media of pamphlets, posters, and motion pictures were again used, but with an increased awareness of the psychology of human behavior. On all sides psychologists were put to work on devising the best methods of appeal, taking into consideration specific cultural and social factors relative to the intended target audience. This was a far cry from the rather "buckshot" approach taken earlier, and indicated the seriousness with which psychological warfare was being waged. On both fronts—the European and the Pacific—American propaganda experts from the various agencies that were created to coordinate domestic and overseas propaganda activities were careful to use scientific methods where possible in devising their campaigns. In particular, there was to be little emphasis on atrocity propaganda, except where this served a deliberate purpose, such as President Roosevelt's delayed announcement of the Japanese execution of the American flyers shot down over Tokyo.

One of the most controversial problems facing historians examining World War II is why the issue of the treatment of German concentration camp victims received such little public acknowledgement until almost the end of the war. The showing of the startling black-and-white newsreel footage of the liberation of these camps was the first time that most Americans had a clear idea of what really happened. Would the earlier revelation of the treatment of the Jews and others in the camps have made a difference in when the United

Figure 5.11. A British poster by Bert Thomas, appealing to the public to avoid unnecessary travel. Such a poster, while highlighting a real problem, also helped to boost the morale of the civilian populations by telling them that they, too, could contribute to the war effort through their everyday actions.

Figure 5.12. An American civilian poster, c. 1943. This poster, produced and distributed by the Texaco Company, was posted on factory and office bulletin boards as a reminder that civilians were also important in the war effort. The caricature of the Japanese soldier is typical of the period.

States entered the war? How much of this indifference can be blamed on a reaction to World War I atrocity propaganda? Was there a strain of anti-Semitism in the United States State Department during the early years of the war that deliberately underplayed the plight of the Jews? These are questions that have not yet been fully answered.

Both sides made much more extensive use of "white" and "black" propaganda through the medium of radio, as the new medium provided the ideal opportunity to establish contact over long distances without necessarily revealing the source of the message. Clandestine radio stations were established that broadcast both true and false information to the enemy, and special commentators were used to create the illusion of broadcasts coming from within their own countries. (The most detailed histories of this interesting subject are Soley, 1989; Soley & Nichols, 1987.) The British, through the services of the British Broadcasting Corporation, were particularly adept at this, establishing several black propaganda stations aimed at both German domestic and military targets. These stations, by essentially broadcasting the truth about wartime conditions, were able to make a considerable impact on the German people, and often caused confusion on the military front (Roetter, 1974). This emphasis on truth, which became the basic philosophy for the British Broadcasting system, proved to be an extremely powerful propaganda weapon, and by the end of the war the German civilian population was listening to these broadcasts in order to find out about conditions in their own country.

On the domestic front, in both Britain and the United States, extensive campaigns were devised to boost homefront morale. Particularly in Britain, where the German Luftwaffe had created chaos with their bombing raids, it was essential that the population be kept from panic. Again, the Ministry of Information, which was charged with this task, realized that truth was their greatest propaganda device, but their experts had a difficult time persuading their government to adopt this tactic. Eventually the ministry won its argument that in fighting totalitarianism, Britain should not borrow its weapons of lies and censorship but instead should rely upon the sensibility and toughness of the British people, taking them into the government's confidence. While the entire truth was not always revealed, in the long run, such propaganda tactics played an important part in maintaining the high morale of the British public, even during the darkest periods early in the war (McLaine, 1979).

In the United States the problems were different, and the major emphasis was placed on providing a clear rationale to the American people as to why they were fighting the war in Europe. (There was no equivocation about why the Pacific War was necessary.) As mentioned in Chapter 4, it was deemed necessary to provide the American fighting man with an orientation to the reasons he was being asked to risk his life. The *Why We Fight* films, discussed in Chapter 4, were compulsory viewing for enlisted men, and the first of these, *Prelude to War*, was also shown to civilian audiences throughout the nation in 1943. It was these films that were the subject of important research into the effects of propaganda messages on specific audiences. Utilizing all of the mass media, the Office of War Information (OWI), the organization charged with handling domestic propaganda before 1943, created immediate antagonism with what had always been a "free press." The American mass media were not used to being told what they could or could not do, and full cooperation with the government only came after a series of delicate negotiations. OWI officials were eager to have the domestic entertainment media use their considerable power to propagandize to the American public in a more blatant fashion than the media executives thought necessary. In the long run, the OWI reduced its demands in the face of congressional disapproval and suspicion that it was being used by President Roosevelt to further his own personal domestic policies. Allan Winkler (1978), in his history of the OWI, suggests that the eventual success of the American propaganda campaigns, both domestic and abroad, was that they "sketched the war as a struggle for the American way of life and stressed the components—both spiritual and material—that . . . made America great" (pp. 156-57).

Post-World War II Conflicts: Korea, Vietnam and the Gulf War

There have been three major wars involving the United States since 1945. In the first two conflicts, Korea and Vietnam, the ideological battle between Communism and capitalism was an underlying factor; in the case of the Gulf War, the United States and its allies decided that Iraq's invasion of Kuwait could not be tolerated within the context of shifting world power (particularly the collapse of the Soviet Union as a protective force for Iraq), as well as emphasizing the need to "protect" the world's oil supply from falling into Saddam Hussein's hands. Each of these conflicts involved using very different propaganda strategies because of the international political alliances then in effect, and the nature of the public response on the homefront. The varied success of these strategies underlined the need to understand the culture of those to whom the propaganda is being directed.

Korea, 1950-1953

The Korean conflict began on June 25, 1950, when the Soviet-backed government of North Korea invaded South Korea. (Even this issue is still in dispute, and there is some evidence that South Korea may have been the initial aggressor. See Aronson, 1970.) The United Nations Security Council met in an emergency session and passed a resolution that demanded withdrawal of the North Korean troops, and also authorized UN members to assist in the execution of the resolution. The Soviet Union had been boycotting the UN and was therefore not present to cast a veto in the Security Council. Eventually the UN Security Council authorized a UN military force "police action" to repel the armed attack, with troops from a number of nations under the command of U.S. General Douglas McArthur. American troops eventually comprised about half of the fighting forces. During the next three years, the opposing armies fought each other up and down the Korean peninsula. On December 31, 1950, about 400,000 Chinese troops entered the war to supplement the 100,000 North Korean soldiers. In a blatant piece of international propaganda, the Communist Chinese government disavowed official participation in the war, claiming that all of the Chinese troops were volunteers who had decided to help their beleaguered North Korean comrades. Eventually, largely through the use of superior air power, the UN forces were able to drive the North Koreans and the Chinese back across the 38th parallel by June of 1951. Truce talks then began that continued until an armistice was signed on July 27, 1953. (These peace talks were, without doubt, the most contentious in the history of warfare!) However, negotiations on the exact conditions of the truce and other issues between the opposing forces continues even today, nearly forty years after the event, and technically the conflict has never really ended.

The propaganda aspects of the Korean conflict were very disturbing for the Americans. Coming out of the propaganda successes of World War II, the U.S. military were suddenly confronted with a very different type of propaganda from the Communists. This time the propaganda battle was being fought in the arena of world opinion, and the vast international audience was divided between the opposing ideological forces of Communism and capitalism. The United States, which for most of the twentieth century had been on the side of "good," suddenly found itself on the defensive after being accused of being the "bad guy." Early in 1952 the Communists charged the UN forces with using germ warfare as a means of explaining the series of epidemics that were then sweeping the civilian and military populations of North Korea. Pictures of insects supposedly dropped by UN planes were shown to the world's press. The North Koreans tried to force captured UN pilots to admit their complicity, and in May 1952 two American pilots "confessed" their guilt. These confessions had come after four months of intensive physical and psychological torture. Of the 78 pilots that were subjected to such pressures, 38 succumbed, while the other 48 resisted all forms of torture. At the end of the war the germ warfare charges were proven to be groundless, and all repatriated pilots repudiated their confessions. However, these reports were widely circulated throughout the world, and even today continue to be part of the Communist mythology about the Korean war. Such accusations, once made, are very difficult to totally eradicate from the historical record, particularly when the audience may be predisposed to accept the veracity of the information.

The issue of prisoner exchanges also proved to be a major propaganda ploy for both sides. The UN captured 171,000 Communist prisoners, of whom slightly more than 20,000 were Chinese. It soon became obvious that more than half of the North Korean prisoners and two-thirds of the Chinese were violently opposed to being repatriated to their Communist homelands. The North Korean armistice negotiators did not wish to acknowledge this, demanding that all prisoners should be repatriated. The Communists even arranged to have trained political agitators deliberately taken prisoner to maintain ideological control among their prisoners, and to foment trouble in the POW camps. The result was that several violent riots took place in the camps in early 1952. (In many cases prisoners were forcibly tattooed with either pro or anti-Communist slogans that turned them into living political billboards, thus making them unacceptable to the other side!) Eventually those prisoners who wanted to return home were allowed to do so after the armistice in July 1953, and nearly 100,000 formerly Communist troops elected not to return to their home countries. 15,000 Chinese prisoners decided to go to Formosa (Taiwan). This issue provided the USIA with a choice propaganda plum, and motion pictures, broadcast interviews, and press features about the defecting prisoners were sent all over the world (Sorensen, 1968).

The most disturbing aspect of the Korean propaganda war for Americans and Britons was that when the prisoners returned home from their ordeals, it was revealed that a substantial portion—perhaps 15% among Americans—had actively collaborated with the enemy, and that only a few—about 5%—had resisted all Communist efforts to indoctrinate them, or to use them for propaganda purposes. The remainder, generally apathetic, had not been collaborators, but had given in to some degree to Communist pressures (Dupuy, 1965). The extensive and expert brainwashing encountered by the Korean War prisoners was an entirely new form of coercive propaganda, and caused much discussion within the U.S. military and among academicians interested in persuasive techniques. This led to a general belief that the men had not been adequately prepared to withstand the psychological and physical tortures that they would encounter, and a reassessment of what ideological training they should have received. This disconcerting aspect of the Korean War, together with the increasing power of world Communism, called into question the ideological strength of the United States. This apparent weakness was a major plank in the anti-Communist platform from which Senator Joseph McCarthy and his followers were able create their national hysteria about the depth of Communist influence in the United States. Among the many far-reaching results of this renewed nationalism was the requirement that teachers and professors sign oaths of loyalty, and the revamping of school and university curricula to emphasize American history and culture (Schrecker, 1986). In the military, the Uniform Code of Military Justice was also rewritten to outline the behavior expected from prisoners subjected to brainwashing by their captors.

The Korean War must be seen as an integral part of the Cold War. As such, it represented a major opportunity for both sides to propagandize on a worldwide scale. In the end, the West may have won the battle, but the prolonged, contentious peace talks, and the strong feelings on both sides engendered by the POW issue, did not bring about a cessation of ideological hostilities. The escalated levels and viciousness of the propaganda battles of the Korean War forced the U.S. government to reexamine its own propaganda techniques and activities, and did much to strengthen the role of the USIA and other agencies charged with shaping America's image at home and abroad.

The Vietnam War

In Vietnam in 1965 the United States launched what is probably the largest propaganda campaign in the history of warfare. The history of the Vietnam conflict is a complex one, having its origins in the almost two-thousand-year-old struggle of the Vietnamese people against outside invaders. First the Chinese and Mongols, and then in the nineteenth century the French tried to turn Vietnam into a colony, but each time the largely peasant armies were eventually able to defeat the intruders. Starting in the 1930s, and continuing throughout the Japanese occupation during World War II, the Vietnamese Communist party (many of whose members had been trained in Moscow in the 1920s) were adroitly able to fashion a program of nationalism that fused anticolonialism and anticapitalism, and which blamed the French colonial system for all of the country's ills. At the conclusion of the war in 1945 the country was split by many competing political factions, but all were opposed to French colonial rule. The Communists took a leading role in the struggle which culminated in the expulsion of the French from Indochina in 1954. This led to a divided Vietnam; the Communists in the North, with their capitol Hanoi, and the non-Communists in the South, with their capitol Saigon. When many diplomatic efforts failed to reunite the country, the National Liberation Front (Viet Cong) was formed to hasten the collapse of the southern Republic and lay the groundwork for reunification. The United States provided "advisors" as well as financial and military aid to bolster the democratic Saigon government, but by 1964 the fighting had escalated to the point that it appeared certain that the Communists would win. It was at this point that the United States decided to send increased numbers of American soldiers to fight with the South Vietnamese.

The direct intervention of the U.S. troops certainly ensured the survival of the South Vietnamese government for the short run, but it also allowed the propaganda of the Communists, both from the North and also inside South Vietnam itself, to claim that once again the country was being invaded by foreigners and colonial oppressors. The long-term Communist propaganda appeal to all of the Vietnamese people was to "Save Vietnam from American Imperialism" (Chandler, 1981, pp. 7-9. This is by far the most detailed book on the propaganda of the Vietnam War). It was this nationalistic, anticolonial appeal, combined with other military factors that eventually triumphed in the face of the far superior fire power of the combined American and South Vietnamese forces.

American propaganda efforts (psychological operations) began in Vietnam in 1954, during the period of transition from French rule, when anti-Communist rumor campaigns were conducted in both North and South Vietnam. As the insurgency escalated, so did the propaganda efforts, and eventually by the early 1960s three special agencies were assisting the South Vietnamese propaganda and psychological warfare programs. These were the United States Information Service (USIS—the overseas arm of the USIA); the State Department's Agency for International Development (USAID); and the Joint Chiefs of Staff's Military Assistance Command (MACV). Although they were supposed to coordinate their efforts, the activities of these three agencies were marked by duplication and inefficiency. To many observers, the "hearts and minds" battle being waged from South Vietnam was simply not working. As a result, on July 1, 1965, the Joint U.S. Public Affairs Office (JUSPAO) became the delegated authority for all propaganda activities. MACV was to continue to operate as the military psychological warfare branch, but under the control of JUSPAO. This organization was under the supervision of the USIA, but operationally subordinate to the U.S. ambassador to the Republic of South Vietnam (Chandler, 1981). JUSPAO was invited to become an active participant in the U.S. Mission Council, the ambassador's highest policymaking body. Chandler (1981) notes that "it was the first meaningful American attempt to integrate the psychological aspect of foreign policy with the political, economic, and military instruments" (p. 27).

JUSPAO had two major propaganda objectives, the first was to undermine and eventually abolish the support for the Communist regime in North Vietnam; the second was to win the "hearts and minds"of the South Vietnamese and solid support for a pro-democratic and nationalistic South Vietnam. To achieve these goals, three audiences were targeted: the first were the Communist soldiers (the Viet Cong) and their supporters within South Vietnam; the second were the masses and elites of North Vietnam; and the third was the non-Communists in South Vietnam.

The propaganda campaign aimed at the Viet Cong was known as *Chieu Hoi*, meaning "open arms." The basic message was "Give up the fight and return to the folds of the government of Vietnam!" Under this program, Viet Cong surrendering to the Republic of Viet Nam were guaranteed protection, medication, and rehabilitation with new jobs in the south. The media used to convey these messages were mainly surrender leaflets and the broadcasts from low flying aircraft. It is estimated that during the seven years it operated in Vietnam, the USIA, supported by the armed forces, dropped nearly 50 billion leaflets—nearly "1,500 for every person in both parts of the country" (Chandler, 1981, p. 3). Five specific propaganda appeals were used in the *Chieu Hoi* program:

- The "fear of death" appeal. The leaflets depicted dead soldiers, including decapitations and severe maimings, under headlines reading, "Continue your struggle against the National Cause, and you will surely die a mournful death like this."
- The hardships endured by Viet Cong. The soldiers were reminded of their poor living conditions, and their desires to be with their families.
- The loss of faith in a Communist victory. Combined with the fear of death, this appeal gave the numbers of Communist dead, and suggested that the Viet Cong were being betrayed by their leaders.
- The soldier's concern for his family and the hardships they faced without him. This appeal was aimed at the central role that the family played in Vietnamese culture, and was one of the most successful. Leaflets typically depicted a worried family or a father playing with his son. The captions stated: "Chieu Hoi means to be reunited with your loved ones. It means escape from your loneliness."
- The last appeal was in reality a combination of all of the others, and coalesced around the theme of disillusionment with the war. This focused on the soldier's insecurities and was supposed to make him question the decisions of the authorities. A typical leaflet read: "Your leaders have deceived you to a lonely death far from your home, your family and your ancestors."

The net effect of these campaigns is difficult to assess. In a special study done of the *Chieu Hoi* propaganda campaign by Ernest and Edith Bairdain of Human Sciences Research, they found that in terms of numbers of defectors the campaign was quite successful, but that these were mainly lower-ranking and the least ideologically motivated individuals. Between 1963 and 1972 more than 200,000 people came over to the South Vietnamese side. Most of these were simply people who had been swept up into Communist service. There were relatively fewer teachers, physicians, division commanders, and so forth. Most important of all, very few North Vietnamese soldiers defected because they were far from their families and believed in the justness of the Communist goal of liberating the south from the American "colonialists." The northern soldiers were also very resistant to surrender proposals and other propaganda appeals, and they were expected to uphold their honor by fighting until they died. In an assessment made of the Vietnam propaganda efforts by the Rand Corporation in 1970, specialist Konrad Kellen noted "neither our military actions nor our political or psywar efforts seem to have made an appreciable dent on the enemy's overall motivation and morale structure" (Chandler, 1981, p. 96).

There were several other factors that mitigated against a successful propaganda effort to capture the hearts and minds of the North Vietnamese, and foremost among these was the decision to try and bomb the North into submission. This bombing destroyed the internal transportation systems and the agriculture of the north, but sustained by heavy support from the Soviet Union and Communist China, the people showed a remarkable ability to withstand these attacks and carry on the war. Chandler suggests that the bombing had a boomerang effect, resulting in a "burst of patriotism" rather than the despair which it was intended to create. "The [Communist] Party adroitly fanned the fires of anger from these attacks and channeled the people's ire toward hatred of the United States and dedication to driving the 'foreign invaders' from Vietnam" (Chandler, 1981, p. 147). Americans had failed to learn the lessons from the blitz on Britain and the saturation bombing of Germany during World War II, namely that a direct, frontal attack on a society tends to strengthen the will of the people to fight back, even under the most trying of circumstances. It also has the effect of increasing the capacity of the society to better prepare itself for future attacks, and to adopt measures that allows it to restore vital functions and effect repairs much faster. The end result was that the "Hate the U.S." propaganda campaign became a very powerful motivating force for the North Vietnamese and is generally credited with helping to bring about the final victory. The North Vietnamese were too dedicated to their cause to be influenced otherwise, while many of the large peasant class in the south simply wanted to be left in peace. In the final assessment, despite the massive propaganda efforts of the United States and the South Vietnamese, these proved to be ineffective in penetrating the "ideological shield" that surrounded the north's population and armed forces.

What lessons can we learn from the propaganda efforts in the Vietnamese War? Chandler (1981) points out that there are interesting parallels between the Vietnamese War and the American Revolutionary War, in that both conflicts saw a relatively small group of backward farmers bring a world superpower to its knees by protracted and unconventional warfare. In both cases the odds for success were minimal, but "psychologically with both patriotism and a vision of the future, the weak prevailed over the mighty—a common denominator in both revolutions was love of country and an uncompromising desire to achieve freedom from foreign rule" (p. 256).

Of course, one of the most interesting aspects of the propaganda efforts in the Vietnam War were the intense propaganda battles waged on the American homefront between those who supported the war and those opposed to it. As disenchantment with the war grew, it became the central focus around which a variety of issues, political, social, and cultural revolved. The Vietnam War provided a focus for a younger generation seeking to break away from the materialist values of their parents; for many young men it also raised the issue of being drafted to fight an "immoral war"; and, eventually, it brought about a major shift in American culture and left a legacy of disillusionment and suspicion of government. The soldiers returning from Vietnam found that the nation had turned its back on them, and they would have to wait until the morally uplifting victory of the Gulf War more than twenty years later before they received their just recognition.

The Gulf War, 1990-1991

The Gulf War, which pitted the U.S.-lead coalition forces against the vaunted army of Iraq under President Saddam Hussein, provided an opportunity for reestablishing the United States as the major world power following the collapse of the Soviet Union. In the minds of the American people the cause was just, for our ally, the tiny, and somewhat helpless Kuwait had been illegally invaded by the brutal forces of the dictator Hussein, and subjected to atrocities. Besides which, this action posed a serious threat to U.S. domestic security by threatening the flow of oil from the Middle East. The war, while of short duration, offered an interesting challenge to propaganda agencies on both sides as they battled to place their respective positions before the court of world public opinion. The propaganda activities of both sides during the Gulf War are the subject of a detailed case study in Chapter 7.

The Cold War, 1945-1985

Once World War II was over, the world had entered a new age; people no longer entertained the naive concept that global conflict could be won or lost by conventional means, for the frightening power of nuclear destruction loomed menacingly over the international scene. While wars of physical destruction continued, there were other types of wars to be fought as the world moved beyond its imperialist-colonial period, and many new nations fought for their rights in the global arena. This generated increased demands for more extensive propaganda activities, particularly as the two great world powers, Russia and the United States, sought to establish their political and cultural hegemony in the rest of the world.

In the struggle for international power, which has become a feature of modern politics, all nations have been forced to adopt new and permanent propaganda strategies as an integral part of their foreign policies. In fact, the use of international propaganda in its many forms is so ubiquitous that the foreign policy of most nations is geared toward both its generation and refutation on a continuous basis. In an age when instantaneous communication is the norm, nations have become conscious of creating and maintaining specific images that they hope to project to the rest of the world; and a vast amount of time, money, and human energy is spent on such activities. The astonishing growth of new communication technologies such as television satellites and transistor radios has created a worldwide audience for what were previously small-scale international activities. Increasingly world leaders are becoming astutely aware that their every action is being critically examined within this new electronic arena, and like the good actors that most politicians are, they are adjusting their postures and policies to make the most of their exposure. Since the end of World War II, there has been an enormous increase in the growth of new forms of propaganda activities, ranging from the traditional foreign policy pronouncements to more subtle, but no less effective, activities such as travel bureaus, sporting events, international trade exhibitions and world expositions, achievements in space and other technologies, and cultural phenomena such as art, fashion, and music. In fact, it would not be inaccurate to say that almost every aspect of human activity can be propagandized in the international arena. The Soviets claim to have the oldest people in the world, the Scandinavians the lowest infant mortality rate, and the Americans the most automobiles per capita. All of these are used, in one form or another, as propaganda. The Olympic Games, in particular, have become a major propaganda event ever since Adolf Hitler used the 1936 Berlin games to showcase his Aryan Reich. (A fine history of the 1936 Olympics is found in Hart-Davis, 1986.) In recent years, both the United States in 1980 (Moscow) and then the Soviets in 1984 (Los Angeles) boycotted the Olympic Games as a means of propagandizing their displeasure over each other's foreign policies. The Soviets went even further, claiming that "criminal elements" would make Los Angeles unsafe for their athletes, hoping to score international propaganda points by drawing attention to the state of domestic and racial conditions in the United States. Ultimately the Los Angeles Games not only proved to be the safest in recent years but also ran at a profit! At this point the Soviets, having been proved wrong, objected that the Americans had subverted the Olympic ideals into a "capitalist sideshow"—and thus are modern propaganda battles waged. In 1988 the games were held in Seoul, South Korea, and became a deliberate, and carefully orchestrated international showcase for the economic development of that Pacific nation.

The emergence of these new communication technologies has often made it possible for those wishing to propagandize to make direct contact with their target audiences, and thus governments have much less control over the flow of information than was possible in the age of print. The consequences of this important historical shift are already noticeable as world public opinion gains influence. There is increasing evidence that the populace in less-developed countries are exhibiting the "frustration of rising expectations." This is caused by a comparison of their own standards of living with the images of the relatively luxurious life-styles in Western democracies as shown daily on worldwide television networks such as CNN. This frustration often manifests itself in hostile acts and bellicose propagandizing against the capitalist nations.

We are also witnessing the emergence of new networks of common interest that cross international boundaries, such as terrorist organizations composed of members of the Irish Republican Army, the Palestine Liberation Organization and other Middle East factions, the Italian Red Brigade, and Japanese radicals, often funded by Libya, Syria or Iran with the oil revenues largely from the European countries. (Whether the defeat of Iraq in the Gulf War will end this type of support remains yet to be seen.) The acts of terror that these various groups engage in are, in fact, their specific forms of propaganda for their differing causes. Capturing an American airplane or an Italian cruise ship can guarantee extensive media coverage that these groups could otherwise not afford. Clearly in cases such as these the terrorists often misjudge the extent of worldwide sympathy for their cause, but these propaganda acts serve an important morale-building function for the groups themselves (Wright, 1990).

This new development in international propaganda activities creates a problem for open societies such as the United States and Great Britain. In recent years the issue of the rights of the free press have been questioned when these rights have run up against the necessity for the government to maintain some sort of secrecy. The U.S. Supreme Court decided by a 6 to 3 vote that the *New York Times* had the right to publish the Pentagon Papers in 1971, even though their exposure would result in an embarrassment for the government and its Vietnam policies. In a closed society, such as the USSR was at that time, there would have been no such public admission of government subterfuge, the press having been under total control of the political system.

In open societies we are constantly faced with negative disclosures in the press that provide ammunition for propaganda attacks. This is one of the tributes that living in a free society extracts; and despite the apparent disadvantages, it seems as if there is greater public confidence in open societies in which the public have some, albeit often skeptical, confidence in their news media. Although there is still a tendency "to kill the messenger" who brings the bad news, this is preferable to receiving managed news or no news at all. As an example, the Soviets were often reluctant to report major catastrophes such as earthquakes, plane crashes, atomic accidents, or natural disasters such as floods or tornadoes. For reasons known only to the Communist psyche, such events were seen as a weakening of their image and a possible source of negative propaganda against Communism as a political and social system. The events at the power station in Chernobyl, Ukraine, on Saturday April 26, 1986 proved to be a turning point in this policy of official secrecy. (An excellent account of the propaganda aspects of this event is Luke, 1989.) It took more than three days to publicly announce what had taken place, and in the meantime the world's press, in the absence of the official "facts" from the Soviet government, made enormous propaganda gains by reporting that more than two thousand people were dead or dying from radiation poisoning. (The *New York Post* ran a headline, borrowed from a New Jersey Ukrainian-language weekly that clearly had its own propaganda agenda and screamed: "MASS GRAVE:— 15,000 reported buried in Nuke Disposal Site.") It was not until May 4 that the Soviet government broadcast any convincing television images of the accident on the evening news program "Vremya," and a full overview did not occur until May 14 when President Mikhail Gorbachev spoke to the nation on this same program. By the time that it was officially announced that 2 people had died "promptly," and that 29 others had died more slowly, with another 300 suffering from radiation sickness, the world's press had become skeptical and accused the Soviets of lying and being untrustworthy. This event, perhaps more than any other, forced the USSR to become more forthcoming about natural and manmade disasters within their borders. It would be almost impossible in the West to "hide" such events from the media for lengthy periods of time.

The emergence of this new international media culture places a great deal of importance on the shaping and channeling of information to gain the maximum advantage; in some ways it has become more important to say what a nation is doing than to really do it. At least we can be thankful for the fact that mass propaganda is now practiced through trade, travel, exchange of culture, and scientific and sporting achievements, and not through warfare. In the war of words that we are all subjected to, nations have taken to trying to "outpeace" each other!

6 How to Analyze Propaganda

A ten-step plan of propaganda analysis includes identification of ideology and purpose, context, identification of the propagandist, investigation of the structure of the propaganda organization, selection of the target audience, understanding of media utilization techniques, analysis of special techniques to maximize effect, audience reaction, identification and analysis of counterpropaganda, and an assessment and evaluation.

The analysis of propaganda is a complex undertaking that requires historical research, the examination of propaganda messages and media, sensitivity to audience responses, and critical scrutiny of the entire propaganda process. There may be a temptation to examine the short-term aspects of propaganda campaigns, but a true understanding of propaganda requires analysis of the long-term effects. Propaganda includes the reinforcement of societal myths and stereotypes that are so deeply embedded in a culture that it is often difficult to recognize a message as propaganda.

As we said in Chapter 1, propaganda is a systematic attempt to shape perceptions, manipulate cognitions, and direct behavior. Its systematic nature requires longitudinal study of its progress. Because the essence of propaganda is its deliberateness of purpose, considerable investigation is required to find out what the purpose is.

We have designed a ten-step plan of analysis that incorporates the major elements of propaganda. This schema makes it difficult to study propaganda in progress because the outcome may not be known for a long time. On the other hand, to study propaganda in progress enables the analyst to directly observe media utilization and audience response in actual settings. Long-range effects may not be known for some time in a contemporary study. Chapter 7 has three case studies of propaganda, two of which are from the past; the other is from the 1991 Persian Gulf War. We believe that contemporary propaganda is different from past propaganda mainly in the use of new media. New technologies must be taken into account, for the forms of media and how they are used have always been significant in propaganda.

The ten stages of propaganda are as follows:

1. the ideology and purpose of the propaganda campaign,
2. the context in which the propaganda occurs,
3. identification of the propagandist,
4. the structure of the propaganda organization,
5. the target audience,
6. media utilization techniques,
7. special various techniques,
8. audience reaction to various techniques,
9. counterpropaganda, if present, and
10. effects and evaluation.

These ten stages take into account the following questions: To what ends, in the context of the times, does a propaganda agent, working through an organization, reach an audience through the media while using special symbols to get a desired reaction? Further, if there is opposition to the propaganda, what form does it take? Finally, how successful is the propaganda in achieving its purpose?

The Ideology and Purpose of the Propaganda Campaign

The ideology of propaganda provides, according to Kecskemeti, "the audience with a comprehensive conceptual framework for dealing with social and political reality" (1973, pp. 849-50). In locating the ideology, the analyst looks for a set of beliefs, values, attitudes, and behaviors as well as ways of perceiving and thinking that are agreed upon to the point that they constitute a set of norms for a society that dictate what is desirable and what should be done. Martha Cooper (1989) describes ideology as a coherent "world view that determines how arguments will be received and interpreted. The common sense of the world view provides the basis for determining what is good, bad, right, wrong, and so forth" (p. 162). Ideology accordingly contains concepts about what the society in which it exists is actually like. It states or denies, for example, that there are classes and that certain conditions are desirable or more

women role in wartime

desirable than others. An ideology is also a form of consent to be a particular kind of social order and conformity to the rules within a specific set of social, economic, and political structures. It often assigns roles to gender, racial, religious, and social groups.

The propaganda analyst looks for ideology in both verbal and visual representations that may reflect preexisting struggles and past situations, current frames of reference to value systems, and future goals and objectives. Resonance of symbols of the past encourages people to apply previously agreed upon ideas to the present and future goals of the propagandist. Cooper cites the example of the ideology of the Old South Plantation Myth from Civil War days being invoked as white supremacy during the Civil Rights movement of the 1960s.

The purpose of propaganda may be to influence people to adopt attitudes that correspond to those of the propagandist or to engage in certain patterns of behavior, for example, to contribute money, join groups, demonstrate for a cause, and so on. Propaganda also has as its purpose to maintain the legitimacy of the institution or organization that it represents and thereby ensure the legitimacy of its activities. Integration propaganda attempts to maintain the positions and interests represented by officials who sponsor and sanction the propaganda messages. Agitation propaganda seeks to arouse people to participate in or support a cause. It attempts to arouse people from apathy by giving them feasible actions to carry out. Kecskemeti said that agitation consists of stimulating mass action by hammering home one salient feature of the situation that is threatening, iniquitous, or outrageous (1973, p. 849).

Mainly, the purpose of propaganda is to achieve acceptance of the propagandist's ideology by the people. Joseph Goebbels said that propaganda had no fundamental method, only purpose—the conquest of the masses.

The Context in Which the Propaganda Occurs

Successful propaganda relates to the prevailing mood of the times; therefore, it is essential to understand the climate of the times. The propaganda analyst needs to be aware of the events that have occurred and of the interpretation of the events that the propagandists have made. What are the expected states of the world social system (war, peace, human rights, and so on)? Is there a prevailing public mood? What specific issues are identifiable? How widely are the issues felt? What constraints exist that keep these issues from being resolved? Is there a struggle over power? What parties are involved, and what is at stake? It has been said that propaganda is like a packet of seeds dropped on fertile soil. To understand how the seeds can grow and spread, analysis of the soil—that is, the times and events—is necessary.

It is also important to know and understand the historical background. What has happened to lead up to this point in time? What deeply held beliefs and values have been important for a long time? What myths are related to the present propaganda? What is the source of these myths? A myth is not merely a fantasy or a lie, but rather it is a model for social action. For example, the mythology of American populism was based on a classic and good hero such as Abraham Lincoln who rose from humble birth to self-made lawyer to the White House. This hero is a Christlike figure because he not only rose from humble beginnings but also was martyred. The model for social action is that a person can rise above difficult circumstances to become a leader who can make significant differences in people's lives. A myth is a story in which meaning is embodied in recurrent symbols and events, but it is also an idea to which people already subscribe; therefore, it is a predisposition to act. It can be used by a propagandist as a mythical representation of an audience's experiences, feelings, and thoughts. Western movies have not only provided a myth about the Old West of the past but a myth of American character for the present. The idea of the yellow ribbons displayed to support the troops in the Persian Gulf War may have come from John Ford's 1949 film *She Wore a Yellow Ribbon*, but the myth of the Western hero (John Wayne) fighting the villain was symbolized in the yellow ribbons as well.

Identification of the Propagandist

The source of propaganda is likely to be an institution or an organization with the propagandist as its leader or agent. Sometimes there will be complete openness about the identity of the organization behind the propaganda; sometimes it is necessary to conceal the identity in order to achieve the goals set by an institution. When identity is concealed, the task of the analyst is a demanding one. It has been quite difficult to detect black propaganda until after all the facts are known. In black propaganda, not only is there deliberate distortion but the identity of the source is usually inaccurate.

Some guidelines for determining the identity of the propagandist are found in the apparent ideology, purpose, and the context of the propaganda message. The analyst can then ask, "Who or what has the most to gain from this?" Historical perspective is also very valuable in making such a determination. The analyst can also look at the broader picture, for, generally speaking, propaganda that conceals its source has a larger purpose than is readily discernible.

When the propagandist is a person, it is easier to identify that person because propagandists usually have what Doob (1966) called "verbal compulsions" (p. 274). Look for the person who speaks frequently and with authority. It is possible, however, for the person to be an agent or front for the actual propagandist, concealing the true identity of the leader or institution.

The Structure of the Propaganda Organization

Nazi regime

Successful propaganda campaigns tend to originate from a strong, centralized, and decision-making authority that produces a consistent message throughout its structure. For this reason, there will be strong and centralized leadership with a hierarchy built into the organization. The apparent leader may not be the actual leader, but the apparent leader espouses the ideology of the actual leader. The analyst can investigate how it was that the leader got the position and try to determine how the leader inspires loyalty and support. The leader will have a certain style that enables him or her to attract, maintain, and mold the members into organizational units. The leadership style may include the mythic elements of the ideology, a charismatic personality, and/or identification with the audience.

Structure also includes the articulation of specific goals and the means by which to achieve them. Furthermore, in relationship to goals, there may be specific objectives and means to achieve them. Goals are usually long range and broader than objectives that are short range and more easily met. For example, a goal could be to stop the construction of nuclear power plants; whereas an objective could be to enlist the support of key figures in the community.

The selection of media used to send the propaganda message is another structural consideration. The analyst needs to look into the means of selecting the media. Often, where propaganda is distributed, the organization owns and controls its own media. Whoever owns the media exercises control over the communication of messages.

The analyst has to determine the makeup of the membership of the propaganda organization. There is a difference between being a follower and a member of an organization. Hitler (1939) wrote in

Mein Kampf, that "the task of propaganda is to attract followers; the task of party organization is to win members. A follower of a movement is one who declares himself in agreement with its aims; a member is one who fights for it" (pp. 474-75). The analyst might then ask, how is entry into membership gained? Is there evidence of conversion and apparent symbols of membership? Does new membership require the adoption of new symbols such as special clothing or uniforms, language, in-group references, and/or activities that create new identities for the membership? Are there rituals that provide mechanisms for conversion or transformation to new identities? Are special strategies designed to increase (or decrease) membership? What rewards or punishment are used to enhance membership in the organization?

The organization can be examined to find out if it has an apparent culture within itself. A culture is a system of informal rules that spells out how people are to behave most of the time. Culture is equal to the social practices that incorporate and form the values that arise among social groups based on their historical conditions and relationships. Values are the bedrock of a culture, thus the propaganda of an organization is based upon a complex system of values in its ideology that will be instrumental in achieving and maintaining all elements of its structure. Meanings are important in culture as are messages that generate meanings.

Beliefs will be talked about; slogans will be used; everyone in the organization will agree with and consistently use these values in many ways. A culture also has heroes and heroines who personify the culture's values. Rituals are the systematic and programmed day-to-day routines in the organization, or they may be anniversary rituals that take place on a grand scale, for example, the parade of the athletes at the Olympics opening ceremony or the inauguration of a president in Washington, D.C. Rituals provide visible and potent examples of what the ideology is.

There will also be a set of formal rules within the organization. The analyst should not only determine what the rules are but how they are sanctioned as well. Is there a system of reward and punishment? How are the rules made known? Who oversees the enforcement of the rules?

An organization network becomes apparent through message distribution. How is the network used to foster communication? How is information disseminated from the leader to the membership? How is information transmitted to the public? Is there evidence that the public is denied access to information that is made available only to the membership or the organization elite?

In order to obtain the data necessary to analyze the structure of a propaganda organization, the analyst should have access to sources that penetrate the organization. Previous investigators (Altheide & Johnson, 1980; Bogart, 1976; Conway & Siegelman, 1982) have either used assistants to feign conversion or have been members of the organization at one time themselves. Often the verbal compulsions of the propagandists result in autobiographic treatment of their roles in the organization (Armstrong, 1979).

Structures of propaganda organizations also vary according to whether the communication is within the organization or directed to the public. The analyst may discern two different and separate structures, one for the hierarchy and the membership and one for the audience and potential members.

The Target Audience

A target audience is selected by a propagandist for its potential effectiveness. The propaganda message is aimed at the audience most likely to be useful to the propagandist if it responds favorably. Modern marketing research enhanced by computer technology enables an audience to be targeted easily. Many facets of an audience are easily determined. Mailing lists can be purchased and coordinated with audience responses to media appeals. For example, if a person responds to a television pledge drive with a contribution, his or her name is put on a mailing list for future mail appeals from the same or other organizations who buy the list.

The traditional propaganda audience is a mass audience, but that is not always the case with modern propaganda. To be sure, mass communication in some form will be used, but it may be used in conjunction with other audience forms such as small groups, interest groups, a group of the politically or culturally elite, a special segment of the population, opinion leaders, and individuals. Bogart (1976) points out that the United States Information agency addresses itself to those in a position to influence others—that is, to opinion leaders rather than to the masses directly. He quotes a USIA report that says, "We should think of our audiences as channels rather than as receptacles" and that "it is more important to reach one journalist than ten housewives or five doctors" (p. 56). Opinion leaders are a target for American propaganda abroad. In the Middle East, for example, the masses can be reached indirectly through reaching the culturally elite 10% of the population.

A distribution system for media may generate its own audience. A television program, a film, or a library may attract a supportive audience. Once that audience is identified, however, it too can be targeted.

Some organizations prefer a buckshot approach to a mass audience. Kecskemeti (1973) claimed that strong propagandist could work the message media in a homogeneous way with a consistent message. Some audience members accept the message more eagerly than others; some reject it.

There are many variations of audience selection, and none should be overlooked by the analyst. It is useful to examine the propagandist's approach to audience selection, noting if there is a correlation between selection practices and success rate.

Media Utilization Techniques

At first, it may not seem difficult to determine how propaganda uses the media. The analyst examines which media are being used by the propagandist. Modern propaganda uses all the media available—press, radio, television, film, computers, fax machines, posters, meetings, door-to-door canvassing, handbills, buttons, billboards, speeches, flags, street names, monuments, coins, stamps, books, plays, comic strips, poetry, music, sporting events, cultural events, company reports, libraries, and awards and prizes. Some well-established honors function as propaganda—for example, the Rhodes Scholarship, the Fulbright Awards Program, and the Soviet Friendship scholarships.

Also, use of tone and sound may have a conditioning effect. In 1950, Dobrogaev, a Russian psychologist, began working with speech tones and sounds for conditioning. In 1954, China began using loud speakers that broadcast official truths in city squares and gathering places. This is still being done in China today. A French fable reminds us, "Man is like a rabbit. You catch him by the ears." Musical anthems and patriotic songs are forms of conditioning, for people walk around whistling these melodies and even sing their children to sleep with them. Musical slogans can become detached from the original composition as were the four opening notes of Beethoven's Fifth Symphony during World War II, which came to signify the V for victory, the sounds of the Morse code for V, dot-dot-dot-dash.

The various messages coming from the same source over the media need to be compared to see if there is a consistency of apparent purpose. All output will be tied to ideology in one way or another.

Describing the media usage alone is insufficient in drawing a picture of media utilization, for the analyst must examine the flow of communication from one medium to another and from media to groups and individuals. Evidence of multistep flow and diffusion of ideas should be sought. The relationship among the media themselves and the relationship between the media and people should be explored.

The main focus should be on how the media are used. The propagandist might show a film and pass out leaflets afterward. This type of practice maximizes the potential of the media. When an audience perceives the media, what expectation is it likely to have? What is the audience asked to do to respond to the message in the media? Does it seem that the audience is asked to react without thinking? Are the media used in such a way as to conceal the true purpose and/or identity of the propagandist?

Propaganda is associated with the control of information flow. Those who control public opinion and behavior make maximum and intelligent use of the forms of communication that are available to them. Certain information will be released in sequence or together with other information. This is a way of distorting information because it may set up a false association. Propaganda may appear in the medium that has a monopoly in a contained area. There may or may not be an opportunity for counterpropaganda within or on competing media. The media should have the capability to reach target audiences, or new technologies may have to be designed and constructed to do so.

The analyst should see what visual images are presented through pictures, symbols, graphics, colors, filmed and televised representations, books, pamphlets, and newspapers. Also, verbal innovations need to be examined for information, slogans, and emotional arousal techniques. The analyst should go beyond interpretation of the message to a closer scrutiny of the ways in which the message is presented in the media. What is the overall impression left with the audience? Essentially, how are the visual and verbal messages consistent with the ideology?

The selection of the media may be related to economics as well as to the most effective access to the audience. An audience that is located in a remote region without access to major media will have to be reached in appropriate ways. Sometimes the ways in which the messages are distributed require acceptance of innovations on the part of the audience. They may be asked to try new technologies or to participate in novel activities.

For analysis of media utilization, every possibility should be examined. Bogart (1976) tells of the faculty members in engineering and medicine at Cairo University who were so intensely sympathetic to Communism that they would not come to the American library or read American material. They would, however, come to see a film about new surgical procedure developed by an American physician or a film about an application of engineering to industry. The overt purpose of the film was to transmit valuable information, but the covert purpose was to get the faculty to observe superior information compared to information from other sources in their professional specialty. They were not expecting propaganda, but they absorbed a good impression of American science. Eventually, they started coming to the American library.

The analyst needs to be aware of unusual and unsavory media utilization as well. In 1954, for example, China began to send opium to Thailand to promote addiction, dependency, passivity, and lethargy, thus rendering a group of people susceptible to takeover.

Special Techniques to Maximize Effect

We have deliberately chosen not to make a comprehensive list of propaganda techniques in the manner of the Institute for Propaganda Analysis (see Chapter 3). Propaganda is too complex to limit its techniques to a short list. There are certain principles, however, that can be elaborated upon to assist the analyst in examining techniques. Aristotle, in discussing rhetoric, advised the persuader to use "all of the available means of persuasion." Goebbels, in discussing propaganda, advised the propagandist that every means that serves the purpose of the conquest of the masses is good. Qualter, in discussing the techniques of propaganda, said that the common slogan of the four basic criteria of successful propaganda should be considered: it must be seen, understood, remembered, and acted upon.

We believe that propaganda must be evaluated according to its ends. Ends may be desired attitude states, but they are more likely to be desired behavior states such as donating, joining, and voting. They may also be aroused enthusiasm manifested in behavior states such as cheering, yelling, and so on.

Predispositions of the Audience: Creating Resonance

Messages have greater impact when they are in line with existing opinions, beliefs, and dispositions. Jacques Ellul (1965 said, "The propagandist builds his techniques on the basis of his knowledge of man, his tendencies, his desires, his needs, his psychic mechanisms, his conditioning" (p. 4). The propagandist uses belief to create belief by linking or reinforcing audience predispositions to reinforce propagandistic ideology or in some cases, to create new attitudes and/or behaviors. Rather than try to change political loyalties, racial and religious attitudes, and other deeply held beliefs, the propagandist voices the propagandee's feelings about these things. Messages appear to be resonant, for they seem to be coming from within the audience rather than from without. Lawrence Weschler (1983), writing about martial law in Warsaw in 1982, quoted John Berger the British art critic, who said that "'propaganda preserves within people outdated structures of feeling and thinking whilst forcing new experiences upon them. It transforms them into puppets—whilst most of the strain brought about by the transformation remains politically harmless as inevitably incoherent frustration'" (p. 69). Of the obvious techniques to look for when analyzing propaganda techniques are links to values, beliefs, attitudes, and past behavior patterns of the target audience.

Messages that are supportive of rather than discrepant from commonly held views of the people are more likely to be effective. Yet the propagandist uses canalization to direct preexisting behavior patterns and attitudes. Once a pattern has been established among a target audience, the propagandist can try to canalize it in one direction or another.

When change does take place, it does so because of a multitude of factors related to the source of the message, the impact of opinion leaders, group interaction, the context in which the message is sent and received, and media utilization.

Source Credibility

Source credibility is one of the contributing factors that seems to influence change. People have a tendency to look up to authority figures for knowledge and direction. Expert opinion is effective in establishing the legitimacy of change and is tied to information control. Once a source is accepted on one issue another issue may be established as well on the basis of prior acceptance of the source.

The analyst looks for an audience's perceived image of the source. How does the audience regard the source? Are the people deferential and do they accept the message on the basis of leadership alone? Is the propaganda agent a hero? Is there evidence that the audience models its behavior after the propagandist? How does the propagandist establish identification with the audience? Does he or she establish familiarity with the audience's locality, use local incidents, share interests, hopes, hatreds, and so on? During the Vietnam conflict, the Viet Cong would move into a hamlet and establish rapport with the local citizenry, taking their time to become integrated into the life of the hamlet. Soon they would enlist help from the villagers; for example, some would prepare bandages; boys would carry messages. Seeing that they were helping the Viet Cong, the villagers would experience cognitive dissonance and have to justify their own behavior by accepting the Viet Cong's view of the world.

Opinion Leaders

Another technique is to work through those who have credibility in a community—the opinion leaders. Bogart (1976) tells how the USIA warned its agents not to offend the opinion leaders in other cultures. They were ordered to avoid taboos, curb criticism of respected leaders, and observe national pride. He said that Americans should sit down when being photographed with Asians in order not to emphasize their shorter stature. Above all, the agents were warned not to patronize opinion leaders in other cultures. The analyst should identify the opinion leaders and examine the ways in which the propagandist appeals to their status and influence.

Face-to-Face Contact

The analyst should look for face-to-face contacts by themselves or following the screening of a film or an event. For example, does the propaganda institution provide local organizations or places to go for information? Is the environment of the place symbolically manipulated? Traditionally, propagandists have provided listening stations, "reading huts," "red corners," libraries, and cultural events. Bogart said that the USIA provided cultural events that were free of political content but that had secondary effects on the people. USIA libraries are used as bait to get people to go in and hear lectures, see films, and listen to tapes. The USIA made special efforts to create a "pretty, inviting place" with flowers and comfortable furniture. One of the authors of this book, Professor O'Donnell, lived in Europe at one time and remembers the American centers and libraries as places to meet important American authors, smoke American cigarettes, drink good bourbon, and eat American food. At the time, these centers were a bit plusher and symbolized a "good life" more than native places did.

Group Norms

Group norms are both beliefs, values, and behaviors that are derived from membership in groups. They may be culturally derived norms or social and professional norms. Research on group behavior has shown that people will go along with the group even when the group makes a decision contrary to privately held beliefs and values (Karlins & Abelson, 1970, Pratkanis & Aronson, 1991). The propagandist exploits people's conforming tendencies, and the analyst should look for examples of this. Conforming tendencies are also used to create a "herd instinct" in crowds. The propagandist may manipulate the environment to create crowded conditions to achieve a more homogeneous effect. It is common practice to hold large meetings in halls too small to accommodate the crowd in order to create the impression of a groundswell of support.

Reward and Punishment

Another way to get people to accept an idea publicly is through a system of rewards and punishments. A propagandist may even use threats and physical inducements toward compliance. "Propaganda of the deed" is when a nonsymbolic act is presented for its symbolic effect on an audience. For example, public torture of a criminal has been practiced for its presumable effect on others. Giving foreign aid with more of an eye to influencing a recipient's attitudes than to building the economy of a country is an example of symbolic reward.

Monopoly of the Communication Source

Whenever there is a monopoly of a communication source, such as a single newspaper or one television network, and the message is consistent and repetitious, people are unlikely to challenge the message. Weschler (1983) said that in Poland prior to the victory of Solidarity, people heard the same thing over and over again. "After a while," he said, "it does get through, and they find themselves thinking. 'Those Solidarity extremists really were bastards.' But the strange thing is that this in no way affects their hatred of the government" (p. 69).

Visual Symbols of Power

The analyst should look at the media messages to examine the visual symbolization of power. Is there an iconographic denotation of power and ubiquity in visual presentations? For example, when a speaker stands in front of a huge flag, there is an emotional association transferred to the speaker. Sometimes a speaker will stand in front of a huge poster of him or herself. This symbolizes a larger-than-life feeling and creates a sense of potency.

Language Usage

Verbal symbolization can also create a sense of power. The use of language associated with authority figures such as parents, teachers, heroes, and gods renders authority to that which the language describes—"the fatherland," "Mother Church," "Uncle Sam." The propaganda agent who can manipulate sacred and authority symbols but avoid detection can define a public view of the social order. Propaganda uses language that tends to deify a cause and satanize opponents. Symbolization affects receivers according to associations that they make with the symbols. Again, it depends on the predispositions of the audience.

In wartime, the enemy is often symbolized as subhuman or animal-like to linguistically soften the killing process. Metaphors of hunting down animals or exterminating vermin were common in the rhetoric of both sides during World War II. Symbols of sex and death are also common in war.

Exaggeration is often associated with propaganda. Goebbels said that outrageous charges evoked more belief than milder statements. There is a great deal of exaggeration associated with the language of advertising. Everything is the "best there is" and "satisfaction is guaranteed." During the Cold War, the Soviets called Americans "imperialists" while referring to the Soviet Union as the "camp of peace and democracy."

Innuendo is also associated with propaganda. Implying an accusation without risking refutation by saying it causes people to draw conclusions. If one says, "The captain was sober today," an audience might draw the conclusion that he is usually drunk.

Arousal of Emotions

Propaganda is also associated with emotional language and presentations. Although this is sometimes true, there are many agents who feel that dispassionate reporting is more effective. The British Broadcasting Corporation has been known for objective and accurate reporting for years. There was outrage when the British government invoked for the first time a little-known clause in the BBC licensing agreement that gives the government the right to take over the BBC transmitters in times of crisis. In 1982 during the Falklands invasion, a BBC-originated program came on the air in the guise of an Argentine radio program. On the program was "Ascension Alice," a sultry-voiced announcer who attempted to demoralize Argentine troops on the Falkland Islands. Alice reported that Argentine president General Leopoldo Galtieri said in a television interview that he was prepared to lose 40,000 men to defend the Falklands. She also played sentimental Latin ballads and a rock song by Queen called "Under Pressure." The Associated Press said that the BBC also broadcast "clearly fake requests from Argentine mothers for their boys at the front" (British Enlist "Alice" in Propaganda War, 1982, p. 10A). Without explaining how they received the requests, they played messages such as a request from Ernesto's mother who said, "Look after yourself son and please come home safely soon." Conservative M.P. Peter Mills said, "We have to win the propaganda war. It's just as important as firing bullets and so far not enough ammunition has been made available" (British Enlist "Alice," 1982, p. 10A).

Bogart (1976) said that emotional propaganda may be appropriate for semi-literate people, but, as previously noted, the USIA tried not to offend opinion leaders. He felt that reporting should not be heavy-handed. Instead of saying, "The Soviet Premier was lying again today when he said '. . . ,'" the Voice of America would report, "Comment on this subject points out . . ."

Audience Reaction to Various Techniques

The analyst looks for evidence of the target audience's response to propaganda. If the propaganda campaign is open and public, the journalists will offer critical reaction to it. This should not be mistaken for the target audience attitudes in opinion polls and surveys reported in the media.

The most important thing to look for is the behavior of the target audience. This can be in the form of voting behavior, joining organizations, making contributions, purchasing the propagandist's merchandise, forming local groups that are suborganizations for the main institution, and crowd behavior. The analyst also looks for the audience's adoption of the propagandist's language, slogans, and attire. Does the target audience take on a new symbolic identity? If so, how do they talk about it? Over time, does the propaganda purpose become realized and part of the social scene?

Counterpropaganda

In a free society in which media are competitive, there is likely to be counterpropaganda. Where the media is completely controlled, counterpropaganda can be found underground. Underground counterpropaganda may take as many media forms as the propaganda itself. There are obvious forms of underground counterpropaganda, such as handbills and graffiti, but other important forms of counterpropaganda are theater, literature, television, films, and poetry. Alternative ideology is presented in the form of entertainment. A. P. Foulkes (1983) presents many examples of both counterpropaganda and propaganda in various literary forms. There are several examples of counterpropaganda to McCarthyism in the 1950s, especially Arthur Miller's play *The Crucible*. Films such as *High Noon* and *Invasion of the Body Snatchers* were also thought to be counterpropaganda to McCarthyism.

Satellite transmission of video counterpropaganda was widely used in Czechoslovakia and Poland to resist the Communist government. Home video cameras and rented satellite dishes enabled the resistance movement to widely broadcast their message.

Counterpropaganda may become as active as propaganda itself. In this case, the analyst would examine it in the same ten stages of analysis for propaganda. The analyst should also attempt to determine if it is clear to the public that counterpropaganda exists to oppose propaganda. Very often both propaganda and counterpropaganda exist apart from mainstream ideology and the beliefs and behaviors of the general public.

Effects and Evaluation

The most important effect is whether the purpose of propaganda has been fulfilled or not. If not the overall purpose, then perhaps some of the specific goals have been achieved. If there has been a failure to achieve goals, the propaganda analyst should try to account for the failure in his or her analysis.

Questions related to growth in membership should also be examined as effects. The analyst must be careful about sources in making determination of membership. Propaganda agents traditionally inflate numbers regarding membership, contributions, and other goals.

Sometimes effects can be detected as adjustments in mainstream society. The analyst looks for the adoption of the propagandist's language and behaviors in other contexts. Legislation may be enacted to fulfill a propagandist's goal, but it may be sponsored by a more legitimate source.

Evaluation is directed to the achievement of goals but also to the means through which the goals were adopted. How did the selection of media and various message techniques seem to affect the outcome? Would a different set of choices have altered the outcome? How did the propagandist manipulate the context and the environment? Would the outcome have been inevitable had there been no propaganda? If the public-at-large changed directions, what seems to account for the swing?

If the analyst can answer the many questions contained within these ten stages, a thorough picture and understanding of propaganda will emerge. It is not always possible, however, to find all of the information one needs to make a complete analysis. Years later, a memoir or a set of papers will appear to fill in missing links and sometimes alter conclusions.

7 Propaganda in Action: Three Case Studies

These three case studies were selected to provide examples of how propaganda has and is being used in our society. The subjects are (a) The U.S. government and industry's unusual efforts to ease the life of women shipyard workers in Vanport, Oregon, during the Second World War, (b) the origins of the antismoking controversy, and (c) the propaganda efforts during the recent Gulf War. Applying the ten-step analysis suggested in Chapter 6, each case study examines the propagandists, the audience, and the various techniques employed. These case studies demonstrate that propaganda is not always successful and can be used in a variety of ways in modern society.

In this chapter the ten stages of propaganda analysis are applied in various ways to what we consider to be three important examples of propaganda in our time. The case studies were chosen for the intensity of their propaganda as well as their relevancy in today's society. The only case study that can be said to be truly over is that of Vanport, although the issue of government support of child care for working women continues. While the Gulf War is over, the full effects of the propaganda efforts during that conflict are still being resolved, and the antismoking campaign continues to devise strategies to combat the earnest efforts of the tobacco industry.

Women and War: Work, Housing, and Child Care

In 1943, the wartime housing project, Vanport City, Oregon, opened. "Vanport" was a contraction of Vancouver, Washington, and Portland, Oregon, for it lay between the two cities. Forty thousand people from all parts of the United States came there to work for the Kaiser shipyards, where the famous Liberty ships were built, and moved into specially built houses and apartments that were paid for by the Federal Housing Authority. Public bus transportation was set up to run on a straight line from the housing past the Kaiser Child Service Center and schools to the job sites for convenience to parents and children.

The Kaiser Child Service Center, specifically designed to assist working mothers in every possible way, had picture windows facing the shipyards so the children could look out and "see where Mommy works," and it was open twenty-four hours a day, seven days a week, twelve months a year. Infirmaries, staffed by doctors and nurses, were available so mothers could work when their children were sick. Child-sized bathtubs, elevated so the Child Service Center staff did not have to strain their backs, were used to bathe the children before their mothers picked them up to go home at the end of the work day. Large professional kitchens, staffed by dieticians and cooks, prepared nutritious meals not only for the children to eat at the Center but also for the mothers to pick up at the end of the work day to take home, heat, and feed the whole family.

Between 1943 and 1945, more than 7,000 women worked for Kaiser in Oregon as shipfitters, machinists, painters, pipefitters, plumbers, sheet metal workers, tank scalers, draftspersons, boilermakers, blacksmiths, slab and flangepersons, electricians, welders, burners, and laborers. They went to work, knowing their children were receiving excellent care and that they could spend quality time with them after work because they were not burdened with household chores. The schools adapted their classes to the women's work shifts, thus children could arrive as early as 5:45 A.M. for early classes or attend afternoon classes and stay until 6:30 P.M. All meals were provided at appropriate hours. Whatever the mother's shift, the school accommodated the children.

When World War II ended, the shipyards closed, the women lost their jobs, and Vanport City, for the most part, was dismantled. A flood in 1948 destroyed what was left, so it no longer exists. There were many wartime communities, some with child care facilities, built and supported by government and industry for the massive wartime effort. This case study analyzes the propaganda of the U.S. government and American industry for one of them, Vanport City. It is unusual in that housing and the features of the child care facility were part of the propaganda techniques.

The Context, Ideology, and Purpose of the Campaign

December 7, 1941, when the Japanese attacked Pearl Harbor, marked the U.S. entry into global war. This military crisis stimulated the government to take extraordinary efforts to maximize industrial production in order to equip the military and its allies. At this time, the prevailing attitudes about women's capabilities and proper roles fixed them as wives and mothers whose primary concerns were about their families and homes. Women, for the most part, were economically dependent upon men and sharply limited in their opportunities to work and influence public affairs. During the Depression women were denied the government relief and participation in recovery programs that were granted to men. Married women who worked during the Depression were viewed as taking jobs away from male breadwinners. "Women's place" was in the home.

When World War II began, at first, defense employers were reluctant to hire women. The federal government's largest training program, Vocational Training for War Production, created no programs for women. However, as millions of men withdrew from jobs to go into military service, a different ideology was born of necessity, and the possibilities for women to receive government training and defense employment increased. By 1942, industry and the government began an intense courtship of women that lasted until 1944. The War Manpower Commission launched national media appeals to women in an effort to get them to go to work (Hartmann, 1982). The ideology of government and industry was that women should fulfill their patriotic duty and hasten victory by joining the work force. Women working, however, was considered a temporary, emergency situation, for they were not regarded as a permanent part of the work force. The propaganda purpose was to achieve maximum production of wartime materials and, in order to recruit women to the workplace, the related purpose was to get women to perceive civilian defense work as glamourous, exciting, and a patriotic duty. This was based on the myth that women could assume men's roles in a time of crisis, although their true mission in life was to be wives and mothers. The most controversial aspect of this view was created by the deeply held beliefs that mothers should stay at home to care for small children. Many attempts were made to alter that belief for the duration of the war, and child care programs were hastily organized. Most were inadequate and poorly staffed (Anderson, 1981), with the exception of Vanport City.

Figure 7.1. Women riveters at Vanport City, Kaiser shipyards, 1943.
SOURCE: Used by permission of the Oregon Historical Society, #OrHi 86502.

Figure 7.2. Vanport Child Service Center, facing the ship-launching site.
SOURCE: Used by permission of the Oregon Historical Society, #OrHi 78700 (cropped).

Figure 7.3. Kaiser Child Service Center staff worker bathing a child in a special tub, 1944.

SOURCE: Used by permission of the Oregon Historical Society, #OrHi 80376.

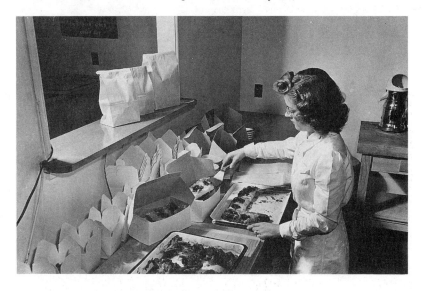

Figure 7.4. Kaiser Child Service Center employee packs meals for mothers to take home when they pick up their children, 1944.

SOURCE: Used by permission of the Oregon Historical Society, #OrHi 80373.

ALL YOU DO IS "HEAT AND EAT" THE FOOD
FROM THE CHILD SERVICE CENTER

Figure 7.5. All you do is "Heat and Eat" the food from the Child Service Center, 1944.

SOURCE: Used by permission of the Oregon Historical Society, #OrHi 86503.

Identification of the Propagandist and
the Structure of the Propaganda Organization

The U.S. government openly conducted a propaganda campaign to alter perceptions of women in the workplace, which has been described in Maureen Honey's *Creating Rosie the Riveter* (1984) and Karen Anderson's *Wartime Women* (1981). The U.S. government as propagandist was assisted by industry, the media, and local groups, thus there was an amazing consistency in the tone of the campaign. In the case of Vanport City, the key propagandist was Edgar J. Kaiser, his management team, and several government agencies.

Kaiser owned the Oregon Shipyard Corporation, which had three huge shipyards. There they built the famous Liberty ships, the first of which was launched on September 27, 1941. The production rate for these ships was so great that seventy-six ships had been built by September 1942. In fact, the *Joseph N. Teal* was built in a record 14 days (Maben, 1987). By the end of 1942, there were 75,000 workers employed in the shipyards with expectations of 100,000 within months. The workers came from all over America, creating a housing shortage of enormous proportions in Portland, Oregon. People slept in cars and tents. Movie theaters started feature films at 2:15 A.M. to accommodate the homeless. Appeals were made to retirees to move to other cities to make room for the workers. To relieve the situation, Kaiser bought 650 acres along the Oregon side of the Columbia River to build a wartime housing project. Funds for wartime housing projects generally came from the Lanham Act appropriations, which were funneled through the National Housing Authority and its subsidiary Federal Public Housing Administration (FPHA), but these funds were already expended. Kaiser went to the U.S. Maritime Commission (USMC) with his plan. The USMC approved it and advanced $26 million to Kaiser, who would build the project that would be supervised by the FPHA. Kaiser signed a cost-plus $2 contract to build his city. This differed from other wartime housing projects because two different government agencies were involved in addition to the Kaiser company. Kaiser was in charge of architectural planning, but the FPHA had to approve the design. A 1943 article entitled "Vanport City" in *Architectural Forum* articulated his goal and called Kaiser "the 'miracle man' of World War II production and the most effective crusader for housing the United States has ever seen. But not for philanthropic reasons" (p. 53). The article quoted Michael Miller, manager of Kaiser's Vancouver shipyard: "The way people live and the way their families are cared for is bound to be reflected in production. If members of his family are sick, the worker worries on the job or stays home to take care of them" (p. 54). Thus, the propaganda goal to be achieved by building the facilities at Vanport City was optimum production.

A Portland architectural firm, Wolff and Phillips was hired to design Vanport City with the following design objectives: (a) to house as many people as possible with the least amount of building materials, (b) to include nursery schools and bus shelters, and (c) to facilitate women's entry into the war (Maben, 1987; Vanport City, 1945). These design objectives were propaganda objectives as well, for the housing facilitated women's work that supported the propagandist's purpose. The city, now dubbed "Kaiserville," for 40,000 new residents, including 9,000 children, was constructed in 10 months, and officially completed on September 26, 1943, although people had begun moving from their tourist cabins, trailer camps, and rented rooms into completed units 10 months earlier. In addition to 10,000 housing units, there were five grade schools, six nursery schools, five social halls, three fire halls, a library, theater, stores, and a hospital.

The Housing Authority of Portland (HAP) was the last link in the structure of the propaganda organization, for it administered the project locally, although neither the city of Portland, Multnomah County, nor the state of Oregon were consulted on any phase of the planning (Maben, 1987). Vanport City had no municipal government, and the residents had no voice in its operation. The propaganda organization functioned as a strong partnership between government and industry.

Target Audience

Men and women were recruited to work in the Kaiser shipyards. The first full-page advertisements appeared in the Portland *Oregonian*, exhorting people in the name of patriotism to work in the shipyards. Recruiters went to New York City to recruit 20,000 workers there, and they provided a seventeen-car train to transport them to Portland. Workers were brought in from so many states that the only states not represented were Rhode Island, New Hampshire, Maine, and Delaware (Maben, 1987). Basically, the recruits were young, married, and they had young children. Shipyard work had been strictly a male bastion, but Kaiser hired women without discrimination. Although other defense industries recruited women in door-to-door solicitation drives in Baltimore, Seattle, and Detroit (Anderson, 1981), there is no evidence that Kaiser did anything but advertise in the newspapers. Certainly, the national media campaign to encourage women to make home front sacrifices comparable to those of the men in the battle zones must have affected the women who decided to work for Kaiser (Anderson, 1981). Some of the women workers came with their husbands who subsequently went to war, thus the women stayed and worked in their places. Other factors were economic necessity, a desire for independence, and loneliness. Many women had to leave their children with friends and relatives to go to work in other shipyards. Those who went to Vanport City took their children with them. This, no doubt, was a major incentive.

Media Utilization Techniques

One form of media utilization is the control of information flow. Vanport City closely resembled the corporation company town of an earlier era. In cooperation with the U.S. government, HAP was the town's operator, and it imposed heavy restrictions and regulations on the occupants. Efforts to change the regulations were effectively squelched. One Vanport couple submitted an article to the *Saturday Evening Post* complaining about the regimentation and bureaucracy. HAP got the *Post* to suspend publication of the article on the grounds that it interfered with the war effort (Maben, 1987). Another regulation required the schools to be operated on a double-shift basis, twelve months of the year. Superintendent James T. Hamilton tried from 1943 to end the double shift for the sake of the children. It was not until 1945 when federal officials, with private knowledge of how well the war in the Pacific was going and that ship production would be phased out, withdrew their objections.

Special Techniques to Maximize Effect

In order to get the workers to give their best energies to production, Kaiser provided the workers' needs for affordable housing, on-site services, and extensive child care services. Dolores Hayden (1986), in her book about architecture, *Redesigning the American Dream*, said that Vanport City "was the most ambitious attempt ever made in the United States to shape space for employed women and their families" (p. 8). Vanport City offered a dazzling array of inducements for mothers with children to take on wartime jobs. James L. Hymes, who was in charge of the child care at Vanport, said, "In the past good nursery schools have been a luxury for the wealthy. The Kaiser Child service centers are among the first places where working people, people of average means, have been able to afford good nursery education for their children" (Hayden, 1986, p. 161). The cost for the child care in a state-of-the-art center with all amenities was seventy-five cents a day. Parents and children went through initial interviews, so each child was given special attention and appropriate placement. The staff was highly trained, and the teacher-student ratio was about 30 to 1. Psychologically, the parents knew their children were well-cared for, and it was convenient to take the children to the center, for the transportation was on a straight line to the shipyards via the Child Service Center. The houses and apartments maximized living quarters and minimized the cooking areas because hot meals could be brought home. These mothers could spend time with their children instead of cooking and doing dishes. The design and support activities symbolized cultural attitudes toward women's work. It was valued, and it was assisted with strong regard for the welfare of the children.

Counterpropaganda

The only semblance of counterpropaganda was squelched, as was seen in the section on Media Utilization Techniques.

Audience Reaction to Various Techniques

People came in droves to Vanport City. They complained about the restrictions related to maintenance and recreation, but the housing units were always filled, and the Child Service Center was a huge success.

Effects and Evaluation

Occupancy of Vanport City reached its highest peak during January 1945. When layoffs began, they were severe. Three thousand were terminated in the first week. By July, 1945, the population had dropped from 40,000 to 26,000. By November, the housing projects were half full. Stabilized by July 1946 at 15,000, demolition, paid for by Lanham Act funds began. Twelve hundred housing units were moved to Bremerton, Washington, for the naval yard. Additional units were used for salvage. At the end 6,396 units remained (Maben, 1987). This was consistent with the rest of the nation as war contracts were cancelled, the men returned from the war, and women lost their jobs.

The housing project at Vanport City met working mothers' needs in a sensitive and helpful way. Never again have the American working women been treated as carefully as they were when women's work was needed for a national emergency.

Between June and September 1945, one of every four women in the United States lost their jobs in the factories, the automobile and steel industries, and in the shipyards. Those who remained in the labor force shifted to clerical, service, and sales positions with reduced earnings (Hartmann, 1982). Another propaganda campaign to remind women of their proper roles was on the horizon.

The Smoking Controversy: Broadcasting, Political Power, and Health

Not all of life's problems have happy endings, and not all propaganda case studies have clear, precise resolutions. This examination of the specific issues surrounding the campaign to remove cigarette advertising from the broadcast media shows that very often propaganda from one side is so powerful and well organized that it simply overwhelms the opposing forces. For many years the tobacco lobby was so powerful in the United States that it appeared virtually untouchable in the halls of Congress; and yet inroads were made, albeit small ones. Most cities have now begun to legislate no smoking areas in the work place; companies such as Pacific Northwest Bell have banned smoking from their office buildings; universities have begun to declare themselves "smoke-free environments"; and all over the United States restaurants are now creating smoke-free areas. This case study demonstrates that sometimes it is the work of one person, aided by the right combination of political and social climate, that can effect changes, even in the face of a massive propaganda structure. This is not a classic case study of propaganda and counterpropaganda; it is an examination of how a combination of personal fortitude, legislative and political maneuvering, and some luck can bring about change. It should be emphasized that the tobacco interests did not really lose this battle; they merely altered their strategies, and their propaganda machine remains as strong and active as ever.

The Historical and Ideological Context

On January 1, 1971, all cigarette advertising disappeared from American radio and television. No longer was the Marlboro man able to light up and show off his tattoo at the same time; the "cool" world of mentholated cigarettes with smoking couples always care-fully depicted in a green pastoral setting ceased to exist; and the recently introduced line of "women's cigarettes"—Virginia Slims—could no longer entertain us with humorous vignettes depicting what happened to women who were caught smoking in the period before the 1930s. In the words of the Virginia Slims slogan, the fight against tobacco advertising on broadcasting had "come a long way, baby!" But to reach this point required a series of actions and reac-tions involving a complex mixture of groups and individuals, both in and outside of Congress, and the development of propaganda campaigns with literally billions of dollars at stake.

There are several ideological bases for the propaganda campaigns created by both sides of the smoking controversy. (In fact, the num-ber of actual interest groups involved in this issue are too numerous to list, but for purposes of this study we will assume that there is a side in favor of smoking and the use of tobacco products, and a side opposed to the consumption of tobacco because it constitutes a health hazard and an environmental nuisance.) First, the tobacco interests in the United States constitute an impressive part of the nation's economy and have established themselves as an important force in American politics. The so-called tobacco coalition includes the eventual clientele who smoke more than $43 billion worth of tobacco products annually, the 22 states in which tobacco is grown, and the approximately 2.5 million jobs of varying types with a payroll of $52 billion supported by the tobacco industry, and the $16.5 billion contribution tobacco makes directly to the nationwide tax base. The industry as a whole accounts for about 2.5% of the nation's Gross National Product. The beneficiaries of this multibil-lion dollar industry include manufacturers, advertising agencies, the mass media, farmers, tax collectors, and shopkeepers (Fritschler, 1983). Clearly there is a lot of money and many other issues involved in any political decisions regarding smoking.

Second, tobacco has an almost mystical role in American history; it was one of the first American crops exported by the early settlers, and was once so valuable that it was even used as currency. This ties in with the third ideological perspective, which concerns the histor-ical antagonism that has traditionally arisen between government and business, especially when the regulation of health or environ-mental matters are the primary issue. In these instances, unless the advantages to the business community involved are very obvious, there is likely to be a great deal of politicking, and the myth of government interference in "free enterprise" is likely to be raised.

Besides which, most Americans do not like to be told what to eat, drink, or smoke.

Fourth—and this is a very complex factor indeed—since 1933 the tobacco producers have been the beneficiaries of federal assistance through the Department of Agriculture, which operates a price support program and market quota rules that enforces a mandatory limit on production. These regulations have driven tobacco prices up and kept the supply down. The contradiction here is obvious, for as Fritschler (1983) in his book *Smoking and Politics* notes, "For the proponents of these tobacco regulations to turn around and fight consumer-health regulation on the grounds that government regulation is unwarranted interference by big brother and bad for the economy is the kind of argument which makes rational people wince" (p. 9). The tobacco industry tends to slide by this conundrum in their antilegislative philosophy. Perhaps this is best exemplified by the statement by Jesse Helms, the conservative Republican senator from the major tobacco state of North Carolina, and a leader of the industry's fight against regulation, when he said, "In North Carolina, tobacco isn't a commodity, it's a religion!" Thus we have a large, powerful industry, determined to preserve its privileges, facing continuous pressure from an equally determined, but much less powerful, somewhat uncoordinated group of individuals, together with various private and governmental health agencies, all of whom are concerned by the growing and very costly health menace that smoking has become.

The final ideological position is the consistent viewpoint put forward by the tobacco industry that, despite the thousands of studies that have established the connection between smoking and various physical ailments such as lung cancer, emphysema, chronic bronchitis, and even heart disease, that the actual causal link between smoking and these medical problems has not been clearly established. Although the health hazards of smoking had been pointed out in the mid-nineteenth century, it took a series of private and government reports between 1954 and 1964 to bring the matter into public arena for political debate. After the initial 1954 study reports done by a private group, the tobacco industry responded by the creation of the Tobacco Industry Research Committee (now called the Council for Tobacco-USA) which distributed fairly substantial funds for scientific research on the use of tobacco and its effects on health. Though this served as a counterpropaganda move, in that the industry began funding its own health-related research thereby demonstrating its concern, this organization was not in a position to directly counter the growing propaganda movement demanding some sort of regulation of public smoking. In 1958, the increased pressure was met head-on with the creation of the Tobacco Institute, Inc., a lobbying public relations group that was supported by large contributions from the various factions making up the tobacco industry. The Tobacco Institute subsequently became the source of most of the industry's propaganda aimed at containing the disorganized array of health groups pushing for the labeling of cigarettes or other regulatory measures.

The Menace of Broadcast Advertising

The emergence of first radio and then television advertising proved to be of immense significance to the growth of the cigarette industry. The use of broadcast advertising was a major propaganda weapon in promoting smoking as an acceptable social behavior (the movies and magazines must also accept major responsibility here), and cigarette brands were widely associated in the public's mind with the sponsorship of many popular radio and then television shows. Brands such as Lucky Strike, Camel, Philip Morris, and Chesterfield became symbols of entertainment as much as commerce during the era of the large radio networks. The emergence of television as a major advertising force in the 1950s brought into prominence brands such as Kent, with its "micronite filter" (later shown to have contained asbestos) and Winston, which "tastes good like a cigarette should," or the Old Gold lady dancing away inside her cigarette box, with only her arms and legs visible. Of all of these new television-promoted brands it was Marlboro, featuring the clean outdoors and the weathered features of the Marlboro Man in his cowboy hat and tattoo, that was most memorable, even though the actor involved later contracted lung cancer from cigarette smoking.

Television was used to promote filter cigarettes, with broad hints (often specific claims) that these were "healthier" than the unfiltered variety. In the late 1940s filter cigarettes accounted for 1.5% of the total market; by 1968 this had grown to nearly 75%. During this same period the number of different brands grew from a half dozen to more than thirty, in all shapes and sizes (Whiteside, 1970). In the latter part of the 1960s the heavy promotion given to new brands of longer 100 millimeter cigarettes was particularly upsetting to those who were beginning to demand government regulation. In 1967, three years after the U.S. Surgeon General had issued a report linking cigarette smoking to lung cancer and other medical problems, the tobacco manufacturers were spending about $217 million on television. In that same year the Public Health Service issued a report that found that "cigarette smokers have substantially higher rates of death and disability than their non-smoking counterparts in the population."

Although the forces opposed to cigarette smoking lacked the structural organization to match the industry's propaganda, they were not without friends in the federal bureaucracy, as well as Congress. After a complex series of legislative steps, fought every step of the way by the tobacco industry, the Federal Trade Commission finally managed to get President Lyndon Johnson's signature on a bill requiring a health warning on cigarette packages on July 27, 1965. This bill also prevented the FTC from any further action against the tobacco industry for four years (the industry wanted a permanent ban), and was seen more as a victory for the propaganda efforts of the Tobacco Institute than a positive health measure. The label was not seen as a serious threat to tobacco sales, whereas removing the FTC from the issue was seen as a major blow for the antismoking group. After examining this battle, one of the lobbyists for the antismoking side characterized the contest between the tobacco industry and the health people as being similar to a match between the Green Bay Packers and a high school football team. It is against this background that the rather unexpected fight to remove cigarette advertising from the broadcast media must be viewed.

The FCC and John Banzhaf III

A young New York lawyer, John Banzhaf III was concerned about the tactics being used to advertise cigarettes, particularly "about the use of the public airwaves to seduce young people into taking up smoking without any attempt to tell the other side of the story on television and radio" (Whiteside, 1970, p. 46). He wrote a letter to WCBS-TV in New York asking for free time to be made available to present the health hazard side of the cigarette story. This request was denied, as Banzhaf had expected, so his next step was to file a petition with the Federal Communications Commission, pointing out that the Surgeon General's report and other scientific findings had shown a relationship between smoking and health, and, further, because this was a controversial issue of public importance, it was therefore proper for the FCC to order radio and television stations to provide reply time under the Fairness Doctrine. This petition was presented early in January 1967, and on Friday, June 2, of that year the FCC—to everyone's surprise—ruled that its fairness doctrine did indeed apply to cigarette advertising on radio and television. The commission dismissed Banzhaf's appeal for "equal time," offering instead a ratio of one antismoking message to three cigarette commercials. Everyone from the tobacco interests to Congress was caught off guard, but it was clear that there would be an appeal of the ruling. Once he had achieved this major victory, Banzhaf expected that he could bow out, and that major private health organizations such as the American Cancer Society, the National Tuberculosis Association, and the American Heart Association—all known propagandists against smoking—would step in and take over. However, he quickly discovered that these groups had serious misgivings about alienating the broadcasters, upon whom they relied for free air time for their own causes and especially for fund-raising activities. The health group support for the FCC decision was quiet, unaggressive, and almost nonexistent during the period when the tobacco industry and the broadcasters appealed the FCC's ruling. Even Senator Robert Kennedy tried to intervene with the health groups on behalf of Banzhaf, but with no success. To their credit, the health agencies felt that the burden of the defense of the original decision lay with the FCC's own legal staff, and eventually they were proved correct. On November 21, 1968, the U.S. Court of Appeals held that the FCC could use its fairness doctrine to require free time for antismoking commercials because this decision was "a public-health measure addressed to a unique danger authorized by official and congressional action."

The result was that a series of antismoking commercials began to appear on radio and television, and this constituted the first major media propaganda campaign against the tobacco interests. The tobacco companies even tried to obtain "right of reply" to the antismoking commercials, but were turned down by the courts. The real importance of getting these antismoking commercials on the air was only realized later, when in February 1969 the FCC issued a public notice that it intended to propose a ruling to ban cigarette advertising from all radio and television broadcasting. This notice was filed four months before the end of the four-year moratorium on the ban that had prevented federal regulatory agencies from taking action against the tobacco industry. The FCC had put Congress on notice that if it did not act by July 1 of that year, the FCC would go ahead with its intentions, and tobacco advertising would disappear from the airwaves.

The tobacco lobby quickly swung into preparation, and several long congressional hearings were held to discuss the whole issue of cigarettes and health, and the proposed FCC action. The National Association of Broadcasters actively joined forces with the Tobacco

Institute to combat the FCC's intention with a barrage of propaganda, claiming that the broadcast industry should be left to regulate itself. Eventually, however, cracks began to appear in this seemingly impregnable alliance, and on July 8, 1969, the NAB announced a plan to phase out all cigarette advertising from the air over a three-and-a-half-year period beginning on January 1, 1970. It is unclear exactly what prompted this decision, but it seems to have been inspired by the fear of having to air both pro and con advertising for tobacco products for the foreseeable future. Moreover, who knew where this might lead with regard to other controversial products. It was far better to bite the bullet and get rid of cigarette advertising lest it contaminate other products. In any case, it was felt that in the three-and-a-half-year interim, the broadcast industry would easily find other customers only too eager to buy into the prime time programs or sporting events that would be made available by the removal of cigarette advertising. The tobacco industry, stung by what they considered to be their betrayal by the broadcasters, went one step further and voluntarily agreed to end all broadcast advertising by September 1970. (Why drag out their impending demise on the air?)

Eventually, acting in a statesmanlike, responsible manner the broadcasters moved the date up to January 1, 1970. The broadcast industry, which stood to lose more than $250 million a year for three years by this decision, became the injured party. Naturally the print media were elated at the prospect of all that additional advertising revenue coming their way. Eventually, after much lobbying by all parties, a compromise was reached, and the final date of January 1, 1971 was set to allow the broadcasters one last chance to extract some revenue from the football bowl games on New Year's Day. (The tobacco industry had to get Congress to exempt it from antitrust action to act in a concerted manner like this.) Congress also managed to extract from the tobacco industry an agreement to strengthen the warning on the package to read: "Warning: The Surgeon General has Determined That Cigarette Smoking Is Dangerous to Your Health."

The Evaluation

Since 1971 there has been no cigarette advertising on radio or television; however, as Fritschler (1983) pointed out, "The cigarette manufacturers were discovering that agreement with the antismoking people was not such a bad thing. The advertising budgets of the manufacturers dropped an estimated 30 percent in 1971, the first year of the television and radio ad ban, and gross sales were up 3 percent" (p. 141). The tobacco industry simply switched their advertising strategy, purchasing more print, billboards, and sponsoring special sporting and other events that gave them clear identification in the media. Kool mentholated cigarettes sponsored a series of jazz festivals; Virginia Slims supported women's tennis tournaments, and numerous other events suddenly found tobacco sponsors.

The propaganda battle between the tobacco industry and the health interests did not cease with the Pyrrhic victory in 1971. Attempts have recently been made to show smoking as being "antisocial" and "unacceptable" to smart, young people; but the number of young smokers has shown no dramatic decrease. (In the fall of 1985, the Surgeon General, Dr. Koop, suggested that by the end of the century, smokers would find their behavior so socially unacceptable that they would have to smoke in private.) Congress also passed laws requiring that health warning labels be placed on other tobacco products such as chewing tobacco and snuff, as well as banning the broadcast advertising of these products. Of particular concern is the increasing amount of smoking among women of all age groups as women move out of the home and into the work force. With this increase in smoking has also come a concomitant rise in tobacco-related illness in women.

The battle between the tobacco industry and its detractors continues unabated. In late 1991 a major study indicated that the cartoon camel logo (Old Joe) used by Camel cigarettes had enormous appeal with children. While R. J. Reynolds, the company that produces this brand claimed that their advertising was intended for adults, the researchers said that the campaign had been "far more successful at marketing Camel cigarettes to children than to adults" (Brody, 1991). As proof for this assertion, the researchers noted that Camel's share of the illegal children's cigarette market had increased from 0.5% to 32.8%, representing sales estimated at $476 million a year. Even without television advertising the children were as familiar with this symbol as they were with the Mickey Mouse logo for the Disney Cable Channel. An additional factor was the extensive promotional campaign offering T-shirts, caps, and other items with the Old Joe logo, which enticed children to purchase this brand. The publication of this study in the prestigious *Journal of the American Medical Association* prompted Congressman Henry Waxman to urge a total ban on all cigarette advertising.

In recent years there have been determined efforts to eradicate smoking by making both the usual health claims, and also by presenting smoking as being socially unacceptable. Antismoking advertisements have gone so far as to depict smokers as ugly, smelly individuals, and also suggesting to teenagers that smoking is "uncool." The tobacco industry's attempts to maintain public recognition by the sponsorship of sports or cultural events has also been criticized. The association between Virginia Slims and professional women's tennis, as well as Philip Morris's sponsorship of the touring show celebrating the 200th anniversary of the Bill of Rights came under fire as a form of surreptitious advertising. The Philip Morris sponsorship was particularly interesting in that questions were raised as to whether the tobacco company was trying to make a point that smokers have rights too.

As indicated earlier, some small victories have been achieved, and the number of adults who smoke has declined since the advertising ban went into force. However, the tobacco lobby remains a powerful force in Congress, able to marshall impressive propaganda forces when required.

The Gulf War: The Mobilization of World Public Opinion

The fighting war in the Persian Gulf lasted for forty-three days, from the first attacks by allied jets on Iraq on the evening of January 17 to the suspension of hostilities on February 28, 1991. These forty-three days of dramatic modern warfare were the focus of intense analysis by military hardware and strategic experts, public opinion analysts and media scholars. However, the war actually began on August 2, 1990, when Iraqi troops stormed the border of Kuwait and took control of that country. In the next five months, leading up to the start of actual combat, the world audience was subjected to a barrage of propaganda from all sides in this conflict. This is an analysis of the propaganda that helped to shape and give definition to the events of the Gulf War. Also, while it was a coalition of countries arrayed against the Iraqis, the emphasis here is essentially on the propaganda strategies of the U.S. forces. Other countries such as Britain, for example, had a quite different set of sociohistorical contexts and circumstances shaping its propaganda strategies.

1. The Ideology and Purpose of the Propaganda Campaign. One of the main purposes of propaganda is to achieve acceptance of the propagandist's ideology by both its own and the other side. In the Gulf War, any analysis of the propaganda must start with an analysis of the ideological objectives of both sides. It is only against this

Figure 7.6. A cartoon by Morin in the *Miami Herald*, showing Saddam Hussein as a vicious spider holding captive the world's oil supply and the American people. Such images help to reinforce the public's image of the "enemy" as a dangerous beast, devoid of human qualities.

SOURCE: Reprinted with special permission of King Features Syndicate.

MORIN, 1991. *MIAMI HERALD.* REPRINTED BY PERMISSION OF KING FEATURES SYNDICATE.

Figure 7.7. In this cartoon from the *Miami Herald,* Morin captures the image of the press as being "managed" by the military. Most polls indicated that there was strong public approval of the tight military control of the press in the Gulf War. This was a legacy left over from the Vietnam War, where it was believed that the way the American press reported the war was responsible for the eventual Communist victory in that country.

SOURCE: Reprinted with special permission of King Features Syndicate.

ideological background that these propaganda strategies make sense. The dominant ideology of the United States is firmly based in the concept of a participatory democratic political structure and a free enterprise capitalist economic structure. These are the ideological tenets of faith that underlie all U.S. perspectives on other countries and cultures. The key ideological term is *freedom*. While the United States does not actively seek to impose its ideology in a militaristic sense, we tend to judge the relative merits of other countries by posing two key questions: How far do other countries deviate from the normative democratic ideology of the United States, and how "free" is their citizenry to express its views without fear of official retribution? The further a country is from the U.S. ideal, the more likely it is that we will view it as politically and culturally immature.

Thus, the dominant ideological approach that governed all propaganda aimed at the Iraqis and its allies was that we were dealing with an enemy that denied basic democratic rights to its own citizens, and especially to those that it had conquered. In the Gulf War the United States was able to claim that the "totalitarian Iraqi dictatorship" had invaded and was attempting to destroy the "freely elected democratic" nation of Kuwait. Little was said about the actual lack of democracy (or women's rights) in Kuwait by official U.S. sources, although this was a key issue for those who opposed the war. In the aftermath of the victory in the desert, the failure to restore any semblance of democracy in Kuwait only serves to underscore this propaganda ploy. It was also a form of ideological propaganda for the United States to appeal directly to the Iraqi people to overthrow their tyrant ruler and restore democracy, and to emphasize that the fight was with Saddam Hussein and not the Iraqi people. A strong ideological belief in democracy always emphasizes that the people are inherently good; it is government institutions that can go bad. Witness our new found love for the Soviet people, but continued suspicion about their armed forces and new government structures.

The Iraqis were much more direct in their ideological propaganda, developing themes that struck deep into the roots of modern history of the Middle East, and which centered around the desire for Pan-Arabic unity, and the need to remove all Western influence from the region. There were few rules in Saddam Hussein's propaganda campaign as he utilized every ploy that he could to gain media attention. First it was claimed that Kuwait had wronged his country by deliberately stealing Iraqi oil; then he claimed that Kuwait was historically part of Iraq; and finally he sought a *Jihad*—a Holy War against the infidel because the American forces were foreign invaders who were "drinking alcohol, eating pork and practicing prostitution" on the holy soil of Islam. These themes played quite well with a small group of Arab countries, particularly in Jordan, where the dislocated Palestinians were eager to back anyone who opposed Israel, but it failed to ignite the Arab world as Saddam had hoped.

In the long run, though each side used its own dominant ideology as a basis for its propaganda efforts, there is little evidence so far that it has had any permanent effect on the Gulf region as a whole. The key victory was on the domestic fronts of the Coalition forces, with the emphasis on the belief that *democracy* will triumph over *totalitarianism*. However, even this victory may be brief if serious domestic problems continue for the foreseeable future.

2. The Context in Which the Propaganda Occurs. Successful propaganda takes into account the prevailing mood of the times, and is conducted within a very specific sociohistorical context. This part of the analysis takes into account the historical events (and its various interpretations) that led up to the propaganda campaign, and includes an analysis of the beliefs and myths that shape historical interpretations. It is also of great importance to understand as fully as possible the various predispositions of the target audiences. Behind the Gulf War there is a vast and complicated history of Arab relations with the West that overarches the entire conflict.

A key factor in examining the sociohistorical contexts of the propaganda for both sides is their previous experiences in warfare. The Iraqis saw their invasion of Kuwait as an extension of the ten-year bitter war with Iran. In this context, there was also the deliberately developed propaganda image of the battle-hardened Iraqi army as a formidable foe for the Coalition forces. This image was also used by the Coalition forces to prepare their own soldiers and their home front publics that this was a "real" war, and not another minor incursion such as Grenada or Panama. Thus the public were prepared for a battle involving what was widely called "the fourth largest standing army in the world," making the eventual victory even more significant and prestigious, even if it was something of an anticlimax after all of the propaganda buildup.

In the United States the issue of Vietnam was central to understanding the propaganda effort, especially that aimed at the home front. The scars of Vietnam are deeply etched into the American mind, and the Gulf War was clearly fought against this gestalt. In a fascinating bibliometric study done by the Freedom Forum (Lamay, 1991a) of about 66,000 news stories in major newspapers, evening television news programs and newsservices between August 1, 1990 and February 28, 1991, it was discovered that the word *Vietnam* appeared 7,299 times overall, "more than any other word or term, and nearly three times as often as the runner-up, 'human shields'" which had 2,588 mentions (p. 41-44). Of course, many of these mentions of Vietnam referred to the previous military experience of the officers, but the specific term *another Vietnam* was "strikingly prevalent," and was nearly two-thirds of the total. The fear of *another Vietnam* was initially a negative metaphor, but it also set the groundwork for developing a strong propaganda campaign aimed at creating a mood in the American public that those experiences would never be repeated again. It was largely against the background of the Vietnam experience that such propagandistic messages as "this time we'll fight to win," "support the troops in the field, even if you don't support the war" and "let's show our gratitude by welcoming home the troops" were successful in marshalling the bulk of American public opinion to support the war.

Also, of course, the Vietnam syndrome has played a major role in the structuring of the current relationship between the U.S. military and the press. In the belief that the press was responsible for the erosion of public support for the earlier conflict, the U.S. (and British) military devised a set of rules for war coverage that was very restrictive. Through the use of supervised "pool" coverage, the military was able to control the information flow to fulfill its own propaganda objectives. It is hoped that with the thoroughness of the victory in the desert demonstrating the obvious superiority of U.S. armed forces on a world scale, that the demoralization of the Vietnam syndrome will abate and be replaced with a more positive public attitude.

An important aspect of context is the actual cultural practices of a group. Experience has shown that in order to be successful those who use propaganda must take into account the culture of their audience. While much analysis of this issue remains to be done, an initial reaction is that both sides in the Gulf War, deliberately or otherwise, failed to take into account the cultural practices of the other. This was particularly true during the period leading up to the start of the actual fighting, when both sides seemed reluctant to engage in the normal tradition of quiet diplomatic negotiation. The Iraqis felt insulted at the tone of the letter that President Bush sent to Saddam Hussein; while the Americans resented the ill-treatment of prisoners and the violent rhetoric emanating from Baghdad. We also need to consider how much of this was due to Bush's determination to publicly exorcise the "wimp factor" with which he had been saddled in his first two years as president.

The predispositions of the public on both sides appeared to incorporate the propaganda strategy that suggested a potential for improvement of their present situations "after the war." However the propaganda on both sides promised more than it could actually deliver in terms of a solution to the region's problems, far more so for the Iraqis. Much work needs to be done to evaluate the prewar moods of the Iraqis and their Arab supporters in order to estimate how much of the propaganda they were offered they believed. Ultimately both the Americans and the Arabs may turn out to be disappointed in the aftermath. In his article in the *London Review of Books*, the noted Arab-American scholar Edward Said (1991) lamented that

> it does no one in it [the Gulf War] any credit, and it will not produce any of the great results which have been predicted, however ostensibly victorious either side may prove to be, and whatever the results may prove to be for the other. It will not solve the problems of the Middle East, or those of America, now in deep recession, plagued by poverty, joblessness, and an urban, education and health crisis of gigantic proportions.

Said's comments, written on the eve of the fighting, have proven to be sadly true. Evaluating the current mood of public opinion against the prewar hopes and aspirations promises to be a rich source for the diligent propaganda analyst.

3. The Identification of the Propagandist. The source of propaganda is likely to be an institution or an organization with the propagandist as its leader or agent. Sometimes there will be complete openness about the identity of the organization behind the propaganda; sometimes it will be necessary to conceal the identity in order to achieve the goals set by the institution. The identification of the propaganda institutions is one of the most difficult tasks that await the propaganda analyst. In the Gulf War there were many organizations on each side, both official and unofficial, that were engaged in formulating and spreading propaganda. Some of these propaganda organizations are quite obvious, such as the various offices of the U.S. armed forces, but many others working behind the scenes are, as yet, unknown. For example, there were many clandestine operations in the Middle East fomenting opposition on both sides, and most of these remain secret. (Both the United States and the British still have not revealed the full extent of their secret operations in World War II!) This is one area where much research remains to be done and it may take many years before most of this information is publicly revealed.

4. The Structure of the Propaganda Organization. The most successful propaganda campaigns tend to originate from a strong, centralized and decision-making authority that produces consistent messages throughout its structure. An examination of the structure of the propaganda organization(s) also includes an articulation of the specific goals of that organization, and the selection of communication media used to further those objectives. This is also a very difficult category to research, because it requires the analyst to have access to information that penetrates the structure of government organizations that may not be readily available.

In the Gulf War the roles of the official propaganda agencies, such as the Voice of America or Radio Baghdad are known, but even here the actual policies formulated for these organizations in the conflict will await further research. On the Iraqi side, the structure of the propaganda agencies remain rather sketchy, and the exact day-to-day role of Saddam Hussein remains a matter of speculation. Who, for instance, made the decision to put the captured airmen on display; or who allowed CNN to stay in Baghdad? (There is some indication that in this latter instance, it was more the result of confused "nondecision" rather than a deliberate propaganda ploy). Solving these mysteries provides a very rich area for propaganda analysis, but it requires perseverance and diligence on the part of the researcher.

5. The Target Audience. A clear vision of the target audience is an essential part of a successful propaganda campaign. The traditional propaganda audience was essentially a mass audience, with little differentiation between groups. The availability of new technologies and market segmentation research has now made a greater selectivity possible. In the Gulf War, there was propaganda aimed at both the mass audience and to specific audiences. For example, what specific target audiences did the Coalition forces define for external propaganda in the Arab world? Such an analysis would show how specific audiences were targeted and the comparative success rate for each group at specific points in time.

There were also clear differences in the securing of the credence of the various audiences, particularly as the war progressed. Initially those who supported the Iraqi position, especially in other Arab countries, gave strong credibility to the Iraqi propaganda about their potential military strength. However, such propaganda lost its credibility once the fighting itself began, and the Iraqi supporters were forced to adopt other justifications, such as "Saddam may be losing, but he has held up under Coalition pressure far longer than anyone anticipated. This is a moral victory for the Arabs." These justifications continued long after the fighting ceased, especially after Saddam Hussein was allowed to continue in office.

The ideological environment for the Coalition audience appeared, in this particular case, to be much more conducive to the implementation of the ultimate propaganda objectives, for after all the Coalition won the war. However, we need to examine the structure of Iraqi society in prewar Iraq to see whether or not the prevailing environment at that time allowed the Iraqi people to seriously believe their leader's propaganda. This requires an understanding of Iraqi and Arab history, as well as a political history of the region. As indicated above, the infrastructure of American society and culture, complete with the accepted ideological tenets of freedom in its many manifestations, clearly provided an ideal environment from which to launch a propaganda campaign against a tyrant such as Saddam Hussein.

One target audience that was not well served by the Coalition side was the large number of Palestinians living in various Arab countries. From all accounts, there was a deliberate attempt made to isolate and even ignore this group because of their support for Saddam Hussein. We will never know whether this represented a lost opportunity to deal with the vexing Palestinian problem by failing to offer a viable alternative to their support of the Iraqis. The postwar efforts being made by the Bush administration to deal with the Palestinian issue suggests that more could have been done during the actual conflict to capture their "hearts and minds."

6. Media Utilization Techniques. This category determines how propaganda uses the media available to it. This would also compare the differences or consistency between the messages carried by various media. Propaganda is associated with the control of information flow, and this analysis would also examine the sequence of such message flow. In the Gulf War, for example, did newspapers have a different series of propaganda messages because they were later in the sequence of information flow? Were specific media used to carry specific propaganda messages; was television used for emotion and print media for ideological justification? These are the types of questions the analyst would ask.

Obviously, given the fact that the conflict was fought out daily in the newspapers and on the television and radio sets of the world, this ensured that the attention of the audience was secured. However, the reactions of this audience to the variety of propaganda messages were varied within each separate culture (the reaction to the CNN broadcasts of civilian bombings in Iraq was received differently in Jordan than it was in the United States), and even within individual cultures themselves (not all Americans agreed with the administration's position).

One very obvious media technique used to maximum effect by the Coalition was the press briefing that appeared on U.S. television every afternoon. This became the focal point of the flow of information for a substantial number of Americans, and was, therefore, one of the most effective sources of propaganda. Through these briefings the public were given a specific structure to the events leading up to the war, and then to the conduct of the war itself. For example, the issue was posed in the Canadian Press that the press briefings often provided deliberate disinformation in order to deceive Saddam Hussein about the relative strengths of the two sides, leading him to think that he could win a ground war (Gwyn, 1991). Another interesting by-product of the press briefings was the public's perception that the reporters were ill-mannered at these briefings. This perception did much to coalesce public support for the military's position on the need to control the press in the combat zone. A key event was a *Saturday Night Live* sketch lampooning the press's behavior at the briefings that convinced White House officials and the president not to ease restrictions on the coverage of the war (DeParles, 1991). Of such events are great administrative decisions made!

7. *Special Techniques to Maximize Effect.* Though propaganda is too complex to limit all of its techniques to a short list, there are, however, certain techniques for "maximum effectiveness" that are worthy of further analysis. These include:

Understanding the predispositions of the audience, and the creation of a "resonance" within the target audience. Clearly both sides in the Gulf War felt that they "knew" what issues would best justify their actions. In a totalitarian society such as Iraq, the control of the systems of communications allowed the government to set the basic agenda, and the various reasons offered for invading Kuwait over the period of several months went largely unchallenged (or so it appears—we still do not have a complete picture of Iraqi public opinion).

It was the Bush administration that on analysis appears to have had the more difficult job of selling the impending conflict to the American public, and several different propaganda strategies were tried before the right combination for achieving a public resonance was found. In the first phase, right after the invasion of Kuwait, there was a great deal of confusion and uncertainty about the administration's position. Were we there to protect the sovereignty of Kuwait, or our oil interests, or the borders of Saudi Arabia? All three reasons were offered, either alone or in combination, and the majority of the American public, though supportive of ousting Saddam Hussein from Kuwait, were not exactly sure of why we were sending massive numbers of troops to the area. The second phase comes after the November 1 speech in which Bush, escalating the verbal offensive, said that Saddam Hussein was more brutal than Adolf Hitler. This at least provided a context in which the public could assess the need to commit troops, and by November 6, the Pentagon released figures that showed that more than 230,000 troops were deployed in Operation Desert Shield.

The third propaganda phase was the most significant. As the conflict escalated toward actual combat, the nature of the news coverage of the Gulf War changed. In a very useful study (Lamay, 1991a) conducted by the Freedom Forum, the findings from the February/March issue of the *Tyndall Report* (which analyzes network television news) were used to demonstrate the emergence of the "yellow ribbon factor." This can be traced to George Bush's strong emphasis in his State of the Union address in early January on the need to support "the boys and the girls" in the Gulf and his avuncular concern for their welfare. This speech was aimed at uniting the defeated supporters of sanctions, the proponents of a continued air war and those who argued for a ground offensive and attracted by far the most rousing applause. Thus was born "yellow ribbonitis"— the notion of supporting the troops regardless of one's feelings about the war itself. In the three weeks prior to January 18, 1991, "controversy" stories dominated yellow ribbon stories on network news by 45 to 8. In the following six weeks, yellow ribbon stories came to the fore 36 to 19 (Lamay, 1991b). Here we have a dramatic quantitative measure of "jumping on the bandwagon" (to use one of the abc's of propaganda developed by the Institute for Propaganda Analysis) in order not to be left behind as the force of public opinion changed in favor of supporting the troops, and going to war. The key questions here are: What issues could the peace movement have used to create their own bandwagon? What were the predispositions of the

American public that made support for the war so overwhelming? What other propaganda techniques did the Bush administration use to successfully bring about this strong coalition of public opinion? Finally, can and will this same bandwagon become part of the presidential election campaign in 1992?

The use of metaphor and imagery. Another important method in maximizing propaganda effectiveness is in the selected use of the metaphors and images that are created to enlist public support for the propagandist's position and to explain events that can shape and manipulate public perceptions. Metaphor is extremely significant in our lives, for as Lakoff and Johnson (1980) point out: "We claim that most of our normal conceptual system is metaphorically structured; that is, most concepts are partially understood in terms of other concepts" (p. 56). Thus the use of specific words and images have a direct bearing on how certain events are structured in the minds of the public. Key images and concepts are evoked by a careful combination of previous experiences with new events. For such metaphorical propaganda to be effective these images must be readily recognizable to the audience that is being propagandized.

In the initial phases of the conflict, even before Iraq occupied Kuwait, the Iraqis had massed thousands of troops on the Kuwaiti border while the negotiations over the "oil rights" issue were underway. (It was the misinterpretation of this Iraqi propaganda ploy by the State Department that has been the cause of much concern about the accuracy of U.S. intelligence gathering.) For reasons that are as yet unclear, the Kuwaitis did not appear to take this propaganda threat seriously. When the official U.S. response to this specific action seemed to be a vague desire for neutrality in the issue, the Iraqis turned the psychological propaganda *threat* into the *reality* of invasion. The question remains, what made Saddam Hussein feel that what had clearly started out as a psychological warfare ploy could be implemented with relative impunity? Did the U.S. government, and the Kuwaitis, misinterpret this as yet another form of posturing, which is so common in the Arab world? (Patai, 1983). Once the invasion of Kuwait had been accomplished, a similar threat was immediately posed to the Saudi Arabian borders, but this time President Bush, setting the stage for his own psychological propaganda, made it very clear that "the integrity of Saudi Arabia" was vital to U.S. interests. On August 8, Bush told the nation and the Iraqis that "a line has been drawn in the sand,"—a metaphor (and a pun, considering the geographic location of the conflict) which has a very precise symbolic meaning for the American public. Derived from countless uses in popular culture, this "don't step over the boundary" image crystallized the logistics of the conflict for the American public, and the rest of the world, and provided a clear signal to the Iraqis that there was a specific point beyond which the United States *would* engage in military action. The message was obviously very clear, for after this statement there were no further Iraqi expansionist military actions.

Once the occupation of Kuwait began, there was a constant stream of psychological propaganda aimed at setting up the specific metaphors by which the conflict would be structured for the world audience. (In this particular instance, because of the role of CNN and the other international television networks, we can consider that there was a worldwide audience for the theater of war.) On August 20, Bush set aside all diplomatic euphemisms and declared that the 3,000 Americans remaining in Kuwait were, in fact, hostages. The word *hostages* conjured up immediate images of the demoralizing impotency experienced during the Iran hostage crisis of a decade earlier; an experience that the American public were in no mood to repeat. In the interim the word had also become synonymous with *terrorism*, and this added to the willingness (even eagerness) of the majority of the American public to finally accomplish something that had frustrated them since Iran, namely to engage terrorists directly in combat. The positioning of the Iraqis as terrorists was a significant factor in coalescing opposition to their actions, and tended to obscure whatever legitimate reasons there might have been for their original disagreement with Kuwait. In addition, the comparison of Saddam Hussein to Hitler was a clear image that had strong public resonance. The ill-advised display of the captured American and Coalition flyers on television for all the world to see simply reinforced the image of the Iraqis as terrorists. The American peace movement, particularly after the appearance of the prisoners, was never able to counter these powerful propaganda images with strong peace metaphors.

The Iraqis had their own metaphors. Saddam Hussein at various times referred to George Bush as: "Criminal Bush," "Oppressor Bush," "Satan," "Criminal Tyrant," "Loathsome Criminal," "Evil Butcher," "America's Satan," and so on. He also called Saudi Arabia's King Fahd, the "Midget Agent," "Traitor Fahd," "Agent Fahd," "Enemy of God," "Ally of the Forces of Evil and Shame," and worst of all, "Jewish" (Pletka, 1991, p. 12). Flowery rhetoric is part of the Arab culture, and when Saddam used phrases like "Americans will swim in their own blood," it meant simply, "we're going to kick ass," (something that George Bush, using his Texas persona, had no difficulty in clearly articulating), but the imagery had more specific and literal connotations to an American audience. It fed directly into the long-established popular culture imagery of bloodthirsty, barbaric Arabs committing atrocities.

Limitations of space preclude an extensive analysis of every potential technique for maximizing the effectiveness of propaganda campaigns, and the reader is referred to Chapter 6 for a list of other useful techniques.

8. Audience Reaction to Various Propaganda Techniques. Here the analyst looks for evidence of the target audience's response to propaganda. If the propaganda campaign is open, then very often it will be discussed by journalists and other commentators. This should not be mistaken for audience reaction, which can be better gauged in shifts in public opinion polls and surveys, as well as overt behavior such as parades or even taking up arms. The analyst looks for the audience's adoption of the propagandist's language and slogans. Does the audience take on a new ideological identity? Over time does the propaganda objective become realized and an integral part of the sociocultural scene?

In the case of the Gulf War, there were literally daily opinion polls on the public's attitude to every phase of the conflict. The administration and the Pentagon were able to use these and their own polls to alter propaganda appeals and strategies to counter any trend which was felt to be harmful to their goals. Future Gulf War propaganda analysts will have the advantage of this having been the most "polled" war in history. The initial reaction is that the administration's propaganda strategies were enormously successful in gaining the majority of public support; the key mystery is how carefully were these strategies planned ahead of time, and who did the planning?

9. Counterpropaganda. In the Gulf War there were serious attempts to counter the propaganda efforts of the U.S. government on the home front by various organizations intent on more peaceful solutions to the crisis. As indicated earlier, these antiwar efforts were dealt a serious blow by the inexplicable actions of the Iraqis, in particular, the parading of "hostages" and then the captured flyers on international television. The nature and the extent of the counterpropaganda that developed in Iraq is still not clear at this time.

10. Effects and Evaluation. The most important effect is obviously whether the objectives of the propaganda campaign have been met or not. If not all of the objectives, then which of the specific goals have been achieved. There are a wide variety of measures possible for assessing the effectiveness of a propaganda campaign, ranging from detailed surveys of public opinion, the success of legislative action, the increase in contributions, or the growth in the membership of specific organizations. Even if the campaign failed, then an evaluation should be able to indicate the reasons for such failure. Also, not all of the effects of propaganda can be seen immediately; some effects are deliberately designed to have a delayed or long-term influence. In the Gulf War the short-term propaganda campaigns on the U.S. home front and internationally were obviously quite effective, but translation of the battle victory into a concept of peace in the Middle East, solving the Saddam Hussein problem, and dealing with U.S. domestic issues has not been as successful. Of course, the most difficult evaluation is the long-term impact on relationships with all of the Arab nations. What new mythologies and images of the West has the war fostered in Arab minds?

By January 1992 some of the propaganda strategies used by the Kuwaiti government to sway American public opinion to their cause were beginning to be revealed. One story, in particular, which had caught the imagination of the American public and politicians during the conflict, was revealed to have been a major propaganda ploy. On October 10, 1990, a fifteen-year-old Kuwaiti girl named "Nayirah" had shocked the Congressional Human Rights Caucus, when she tearfully asserted that she had watched as Iraqi soldiers took 15 babies from their incubators in Al-Adan hospital in Kuwait City, and "left the babies on the cold floor to die." Nayirah's true identity was kept a secret to protect her family from reprisals in occupied Kuwait. On January 6, 1992, John R. MacArthur revealed in the *New York Times* that Nayirah was, in fact, the daughter of the Kuwaiti ambassador to the United States, Suad Nasir al-Sabah, a member of the Kuwaiti ruling family. Once the Gulf War had ended, all attempts to verify the story by independent groups such as Amnesty International and Middle East Watch failed to turn up any evidence that the incident had, in reality, taken place.

MacArthur (1992) also revealed the significant role played by the major public relations firm of Hill and Knowlton in their work for the Citizens for a Free Kuwait organization. Ostensibly a group of concerned private citizens, in reality Citizens for a Free Kuwait received more than 95% of its funding directly from the Kuwaiti government, and worked to lobby Congress for military intervention as well as playing a major role in swaying American public opinion in favor of such intervention. Hill and Knowlton received more than $6 million for their efforts, which included writing speeches for Kuwaitis and coaching them on their appearances before the media and public. Of special interest was their use of focus group techniques to pinpoint those issues that would have the most resonance for the American public. These focus groups, conducted by the Werthlin Group, revealed that atrocity stories were very likely to sway public opinion in favor of going to war. MacArthur claims that the "dead babies" story was a defining moment in the propaganda campaign to prepare the American public for the need to go to war. President George Bush used the dead babies story more than ten times in the 40 days following Nayirah's testimony, and in the Senate debate on whether to approve military action, seven senators specifically focused on the story. The final margin of victory in favor of military intervention was five votes.

Despite the obvious manipulation of the emotions of the American public, the revelation of the propaganda aspects of the dead babies on both ABC (20/20) and CBS (60 Minutes), as well as in MacArthur's New York Times article failed to elicit a major public outcry. Although this incident is reminiscent of George Creel's revelations in How We Advertised the War after World War I, the American public, mired in an economic depression, clearly did not care that they had, once again, been duped by skillful professional manipulators. In early February, the U.S. government claimed that the U.S. ambassador to Kuwait had been able to locate several eyewitnesses to this incident, but the details of the story were still very sketchy. (There is no doubt that long after this book has been published, there will still be disagreements as to exactly what did happen in the dead babies incident.) The pivotal role played by Hill and Knowlton in the creation and dissemination of the dead babies story and the manipulation of American public opinion is of particular concern to the propaganda analyst. It is highly likely that further propaganda strategies will gradually be revealed in the next few years.

The Gulf War was important politically, but it was also a major event in the history of propaganda because of the widescale application of new communications technologies in the battle for the hearts and minds of the public. Many years will be spent before we will have anything approaching an accurate assessment of the role and effectiveness of the various propaganda activities of this conflict.

8 How Propaganda Works in Modern Society

Propaganda is a form of communication and can, therefore, be depicted as a process. A model of the propaganda process includes the sociohistorical context; a cultural rim made up of government, economy, events, ideology, and myths of society; the propaganda institution; the propaganda agents; media methods; the social network; and the public. Generalizations about propaganda in modern society are based on the events and concepts discussed throughout this book.

This chapter presents a model of propaganda and several generalizations that have evolved from the events, ideas, and concepts that have been discussed in previous chapters. This chapter also reaffirms our position that propaganda is a form of communication that can be depicted as a process.

Model of the Process of Propaganda

As one looks at the model of propaganda (Figure 8.1), the development of propagandistic communication as a process within a social system is illustrated. The model is complex because, as we have seen in the preceding chapters, propaganda itself is complex. The process of propaganda takes the form of a message flow through a network system that includes propaganda agents, various media, and a social network, originating with an institution and ending with the possibility of response from the public or a target audience within the public. The message flow is contained within a cultural rim that is itself placed within a sociohistorical context. The model, therefore, depicts the necessity of examining the process of propagandistic communication within the multitude of features contained within a social-historical-cultural framework. The flow of propaganda from institution to public has several canals that feed into or are fed by the elements of the cultural rim, to and from the institution itself, to and from the media, and to and from the public. This indicates that as propaganda occurs it has a potential impact on the culture at any point during the process, and of course, the culture has, in turn, an impact upon the process of propaganda.

Social-Historical Context

Propaganda as a process is socially determined. The sociohistorical context provides a heritage that gives a propagandist motivation and even a style of communication. In order to understand how propaganda works, it is necessary to consider how the existing sociohistorical context allows it to work. The propaganda that emerges is the product of forces established long before the activity originated and is controlled by those forces. That is why the uses and methods by which propaganda emerges differ from society to society.

The propagandist is influenced by past models through allusions to historical figures, methods, and impulses for current propaganda activity. For example, the idea that freedom is worth dying for was the basis for Patrick Henry's Give me Liberty or Give Me Death speech in the time of the American Revolution. The same idea provided the impulse for the anti-Communist slogan, Better Dead Than Red almost 200 years later. In another culture, the Middle East, present-day propaganda can be traced back to the sociohistorical context of the origins of Mohammedanism in the seventh century and the subsequent spread of the Islamic religion. Thirteen centuries later, Mohammed's charge to his disciples to convert the infidels and be willing to die fighting for the faith still shapes the content that takes form through modern technologies. When the Palestinians commit what Americans may think are suicidal acts, they do so believing that a death for the cause will assure them a place on the right hand of God. Each incident of propaganda is, thus, historically based; yet each act of propaganda also takes place at a specific time in history and is a product of its time. It is highly unlikely that the propaganda of Adolf Hitler would have worked in Germany during a time of prosperity. Time, both past and present, shapes the internal dynamics of the model.

The flow of propaganda to and from an institution depends upon the conditions of the times and upon the availability of the media.

SOCIAL-HISTORICAL CONTEXT

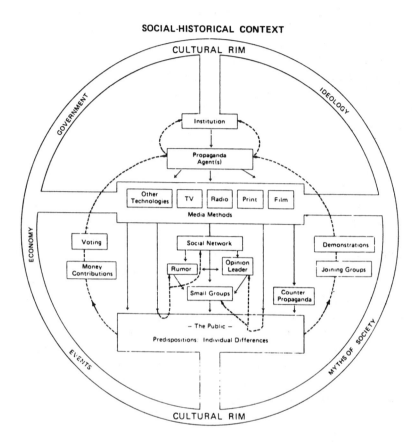

Figure 8.1. Model of the process of propaganda.

For example, conditions in the 1950s in America tended to be more restrictive than the 1960s due to the Red Scare and McCarthyism. In the sixteenth century, Martin Luther's ability to reach his audience was made possible by the development of the printing press. If the times and the conditions are right, to paraphrase Nietzsche, the propagandist is a hero who does nothing but shake the tree when the fruit is ripe.

Cultural Rim

Culture includes the sociohistorical context. We have depicted culture within the sociohistorical context only for purposes of clarifying the concepts presented here. In the model, the elements of culture are depicted as a rim surrounding the flow of propaganda with canals leading to and from the process and the cultural rim. The cultural rim is the infrastructure that provides the material context in which messages are sent and received. How propaganda is developed, used, and received is cultural specific. The elements of a culture—its ideologies, societal myths, government, economy, and specific events that take place—influence propaganda. Take, for example, whether a society is open or closed. A closed society such as China controls the media, preventing messages from the outside from coming into the system. American newspapers cannot be freely sold. The Chinese are not only forced to rely on national newspapers and television for news but for interpretation of events as well. Unless the situation changes, future generations may never know that university students and workers peacefully demonstrated against the government in Tiananmen Square in Beijing in 1989. As far as the Chinese media was concerned, "no one died in Tiananmen Square" (Lutz, 1989).

An open society, on the other hand, tends to have more flexible, accessible media systems that accept or reject messages without having to refer to higher authorities. In the fall of 1985, the American Broadcasting Company and the producers of the program 20/20 chose to reject a program segment about the death of Marilyn Monroe and a connection with Robert Kennedy because of the producer's personal friendship with the Kennedy family. The British Broadcasting Corporation, however, chose to broadcast the story. In open systems, the variety of channels in the media, competing images, and easy access to them tend to make audiences less suspicious but also more discerning and concerned about the potential for propaganda.

The economy dictates the flow of propaganda relative to the sale or consumption of goods. Advertising certainly dictates the structure of the mass media system in the United States. In the nineteenth century, the economy even dictated the attainment of literacy. If a nation needed laborers, it was less likely to support education of the masses.

As we said before, culture is a system of formal and informal rules that tell people how to behave most of the time. People's behavior, in turn, can alter the culture by creating new societal myths or changing ideologies. As James Carey (1988) has pointed out, "Culture as a system of construed meanings changes in relation to other cultural objects such as technologies and economic practices or other social processes such as conflict and accommodation, such changes are transformations on a given cultural tradition, a tradition that insists on reasserting itself" (p. 11).

The Process of Propaganda

Institution

An institution generally initiates and fosters propaganda due to its organizational and financial powers. The propaganda may be to maintain the institution's legitimacy, its position in society, and its activities. An institution that is outside of the established order may also initiate propaganda to agitate in order to demonstrate support for a counterideology or concern over an issue. Institutional affiliation may not be revealed by the propagandists, who may act as fronts or agents for the source. This is often the case during wartime or for espionage activity.

Propaganda Agents

Propaganda agents are the people who facilitate messages directly and through the media for an institution. Sometimes they are powerful and charismatic figures; other times they are bureaucrats or low-keyed disseminators of information. Their purpose is to send out ideology with a specific objective to a target audience for the benefit of the institution but not necessarily for the good of the receivers. There is likely to be a hierarchy of agents with a chain of command to ensure that the message will be homogeneous.

Media Methods

The propaganda agents select and use the available media to send the message to the target audience. The development of new technologies affects the nature of propaganda and has been seen to be the major factor in the use of propaganda. Short-wave radio has enabled the major governments of the world to broadcast ideology to remote places. Satellite dishes and cable television have enhanced religious television, giving it access to virtually every American home. Direct mail and the storage and speed of computer usage has produced a steady and regulated stream of messages to target addresses. Fax machines have become so commonplace that they too are being used for propaganda messages.

Media utilization is vital to a propaganda campaign. Access to and control of the media literally means access to and potential control of public opinion. The type of media selected by the propagandist is appropriate to the audience that needs to be reached. Media are used to disseminate information to the membership of a propaganda organization as well as to those whose support is solicited. Where the media are not owned, the propagandist runs the risk of the information being filtered through the media or being released in an inappropriate fashion.

The media message should be homogeneous with a consistency of purpose in order for the propaganda to be effective. Less control over the media means less control over the homogeneity of the message.

Mass media has become so extensive and influential that it affects the culture. Although the propagandist's intent is to reach a target audience, the media usage can influence culture along the way to the target audience. Likewise, the culture influences the media. An open society allows competing messages to come from the media, thus the propagandist's message, when mediated by unsympathetic or critical people, can be diffused. On the other hand, the worldwide media is avaricious for sensational news. This enables propagandists to receive worldwide exposure at no cost. Certainly, terrorist hijackings of airplanes and ships and the subsequent media coverage have promulgated messages that otherwise would have remained unheard or unseen. Conversely, media coverage of a competing event can completely diffuse the impact of a propaganda event, such as in 1968 when the North Koreans released the *Pueblo* crew while the media covered Apollo 8's journey to the moon.

Media also affect the propaganda agents and the institution. Too much exposure may be harmful, causing the propagandist to have to change strategies. Unwanted publicity can lessen the credibility of an agent or institution. The peculiarities of the medium itself may not be understood well enough. Richard M. Nixon discovered that television caused him to appear unshaven and unattractive in the 1960 debates with John F. Kennedy because he wore improper makeup and the wrong color suit. Before his 1969 campaign appearances on television, Nixon hired Johnny Carson's makeup man to make sure that his appearance was appropriate for the televised image.

Sometimes the target audience receives the message directly from a medium or combination of media; sometimes selected audiences function as channels of communication to broader audiences through a social network.

Social Network

A social network is made up of the following: opinion leaders who may influence an audience because of their position with the social network; small groups of people that may include opinion leaders and/or propaganda agents; and people who facilitate rumors innocently or deliberately throughout a social network. In the multistep flow of communication, a social network receives information from the media that is, in turn, disseminated throughout a community by leaders within it. Likewise, the public may receive information from the media and carry it back to the opinion leaders for explanation or confirmation.

As we have seen, in institutions such as the United States Information Agency, information may be sent directly from the propaganda agent to opinion leaders, sidestepping the media altogether. Although the process model of propaganda depicts the flow of information from the propaganda agent through the media to the social network, it is possible for the message to bypass the media and go directly to opinion leaders or small groups. For the most part, however, the media are used heavily by agents of propaganda with the social network coming into play as a mediating influence.

The Public

The propagandist's audience may be the general public or a segment of the public targeted for a specific set of responses. As we have seen in Chapter 6, the predispositions of the audience are canalized by the propaganda message, having the effect of resonance. Media experiences create shared experiences, thus the public may form communities related to the propaganda message. For example, the abortion controversy has created moral communities among those who oppose abortion.

Public response to propaganda messages takes many forms. The public may fail to receive a message; it may choose to ignore it; it may be skeptical and suspicious; it may take sides for and against; it may respond in desired ways. Desired behavioral responses are voting, contributing money, purchasing products, joining groups, engaging in demonstrations, and putting pressure on elected officials through letters, telegrams, and phone calls. Such responses can be observed and measured, enhancing the propagandist's effectiveness. The same responses can also be fed back into the cultural rim, creating new events, affecting the economy, creating new myths, electing new government officials, and altering ideology over time.

The model of the process of propaganda is an interactive and cyclical model with each segment having the potential of interacting with another. Propaganda is a communicative form with potential to create change. This book has demonstrated changes throughout history, but, more important, it should equip the reader with the ability to recognize and evaluate propaganda in modern society. We have learned more about propaganda in writing and revising this book, and the following generalizations, though few in number, may constitute new ways of looking at a very old subject.

Generalizations About Propaganda

1. Propaganda creates and is created by strange and powerful bedfellows. Special interests cause groups that are normally diverse to unite in a common cause. The abortion controversy has brought the far right and the Roman Catholics together. The antipornography movement united the moral majority and feminists.

2. Propaganda serves an informative function in that it tells people what to think about and how to behave. Because people turn to the media in order to understand events and find out what to do about them, they unwittingly expose themselves to propaganda and may become willing or naive supporters of an invisible institution.

3. Even when it is obvious that a message is propaganda, people will respond favorably to it. Knowledge that communication is propagandistic does not necessarily neutralize people's reaction to it.

4. People tend to divide into opposing camps in response to propaganda, and public communities are formed that create powerful armies to fight for and support a cause. The media can instantly transmit information, and the community responds with instantaneous reactions.

5. New technologies are powerful allies of propagandists. Satellite dishes and home video cameras have assisted the transmission of counterpropaganda in societies in which media is controlled. Twenty-four hour worldwide television broadcasts reach nearly all areas of the world. Instant information is readily available at all times. Computer technology and fax machines have created an unexpected force in direct mail propaganda. People's predispositions are easily identifiable through market research, making them easy targets for propaganda.

6. External propaganda may be created for internal consumption. Displays of aggression toward an enemy may not faze the enemy, but they can bolster morale at home.

7. Propaganda is not necessarily an evil thing. It can only be evaluated within its own context according to the players, the played upon, and its purpose.

This examination of propaganda has, we hope, made you more aware of how much this activity has shaped our lives and helped to form the attitudes we have on so many subjects. Propaganda by itself is a natural outgrowth of the development of sophisticated media of communication; it will always be with us, in one form or another and individuals can accept or reject it as they wish. Propaganda should not be feared, for in a free society, somewhere, somehow, alternate message systems always appear. As this book was being revised in 1991, the world saw a series of remarkable events—the fall of the Berlin Wall and the reunification of Germany, the demise of Communism in most of Eastern Europe, and the breakup of the Soviet Union with a subsequent and failed coup. The world is very different now, but other events will occur. As long as people care, propaganda's powers can be controlled. If people give up their right to free speech, for whatever reason, then have they lost control of propaganda systems. The 200th anniversary of the Bill of Rights to the United States Constitution also fell within 1991. The First Amendment to the Bill of Rights guarantees the freedom of speech and the press as well as the right to petition the government to redress grievances. In the long run, these freedoms in a free and open society are the greatest deterrents to the misuse of propaganda.

References

Advisory Board for Cuba Broadcasting (1989). Report for 1989. Washington, DC.

Ajemian, R., Goodgame, D., & Kane, J. J. (1991, February 18). Can the pro-war consensus survive? *Time*, pp. 32-34.

Ajzen, I. & Fishbein, M. (1980). *Understanding attitudes and predicting social behavior*. Englewood Cliffs, NJ: Prentice-Hall.

Alexandre, L. (1988). *The Voice of America from detente to the Reagan doctrine*. Norwood, NJ: Ablex.

Allport, G. W. (1935). Attitudes. In C. Murchison (Ed.), *The handbook of social psychology* (pp. 798-884). MA: Clark University Press.

Allport, G. W. (1968). The historical background of modern social psychology. In G. Lindzey & E. Aronson (Eds.), *The handbook of social psychology* (Vol. 1, pp. 1-280). Reading, MA: Addison-Wesley.

Altheide, D. L., & Johnson J. M. (1980). *Bureaucratic propaganda*. Boston: Allyn & Bacon.

Anderson, J. A. (1991). *Communication yearbook 14*. Newbury Park, CA: Sage.

Anderson, K. (1981). *Wartime women: Sex roles, family relations, and the status of women during world war II*. Westport, CT: Greenwood.

Armstrong, B. (1979). *The electronic church*. Nashville: Thomas Nelson.

Aronson, J. (1970). *The press and the cold war*. Indianapolis: Bobbs-Merrill.

Aronson, E. (1980). *The social animal*. San Francisco: W. H. Freeman.

Bailyn, B. (1967). *The theological origins of the American revolution*. Cambridge, MA: Harvard University Press.

Ball-Rokeach, S. J., & DeFleur, M. L. (1976). A dependency model of mass-media effects. *Communication Research, 3*, 3-21.

Bandura, A. (1977). *Social learning theory*. Englewood Cliffs, NJ: Prentice-Hall.

Bandura, A. (1986). *Social foundations of thought and action: A social cognitive theory*. Englewood Cliffs, NJ: Prentice-Hall.

Barnouw, E. (1968). *The golden web: A history of broadcasting in the United States, 1933-1953*. New York: Oxford University Press.

Barrett, E. W. (1953). *Truth is our weapon*. New York: Funk & Wagnalls.

Bem, D. J. (1970). *Beliefs, attitudes and human affairs*. Belmont, CA: Brooks/Cole.

Benson, T. W., & Prosser, M. H. (1969). *Readings in classical rhetoric*. Boston: Allyn & Bacon.

Berelson, D. (1956). *Reader in public opinion and communication.* New York: Free Press.

Biddle, P. R. (1966). *An experimental study of ethos and appeal for overt behavior in persuasion.* Unpublished doctoral dissertation, University of Illinois, Urbana.

Blumer, H. (1933). *Movies and conduct.* New York: Macmillan.

Bogardus, E. S. (1925). Measuring social distance. *Journal of Applied Sociology, 9,* 299-308.

Bogart, L. (1976). *Premises for propaganda: The U.S. Information Agency's Operating Assumptions in the Cold War.* New York: Free Press.

Bohn, T. (1977). *An historical and descriptive analysis of the "why we fight" films.* New York: Arno.

Bonner, R. J. (1933). *Aspects of Athenian democracy.* Berkeley: University of California Press.

Boster, R. J. & Mongeau, P. (1984). Fear-arousing persuasive messages. In R. N. Bostrum & B. H. Westley (Eds.), *Communication Yearbook 8* (pp. 330-375). Beverly Hills, CA: Sage.

Bramson, L. (1961). *The political context of sociology.* Princeton, NJ: Princeton University Press.

Brody, G. H., & Stoneman, Z. (1983, June). The influence of television viewing on family interaction: A contextualist framework. *Journal of Family Issues, 4*(2), 329-348.

Brinkley, A. (1982). *Voices of protests: Huey Long, Father Coughlin and the Great Depression.* New York: Vintage.

British enlist "Alice" in propaganda war. (1982, May 23). *Dallas Morning News,* p. 10A.

Brody, J. E. (1991, December 11). Smoking among children is found linked to cartoon advertisements. *New York Times,* p. A16.

Brown, J. A. C. (1963). *Techniques of persuasion: From propaganda to brainwashing.* Baltimore: Penguin.

Browne, R. W. (1850). *The Nichomachean Ethics of Aristotle* (Vol. 2). (Trans.). London: H. G. Bohn.

Brownfield, A. C. (1984, May 4). *Washington Inquirer,* p. 6.

Brownstein, R. (1990). *The power and the glitter: The Hollywood-Washington connection.* New York: Pantheon.

Bruntz, G. G. (1938). *Allied propaganda and the collapse of the German empire in 1918.* Stanford, CA: Stanford University Press.

Bryant, D. C. (1953, December). Rhetoric: Its function and scope. *Quarterly Journal of Speech, 39,* 401-424.

Bumpus, B., & Skelt, B. (1985). *Seventy years of international broadcasting.* Paris: Unesco.

Burke, K. (1973). *The philosophy of literary form.* Berkeley: University of California Press.

Burnett, N. F. S. (1989). Ideology and propaganda: Toward an integrative approach. In T. Smith III (Ed.), *Propaganda: A pluralistic perspective* (pp. 115-26). New York: Praeger.

Campbell, C. W. (1985). *Reel America and World War I.* Jefferson, NC: McFarland.

Carlson, J. (1983, October). Crime-show viewing by pre-adults: The impact on attitudes toward civil liberties. *Communication Research, 10,* 529-552.

Cary, H. (1854). *Plato: Works of Plato* (Vol. 1). (Trans.). London: H. G. Bohn.

Carey, J. W. (1989). *Communication as culture: Essays on media and society.* Boston: Unwin Hyman.

Carey, J. W. (Ed.). (1988). *Media, myths, and narratives: Television and the press.* Newbury Park, CA: Sage.

CBS Spreads Disinformation on Aids. (1987, April 13). *AIM report,* pp. xvi-8.

Chaiken, S., & Stangor, C. (1987). Attitudes and attitude change. *Annual Review of Psychology, 38,* 575-630.

Chandler, R. W. (1981). *War of ideas: The U.S. propaganda campaign in Vietnam.* Boulder: Westview.

Choukas, M. (1965). *Propaganda comes of age.* Washington, DC: Public Affairs Press.

Christenson, R. M., & McWilliams, R. (Eds.). (1967). *Voice of the people: Readings in public opinion and propaganda.* New York: McGraw-Hill.

Cohn, J. (1989). *Creating America: George Horace Lorimer and the Saturday Evening Post.* Pittsburgh: University of Pittsburgh Press.

Cole, R. (1986). *The political life of children.* Boston: Houghton Mifflin.

Comstock, G. (1980). *Television in America.* Beverly Hills, CA: Sage.

Conway, F., & Siegelman, J. (1982). *Holy terror: The fundamentalist war on America's freedoms in religion, politics and our private lives.* New York: Doubleday.

Cooper, L. (1932). *The rhetoric of Aristotle.* (Trans.). New York: Appleton-Century-Crofts.

Cooper, M. (1989). *Analyzing public discourse.* Prospect Heights, IL: Waveland.

Costello, J. (1985). *Love, sex and war: 1939-1945.* London: Pan Books.

Creel, G. (1920). *How we advertised America.* New York: Harper & Row.

Cushman, D. P., & McPhee, R. D. (1980). *Message-Attitude-Behavior relationship: Theory, methodology, and application.* New York: Academic Press.

Crouthamel, J. L. (1989). *Bennett's New York Herald and the rise of the popular press.* Syracuse: University of Syracuse Press.

Czitrom, D. J. (1982). *Media and the American mind.* Chapel Hill: University of North Carolina Press.

Davison, W. P. (1971, November). Some trends in international propaganda. *Annals of the American Academy of Political and Social Science, 398,* 1-13.

DeFleur, M., & Ball-Rokeach, S. (1982). *Theories of mass communication.* New York: Longman.

Delia, J. (1971). Rhetoric in the Nazi mind: Hitler's theory of persuasion. *Southern Speech Communication Journal, 37*(2), 136-49.

Delia, J. G. (1987). Communication research: A history. In C. R. Berger & H. Chaffee (Eds.), *Handbook of Communication Science* (pp. 20-98). Newbury Park, CA: Sage.

DeParles, J. (1991, May 5). Long series of military decisions led to Gulf War news censorship. *New York Times,* p. A1.

Dewey, J. (1927). *The public and its problems.* Chicago: Swallow Press.

Dewey, J. (1935). *Liberalism and social action.* New York: G. P. Putnam's Sons.

Dickens, A. G. (1968). *Reformation and society in sixteenth century Europe.* New York: Harcourt Brace Jovanovich.

Dondis D. (1981). Signs and symbols. In R. Williams (Ed.), *Contact: Human communication and its history* (pp. 71-86). New York: Thomas & Hudson.

Donnerstein, E., & Malamuth, N. (Eds.). (1984). *Pornography and sexual aggression.* New York: Academic Press.

Doob, L. W. (1948). *Public opinion and propaganda.* New York: Henry Holt & Co.

Doob, L. W. (1966). *Public Opinion and Propaganda* (2d Ed.). Hamden, CT: Archon.

Doob, L. W. (1989). Propaganda. In E. Barnouw et al. (Eds.), *International Encyclopedia of Communications* (Vol. 3, pp. 374-78). New York: Oxford.

Dowd, M. (1991, July 5). An Old-Fashioned Day of Patriotism. *New York Times,* p. C7.

Duffey, B., & Walsh, K. T. (1991, March 4). The Gulf War's Final Curtain. *U.S. News & World Report,* pp. 24-34.

Dupuy, T. N. (1965). Korean War. In Encyclopedia Britannica (Vol. 13, pp. 467-75). Chicago: Encyclopedia Britannica.

Ebon, M. (1987). *The Soviet propaganda machine.* New York: McGraw-Hill.

Editor (1937, January). Editorial Foreword. *Public Opinion Quarterly, 1,* 3.

Edwards, W. (1954). The theory of decision making. *Psychological Bulletin, 51,* 390-417.

Ellul, J. (1965). *Propaganda: The formation of men's attitudes.* New York: Knopf.

Emery, E., & Emery, M. (1984). *The press and America.* Englewood Cliffs, NJ: Prentice-Hall.

Ewen, S., & Ewen, E. (1982). *Channels of desire: Mass images and the shaping of American consciousness.* New York: McGraw-Hill.

Festinger, L. (1957). *A theory of cognitive dissonance.* Stanford, CA: Stanford University Press.

Fielding, R. (1972). *The American newsreel.* Norman: University of Oklahoma Press.

Fishbein, M., & Ajzen, I. (1975). *Beliefs, attitudes, intentions, and behavior: An introduction to theory and research.* Reading, MA: Addison-Wesley.

Fleming, D., & Bailyn, B. (Eds.). (1969). *The intellectual migration, Europe and America, 1930-1960.* Cambridge: Harvard University Press.

Forman, C. W. (1979). Christian missions in the ancient world. In Lasswell, D. Lerner, & H. Speier (Eds.), *Propaganda and communication in world history (Vol. 1, pp. 330-47): The symbolic instrument in early times.* Honolulu: University Press of Hawaii.

Foulkes, A. P. (1983). *Literature and propaganda.* London: Methuen.

Freemantle, A. (1965). *The age of faith.* New York: Time-Life Books.

Frotschler, A. L. (1983). *Smoking and politics.* Englewood Cliffs, NJ: Prentice-Hall.

Furhammer, L., & Isaksson, F. (1971). *Politics and film.* New York: Praeger.

Galimore, T. (1991). *Radio Marti: A study of U.S. international broadcasting policy and the ban on domestic dissemination of government information.* Paper presented at the ICA, Chicago.

Gerbner, G., Gross, L., Signorelli, N., Morgan, M. & Jackson-Beeck, M. (1979, Summer). The demonstration of power: Violence profile no. 10. *Journal of Communication, 29,* 177-96.

Ginsberg, B. (1986). *The captive public: How mass opinion promotes state power.* New York: Basic Books.

Graff, H. J. (Ed.). (1981). *Literary and social development in the West.* Cambridge: Cambridge University Press.

Grandin, T. (1939). *The political uses of radio.* Geneva: Geneva Research Center.

Greenberg, B. S. (Ed.). (1980). *Life on television.* Norwood, NY: Ablex.

Griffith, W. W. (1980).

Gruening, E. (1931). *The public pays: A study of power propaganda.* New York: Vanguard.

Gustainis, J. (1989). Propaganda and the law: The case of three Canadian films. In T. Smith III (Ed.), *Propaganda: A pluralistic perspective* (pp. 115-26). New York: Praeger.

Gwyn, R. (1991, February 26). Saddam tricked into thinking that he could win. *Toronto Star,* p. A1.

Hale, J. (1975). *Radio power.* Philadelphia: Temple University Pres.

Hall, S. (1977). The hinterland of science: Ideology and the sociology of knowledge. In Centre for Contemporary Cultural Studies, *On Ideology.* London: Hutchinson.

Hall, S. (1980). Cultural studies: Two paradigms. *Media, Culture, and Society, 2*(1).

Hall, S. (1984, January). The culture gap. *Marxism Today,* 18-22.

Hanke, H. (1990). Media culture in the GDR: Characteristics, processes and problems. *Media Culture and Society, 12*(2), 175-93.

Hardt, H. (1989). The return of the "critical" and the challenge of radical dissent: Critical theory, cultural studies, and American mass communication research. In J. A. Anderson (Ed.), *Communication Yearbook 12* (pp. 558-600). Newbury Park, CA: Sage.

Hart-Davis, D. (1986). *Hitler's games: The 1936 Olympics.* New York: Harper & Row.

Hartmann, S. M. (1982). *The home front and beyond: American women in the 1940s*. Boston: Twayne.

Hayden, D. (1986). *Redesigning the American dream: The future of housing, work, and family life*. New York: Norton.

Heider, F. (1946). Attitudes and Cognitive Organization. *Journal of Psychology, 21,* 107-12.

Heilbroner, R. L. (1985, January). Advertising as agitprop. *Harper's,* 71-76.

Herzstein, R. (1978). *The war that Hitler won*. New York: G. P. Putnam's Sons.

Hess, S., & Kaplan, M. (1975). *The ungentlemanly art*. New York: Macmillan.

Hitler, A. (1939). *Mein Kampf*. New York: Reynal & Hitchcock.

Honey, M. (1984). *Creating Rosie the Riveter: Class, gender, and propaganda during World War II*. Boston: University of Massachusetts Press.

Hovland, C. I., & Mandell, W. (1952). An experimental comparison of conclusion drawing by the communicator and by the audience. *Journal of Abnormal and Social Psychology, 47,* 581-88.

Hovland, C. I., Janis, I. L., & Kelly, H. H. (1953). *Communication and persuasion: Psychological studies of opinion change*. New Haven, CT: Yale University Press.

Hovland, C. I., Lumsdaine, A. A., & Sheffield, F. D. (1949). *Experiments on mass communication (vol. 3), Studies in social psychology in World War II*. Princeton, NJ: Princeton University Press.

How to detect propaganda. (1937). *Propaganda Analysis, 1.2,* 5-8.

Hunt, E. L. (1925). Plato and Aristotle on rhetoric and rhetoricians. In E. L. Hunt (Ed.), *Studies in rhetoric and public speaking* (pp. 3-60). New York: Century.

Jones, D. B. (1945). Hollywood war films. *Hollywood Quarterly, 1*(1), 1-19.

Jones, M. (1990). Fake? The Art of Deception. London: British Museum Publications.

Jowett, G. S. (1976). *Film: The democratic art*. Boston: Little, Brown.

Jowett, G. S. (1982). They taught it at the movies: films on models for learned sexual behavior. In S. Thomas (Ed.), *Film/Culture* (pp. 209-221). Metuchen, NY: Scarecrow Press.

Jowett, G. S. (1987). Propaganda and communication: The re-emergence of a research tradition. *Journal of Communication, 37*(1), 97-114.

Jowett, G. S. (in press). Social science as a weapon: The origins of the Payne Fund studies, 1926-1929. *Communication*.

Joyce, W. (1963). *The propaganda gap*. New York: Harper & Row.

Kapferer, J. N. (1990). *Rumors: Uses, interpretations, and images*. New Brunswick, NJ: Transactions Press.

Karlins, M., & Abelson, H. I. (1970). *Persuasion: How opinions and attitudes are changed*. New York: Springer.

Katz, E., & Lazarsfeld, P. (1955). *Personal influence: The part played by people in mass communication*. Glencoe, IL: Free Press.

Katz, E., & Szecsko, T. (Eds.). (1981). *Mass media and social change*. Beverly Hills, CA: Sage.

Kecskemeti, P. (1973). Propaganda. In I. D. Pool et al. (Eds.), *Handbook of communication* (pp. 844-70). Chicago: Rand McNally.

Kelman, H. C., & Hovland, C. I. (1953). "Reinstatement" of the communicator in delayed measurement of opinion change. *Journal of Abnormal and Social Psychology, 48,* 3.

Kneitel, T. (1982, December). Secrets of Propaganda Broadcasting. *Popular Communication: The Monitoring Magazine,* pp. 8-21.

Kubey, R., & Csikszentmihalyi, M. (1990). *Television and the quality of life: How viewing shapes everyday experience*. Hillsdale, NJ: Lawrence Erlbaum.

Lakoff, G., & Johnson, M. (1980). *Metaphors we live by*. Chicago: University of Chicago Press.

Lamay, C. (1991a). By the numbers I: The bibliometrics of war. In *The media at war: The press and the Persian Gulf conflict* (pp. 41-44). New York: Freedom Forum.

Lamay, C. (1991b). By the numbers II: Measuring the coverage. In *The media at war: The press and the Persian Gulf conflict* (pp. 45-50). New York: Freedom Forum.

Land, R. E., & Sears, D. O. (1964). *Public opinion*. Englewood Cliffs, NJ: Prentice-Hall.

Lang, J. S. (1979, August 27). The great American bureaucratic propaganda machine. *U.S. News and World Report*, pp. 43-47.

Lang, K. (1989). Communications research: Origins and development. In E. Barnouw, G. Gerbner, W. Schramm, T. L. Worth, & L. Gross, *International Encyclopedia of Communications* (Vol. I, pp. 369-74). New York: Oxford University Press.

LaPiere, R. T. (1934). Attitude versus actions. In M. Fishbein, *Readings in attitude theory and measurement* (pp. 26-31). New York: John Wiley.

Laski, H. J., et al. (1970). *Where stands democracy: A collection of essays*. Freeport, NY: Books for Libraries Press.

Lasswell, H. (1927). *Propaganda technique in the world war*. New York: Knopf.

Lasswell, H. (1935). *Propaganda and promotional activities*. Minneapolis: University of Minnesota Press.

Lasswell, H. (1938). Foreword. In G. G. Bruntz, *Allied propaganda and the collapse of the German empire in 1918* (pp. v-viii). Stanford, CA: Stanford University Press.

Lasswell, H., & Blumsenstock, D. (1939). *World revolutionary propaganda: A Chicago study*. New York: Knopf.

Lasswell, H. D. (1951). Political and Psychological Warfare. In D. Lerner, (Ed.), *Propaganda in war and crisis* (pp. 261-77). New York: George W. Stewart.

Lasswell, H. D., Lerner, D., & Speier, H. (Eds.). (1979). *Propaganda and communication in world history (Vol. 1): The symbolic instrument in early times*. Honolulu: University Press of Hawaii.

Lasswell, H. D., Lerner, D. & Speier, H. (Eds.). (1980). *Propaganda and communication in world history (Vol. 2): The emergence of public opininon in the West*. Honolulu: University of Hawaii Press.

Lazarsfeld, P. L., Berelson, & Gaudet, H. (1948). *The people's choice: How the voter makes up his mind in a presidential campaign*. New York: Duell, Sloan, & Pearce.

Lazarsfeld, P. L., & Stanton, F. N.(Eds.). (1944). *Radio research, 1942-43*. New York: Duell, Sloan, & Pearce.

Lee, A. M., & Lee, E. B. (1979). *The fine art of propaganda*. San Francisco: International Society for General Semantics.

Lee, C. (1980). *Media imperialism reconsidered: The homogenization of television culture*. Beverly Hills, CA: Sage.

Lerner, D. (Ed.). (1951). *Propaganda in war and crisis: Materials for American policy*. New York: G. W. Stewart.

Lerner, D. (1951). Effective propaganda: Conditions and evaluation. In D. Lerner (Ed.). *Propaganda in war and crisis: Materials for American policy* (pp. 344-54). New York: G. W. Stewart.

Lerner, D., & Nelson, L. M. (Eds.). (1977). *Communication research: A half century appraisal*. Honolulu: University Press of Hawaii.

Liebert, R. M., Neale, J. M., & Davidson, E. S. (1973). *The early window: Effects of television on children and youth*. New York: Pergamon Press.

Likert, R. (1932). A technique for the measurement of attitudes. *Archives of Psychology*, No. 140. New York

Linebarger, P. M. A. (1954). *Psychological warfare.* New York: Duell, Sloan, and Pearce.

Lippmann, W. (1922). *Public opinion.* New York: Free Press. (Reprinted 1960, Macmillan)

Lippmann, W. (1925). *The phantom public.* New York: Harcourt Brace.

Littlejohn, S. W. (1989). *Theories of human communication.* Belmont, CA: Wadsworth.

Lowenthal, L. (1949). *Prophets of deceit: A study of the techniques of the American agitator.* New York: Harper.

Lowery, S. A., & DeFleur, M. L. (1983). *Milestones in mass communication research.* New York: Longman.

Lowery, S. A., & DeFleur, M. L. (1988). *Milestones in mass communication research.* New York: Longman.

Luke, T. W. (1989). *Screens of power: Ideology, domination and resistance in informational society.* Urbana: University of Illinois Press.

Lutz, W. (1989, July 12). No one died in Tiananmen square. *New York Times,* pp. A1, A9.

Maben, M. (1987). *Vanport.* Portland: Oregon Historical Society Press.

MacArthur, J. R. (1992, January 6). *New York Times,* p. A11.

MacCunn, J. (1906). The ethical doctrine of Aristotle. *International Journal of Ethics, 16,* 301.

Mannheim, K. (1943). *Diagnosis of our time.* London: Routledge, Kegan, Paul.

Martin, L. J. (1971, November). Effectiveness of international propaganda. *Annals of the American Academy of Political and Social Science, 398,* 61-70.

Marwell, G., & Schmitt, D. R. (1967). Dimensions of compliance gaining behavior: An empirical analysis. *Sociometry, 30*(3), 340-64.

Maxwell, B. W. (1936). Political propaganda in Soviet Russia. In H. L. Childs (Ed.), *Propaganda and dictatorship* (pp. 61-79). Princeton, NJ: Princeton University Press.

McBride, S. (1980). *Many voices, one world.* New York: Unipub.

McCroskey, J. C. (1969). A summary of the effects of evidence in persuasive communication. *Quarterly Journal of Speech, 55*(1), 169-76.

McGuire, W. J. (1964). Inducing resistance to persuasion: some contemporary approaches. In L. Berkowitz (Ed.), *Advances in experimental social psychology* (Vol. 1). New York: Academic Press.

McGuire, W. J. (1968). Personality and attitude change. In A. G. Greenwald, T. C. Brock, & T. M. Ostrom, (Eds.), *Psychological foundations of attitudes* (pp. 171-96). New York: Academic Press.

McGuire, W. J. (1969). The nature of attitudes and attitude change. In G. Lindzey & E. Aronson (Eds.), *The Handbook of social psychology,* (Vol. 3, pp. 136-314). Reading, MA: Addison-Wesley.

McGuire, W. J. (1985). Attitudes and attitude change. In G. Lindzey & E. Aronson (Eds.), *Handbook of Social Psychology* (Vol. 2, pp. 233-346). New York: Random House.

McLaine, I. (1979). *Ministry of morale: Home front morale and the Ministry of Information in World War II.* London: George Allen & Unwin.

McQuail, D. (1975). *Communication.* New York: Longman.

McQuail, D. (1984). With the benefit of hindsight: Reflections on uses and gratifications research. *Critical Studies in Mass Communication, 1*(2), 177-93.

Merton, R. (1968). *Social theory and social structure.* New York: Free Press.

Meyerhoff, A. E. (1965). *The strategy of persuasion: The use of advertising skills in fighting the cold war.* New York: Coward McCann.

Miller, G. (1980). Foreword. In D. P. Cushman & R. D. McPhee, *Message-Attitude-Behavior relationship: Theory, methodology, and application.* New York: Academic Press.

Mitchell, M. (1970). *Propaganda, polls, and public opinion: Are the people manipulated?* Englewood Cliffs, NJ: Prentice-Hall.

Morley, D. (1988). *Family television: Cultural power and domestic leisure.* London: Comedia.

Naisbitt, J. (1982). *Megatrends*. New York: Warner.

National Public Radio. (1991, June 26).

Negrine, R., & Papathanassopolous, S. (1990). *The internationalization of television*. London: Pinter Publishers.

Nelson, R. A. (1981). Propaganda. In M. T. Inge (Ed.), *Handbook of American popular culture* (Vol. 3). Westport, CT: Greenwood.

Noelle-Neumann, E. (1991). The theory of public opinion: The concept of the spiral of silence. In J. A. Anderson (Ed.), *Communication yearbook 14* (pp. 256-287). Newbury Park, CA: Sage.

Nordenstreng, K. (1982, Summer). U.S. policy and the third world: A critique. *Journal of Communication, 32*, 54-59.

Nordenstreng, K., & Schiller, H. I. (1979). *National sovereignty and international communication*. Norwood, NJ: Ablex.

Nye, G. P. (1941, September 15). Our madness increases as our emergency shrinks. *Vital Speeches, 7*, 722.

O'Donnell, V., & Kable, J. (1982). *Persuasion: An interactive dependency approach*. New York: Random House.

O'Donnell, V., & Jowett, G. (1989). Propaganda as a form of communication. In T. J. Smith (Ed.) *Propaganda: A pluralistic perspective*. New York: Praeger.

Oh, What a Censored War! (1991, May). *Newsletter on Intellectual Freedom, 40*(69), 93-97.

O'Neill, W. L. (1982). *A better world*. New York: Simon & Schuster.

Osgood, C. E., Suci, G. J., & Tannenbaum, P. G. (1957). *The measurement of meaning*. Urbana: University of Illinois Press.

Packard, V. (1957). *The hidden persuaders*. New York: D. McKay.

Patai, R. (1983). *The Arab mind*. New York: Scribners.

Payne, D. (Ed.). (1965). *The obstinate audience*. Ann Arbor, MI: Foundation for Research on Human Behavior.

Pearl, D., Bouthilet, L., & Lazar, J. (Eds.) (1982). *Television and behavior: Ten years of scientific progress and implications for the eighties*. Washington, DC: Government Printing Office.

Petty, R. E., & Cacioppo, J .T. (1986). The elaboration likelihood model of persuasion. *Advanced Experimental Psychology, 19*, 123-205.

Petty, R. E., & Cacioppo, J. T. (1986). *Communication and persuasion: Central and peripheral routes to attitude change*. New York: Springer-Verlag.

Phillippe, R. (1980). *Political graphics: Art as a weapon*. New York: Abbeville.

Pletka, D. (1991, March 4). Swimming in Blood and Other Flowery Phrases. *Insight*, 14.

Pool, I. D., Frey, F. W., Schramm, W., MacCoby, N., & Parker, E. B. (Ed.s.). (1973). *Handbook of communication*. Chicago: Rand McNally.

Pope, D. (1983). *The making of modern advertising*. New York: Basic Books.

Pratkanis, A., & Aronson, E. (1991). *Age of propaganda: The everyday use and abuse of persuasion*. New York: W. H. Freeman.

Pratkanis, A. R., & Greenwald, A. G. (1985). A reliable sleeper effect in persuasion: Implications for opinion change theory and research. In L. S. Alwit & A. A. Mitchell (Eds.), *Psychological processes and advertising effects* (pp. 157-73). Hillsdale, NJ: Lawrence Erlbaum.

Psy-Ops Bonanza, A. (1991, June 17). *Newsweek*, 23-24.

Qualter, T. H. (1962). *Propaganda and psychological warfare*. New York: Random House.

Qualter, T. H. (1985). *Opinion control in the democracies*. New York: St. Martin's Press.

Qualter, T. H. (1991). *Advertising and democracy in the mass age*. New York: St. Martin's Press.

Randall, R. S. (1968). *Censorship of the movies*. Madison: University of Wisconsin Press.

Read, J. (1941). *Atrocity propaganda, 1914-1919*. New Haven, CT: Yale University Press.

Reeves, N. (1986). *Official British film propaganda during the First World War*. London: Croom Helm.

Reinard, J. C. (1988, Fall). The empirical study of the persuasive effects of evidence: The status after fifty years of research. *Human Communication Research, 15*, 3-59.

Roberts, D. F., & Maccoby, N. (1985). Effects of mass communication. In G. Lindzey & E. Aronson (Eds.), *Handbook of social psychology* (Vol. 2, pp. 539-98). New York: Random House.

Roelker, N. L. (1979). The impact of the reformation era on communication and propaganda. In H. D. Lasswell, D. Lerner, & H. Speier (Eds.), *Propaganda and communication in world history (Vol. 1): The symbolic instrument in early time* (pp. 41-84). Honolulu: University Press of Hawaii.

Roetter, C. (1974). *The art of psychological warfare, 1914-1945*. New York: Stein & Day.

Rogers, E. M. (1982). *Diffusion of innovations*. New York: Free Press.

Rogers, E. M., & Kincaid, D. L. (1981). *Communication networks: Toward a new paradigm for research*. New York: Free Press.

Rogers, E. M., & Shoemaker, F. F. F.(1971). *Communication of innovations: A cross-cultural approach*. New York: Free Press.

Roloff, M. E., & Miller, G. R. (Eds.). (1980). *Persuasion: New directions in theory and research*. Beverly Hills, CA: Sage.

Ronalds, F. S., Jr. (1971, November). The future of international broadcasting. *Annals of the American Academy of Political and Social Science, 398*, 31-80.

Rosenberg, H. L. (1983). For your eyes only. *American Film, 8*(9), 40-43.

Rosenthal, S. P. (1934). Changes of Socio-Economic Attitudes Under Radical Motion Picture Propaganda. Archives of Psychology, No. 166. New York.

Rubin, A. M., & Windahl, S. (1986). The Uses and Dependency Model of Mass Communication. *Critical Studies in Mass Communication, 3*(2), 184-99.

Rubin, B. (1973). *Propaganda and public opinion: Strategies of persuasion*. Columbus, OH: Xerox Education.

Rutherford, W. (1978). *Hitler's propaganda machine*. London: Bison Books.

Said, E. (1991, March 7). Writes on the Eve of the Iraqi-Soviet Talks. *London Review of Books*, pp. 7-8.

Schiller, H. I. (1970). *Mass communication and American empire*. New York: Augustus M. Kelly.

Schrecker, E. W. (1986). *No ivory tower: McCarthyism and the universities*. New York: Oxford University Press.

Schreiner, S. A., Jr. (1977). *The condensed world of Reader's Digest*. New York: Stein & Day.

Schudson, M. (1978). *Discovering the news*. New York: Basic Books.

Schudson, M. (1984). *Advertising, the uneasy persuasion*. New York: Basic Books.

Sereno, K., & Martensen, C. D. (1974). *Foundations of communication theory*. New York: Harper & Row.

Shannon, C., & Weaver, W. (1949). *The mathematical theory of communication*. Urbana: University of Illinois Press.

Shaw, J. F. (Trans.). (1873). On Christian doctrine. In Rev. M. Dodds (Ed.), *The works of Aurelius Augustine, bishop of Hippo*. Edinburgh: T. & T. Clark.

Shibutani, T. (1966). *Improvised news*. Indianapolis: Bobbs-Merrill.

Short, K. R. M. (1990). *International broadcasting and "the best interests of mankind"—A historical perspective*. (unpublished)

Shulman, H. C. (1990). *The Voice of America: Propaganda and democracy, 1941-1945*. Madison: University of Wisconsin Press.

Shultz, R. H., & Godson, R. (1984). *Dezinformatsia: Active measures in Soviet strategy.* Washington, DC: Pergamon-Brassey's.

Smith, B. L. (1958). Propaganda. In D. L. Sills (Ed.), *Encyclopedia of the Social Sciences* (Vol. 12, pp. 579-88). New York: Macmillan.

Smith, T. J. (1989). *Propaganda: A pluralistic perspective.* New York: Praeger.

Soley, L. C. (1989). *Radio warfare: OSS and CIA subversive propaganda.* New York: Praeger.

Soley, L. C., & Nichols, J. S. (1987). *Clandestine radio broadcasting.* New York: Praeger.

Sorenson, T. C. (1968). *The word war.* New York: Harper & Row.

Sparks, A. (1990). *The mind of South Africa.* New York: Knopf.

Special Report by the Advisory Council for Cuba Broadcasting on TV Marti. (1991). Washington, DC.

Speer, A. (1970). *Inside the Third Reich.* New York: Macmillan.

Speier, H. (1950, January). The historical development of public opinion. *American Journal of Sociology, 55,* 376-88.

Speier, H. & Otis, M. (1944). German radio propaganda in France during the Battle of France. In P. Lazarsfeld & F. Stanton (Eds.), *Radio Research, 1942-1943* (pp. 208-47). New York: Duell, Sloan, & Pearce.

Sproule, J. M. (1983). The institute for propaganda analysis: Public education in argumentation, 1937-1942. In D. Zarefsky, M. O. Sellers, & Jack Rhodes (Eds.), *Proceedings of the Third Summer Conference on Argumentation* (pp. 486-99). Annandale, VA: Speech Communication Association.

Sproule, J. M. (1987). Propaganda studies in American social science: The rise and fall of the critical paradigm. *Quarterly Journal of Speech, 73,* 60-78.

Sproule, J. M. (1989). Progressive propaganda critics and the magic bullet theory. *Critical Studies in Mass Communication, 6*(3), 225-46.

Sproule, J. M. (1991). Propaganda and American ideological critique. In J. A. Anderson (Ed.), *Communication Yearbook,* (Vol. 14, pp. 211-38). Newbury Park, CA: Sage.

Statistical Abstracts of the United States (1991). Washington, DC: Government Printing Office.

St. Hill, T. N. (1974). *Thomas Nast: Cartoons and illustrations.* New York: Dover Press.

Steele, R. W. (1985). *Propaganda in an open society: The Roosevelt administration and the media, 1933-1941.* Westport, CT: Greenwood.

Stein, A. H., & Friedrich, L. K. (1972). Television content and young children's behavior. In J. P. Murray, E. A. Rubenstein, & G. A. Comstock (Eds.), *Television and social behavior, vol. II: Television and social learning.* Washington, DC: Government Printing Office.

Stone, P. H. (1979, April 14). Muldergate on Madison Avenue. *The National,* 390-93.

Szanto, G. H. (1978). *Theater and propaganda.* Austin: University of Texas Press.

Taylor, R. (1979). *Film propaganda: Soviet Russia and Nazi Germany.* London: Croom Helm.

Tebbel, J. (1969). *The American magazine: A compact history.* New York: Hawthorn Books.

Thomas, W. I., & Znaniecki, F. (1918). *The Polish peasant in Europe and America* (Vol. 1). Boston: Badger.

Thomson, O. (1977). *Mass persuasion in history.* Edinburgh: Paul Harris.

Thurstone, L. L. (1929). *The measurement of attitudes.* Chicago: University of Chicago Press.

Triandis, H. C. (1977). *Interpersonal behavior.* Monterey, CA: Brooks/Cole.

U.S. Information Agency (1991). *USIA fact sheet.* Washington, DC.

Valins, D. (1966). Cognitive effects of false heart-rate feedback. *Journal of Personality and Social Psychology, 4*(4), 400-408.

Vanport City. (1943, August). *Architectural Forum, 9*, 53-62.

Vaughn, S. L. (1980). *Holding fast the inner lines: Democracy, nationalism, and the committee on public information.* Chapel Hill: University of North Carolina Press.

VOA in 1989 and Beyond. (1989). Washington, DC: Voice of America.

Wanger, W. (1941, November). The role of movies in morale. *American Journal of Sociology, 47*, 375-83.

Ward, L. N. (1985). *The motion picture goes to war: The U.S. government film effort during World War I.* Ann Arbor: University of Michigan Research Press.

Weisman, S. R. (1991, December 5). Japanese regrets over war unlikely after Bush's stand. *New York Times*, pp. A1, 12.

Weschler, L. (1983, April 11). A state of war—1. *New Yorker*, 45-102.

Westley, B. H., & Maclean, M. S., Jr. (1977). A conceptual model for communications research. In K. K. Sereno & C. D. Mortensen (Eds.), *Foundations of communication theory* (pp. 73-83). New York: Harper & Row.

Wheeless, L. R., Barraclough, R., & Stewart, R. (1983). Compliance-gaining and power in persuasion. In R . N. Bostrom (Ed.), *Communication Yearbook 7* (pp. 105-145). Beverly Hills, CA: Sage.

Whitfield, S. J. (1991). *The culture of the cold war.* Baltimore: Johns Hopkins Press.

Whiteside, T. (1970, December). Cutting down. *New Yorker*, pp. 42-95.

Whiteside, T. (1971, March 27). Selling death. *New Republic*, pp. 15-17.

Williams, F. (1989). *The new communications* (2d ed.). Belmont, CA: Wadsworth.

Williams, R. (1958). *Culture and society: 1780-1950.* New York: Columbia University Press.

Williams, R. (1961). *The long revolution.* New York: Columbia University Press.

Williams, R. (1966). *Communications.* London: Chatto & Windus.

Williams, R. (1973). *The country and the city.* London: Chatto & Windus.

Wilkerson, M. M. (1932). *Public opinion and the Spanish-American War.* Baton Rouge: Louisiana State University Press.

Winkler, A. (1978). *The politics of propaganda: The Office of War Information, 1942-1945.* New Haven, CT: Yale University Press.

Wisan, J. E. (1934). *The Cuban Crisis as reflected in the New York press.* New York: Columbia University Press.

Wish, H. (1950). *Society and thought in Early America.* New York: David McKay.

Wright, J. (1990). *Terrorist propaganda.* New York: St. Martin's.

Zajonc, R. B. (1968). Attitude effects of mere exposure. *Journal of Personality and Social Psychology Monograph, 9*(2), pt. 2.

Zajonc, R. B. (1980). Feeling and thinking: Preferences need no inferences. *American Psychologist, 35*, 151-75.

Zimbardo, P. G., & Leippe, M. R. (1991). *The psychology of attitude change and social influence.* New York: McGraw-Hill.

Zeman, Z. A. B. (1973). *Nazi propaganda.* New York: Oxford University Press.

Zeman, Z. A. B. (1978). *Selling the war: Art and propaganda in World War II.* London: Orbis.

Zimbardo P. G., Ebbeson, E., & Maslach, C. (1977). *Influencing attitudes and changing behavior.* Reading, MA: Addison-Wesley.

Zimbardo, P. G., & Leippe, M. (1991). *The psychology of attitude change and social influence.* New York: McGraw-Hill.

Index

"ABCs of Propaganda Analysis", 182-183, 257

Abelson, H. I., 154, 224

Adams, Samuel, 64-69, 70; *Boston Gazette*, 69; Committee of Correspondence, 69

Adorno, T., 128

Adventist World Radio, 107

Agency for International Development (USAID), 204

Agenda-setting, 146

Agitational-Propaganda Section of the Central Committee of the Communist Party (Agitprop), 176

AIDS (Acquired Immune Deficiency Syndrome), 14

Ajzen, Il, 23, 138

Alexander Nevsky, 94

Alexandre, L., 15

All Asia Radio Service (Sri Lanka), 106

Allport, Gordon, 126; definition of attitude, 126

al-Sabah, Suad Nasir, 261

Althiede, D. L., 32, 33, 218

American Alliance for Labor and Democracy, 123

American Broadcasting Company (ABC), 266

American Federation of Labor (AFL), 123

American Heart Association, 244

American Revolution, 51-71, 156, 264

Anderson, F., 130

Anderson, J., 146, 221

Anderson, K., 231, 235, 236, 237

Apollo 8, 130

Architectural Forum, 235

Aristotle, 18,27,28; *Rhetoric*, 27, 28; *Nicomachean Ethics*, 28

Armored Attack (formerly *North Star*), 98

Armstrong, B., 218

Aronson, E., x, 3, 20, 224

Aronson, J., 200

"Ascension Alice," 226

Asquith, Herbert (P. M.), 163

Atlantic Monthly, 88

Attitude, 126; study of, 126-127

Bacon, Sir Francis, 29

Bailyn, Bernard, 128

Bairdain, Ernest and Edith, 205

Ball-Rokeach, S., 146

Bandura, A., 24, 138, 139, 140, 142

Banzhaf, John, III, 243-244

Baptism of Fire, 96

Barnouw, E., 179, 181

Barraclough, R., 140

Battle Cry of Peace, 92

Battle of Britain, 9

Battleship Potemkin, 94

Bay of Pigs, 13
Beethoven, Ludvig von, 219
Behavior, affective, 34; attributive, 34
Bem, D., 5, 25, 134
Bennett, James Gordon, 80; *New York Herald*, 80
Benson, T., 29
Berelson, D., 131
Berger, J., 222
Berkowitz, L., 142, 143
Biddle, P. R., 31
Big Jim McClain, 98
Bittman, Ladislav, 14
Blackton, J. Stuart, 92
Blakenhorn, Heber (Capt.), 165
Blumenstock, D., 86
Blumer, H., 90; *Movies and Conduct*, 90
Boer War, 156
Bogardus, E. S., 125, 126
Bogart, L., 4, 7, 218, 220, 223, 226
Bonner, R. J., 27
Boster, R. J., 133
Boston Massacre, 63
Boston Tea Party, 69
Bradford, William, *Pennsylvania Journal*, 64
Brainwashing, 2, 77, 201-202
Bramson, L., 82
Brande, W. T., 54
Brawn, Max, 187
Brinkley, A., 178, 179, 180, 181
British Broadcasting Corporation (BBC), 9, 198, 225, 226, 266
Brodie, J., 145
Brown, J. A. C., 109
Browne, R. W., 28
Brownfield, Allan C., 14
Brownstein, R., 99-100
Bruntz, G. G., 163
Bryant, D. C., 30-31
Bryce Commission Report, 172
Bulwer, John, 29
Bumpus, B., 103, 106
Bureau of Applied Social Research, 128
Burke, Kenneth, 30; "The Rhetoric of Hitler's 'Battle,'" 30; dramatistic pentad, 30
Burnett, N. F. S., 1
Bush, George, 5, 8, 160, 252-253, 257, 259, 262
Butsch, R., 145

Cacioppo, J. T., 137
Caesar, Julius, 38-39, 73, 185; propaganda techniques, 37-39
Campbell, C. W., 92
Canalization, 222
Capra, Frank, 129
Carey, J., 266
Carey, J. W., 152, 266
Carlson, J., 144
Carson, Johnny, 268
Carson, Rachel, 89; *Silent Spring*, 89
Cary, H., 27
Cato, Marcus, 29
Cavell, Edith, 171
CBS Evening News, 14
Ceausescu, Nicholae, 7
Central Committee for National Patriotic Associations (Br.), 163
Central Intelligence Agency (CIA), 10, 13, 15
Chandler, R. W., 203-206
Charlamagne, 39
Charles V, Emperor, 49
Chansons de Geste, 47
Chieu Hoi program (Vietnam), 204
The China Syndrome, 97
Chinese-Japanese War (1894-95), 40
Choukas, M., 125
Cicero, Marcus, 29
Citizens for a Free Kuwait, 261
Civil War (U.S.), 7
CNN, 254, 256, 259
Cognitive dissonance, theory of, 134
Cohn, J., 87
Coles, R., 34
Coleman, J., 136
Comenius, Alexius, 44
Committee of Correspondence, 69
Committee on Public Information, 92, 123, 124
Communication, defined, 18, 19
"Compliance-gaining" strategies, 140
Comstock, G., 144
Confessions of a Nazi Spy, 95
Confucius, 36; *Analects*, 36
Constantine I, Emperor, 43
Conway, F., 218
Cooper, L., 27
Cooper, M., 213-214
Cortez, 156

Costello, J., 10
Coughlin, Father Charles E., xi, 177, 179-181; *Social Justice*, 181; National Union of Social Justice, 180-181
Council for Tobacco—U.S.A. (formerly Tobacco Industry Research Committee), 241
Council of Cleremont, 44
Council of the People's Commissars Radio, 102
Counterpropaganda, 227, 238
Cox, Leonard, 29
Cranach, Lucas, 50, 51
Creel, George, 123, 124, 125; *How We Advertised America*, 124
Critical Studies in Mass Communication, 152
Crouthamel, J. L., 81
The Crucible, 227
Crusades, the, xi, 44-47
Csikszentimihalyi, M., 146
Cultural Studies, 151-152
Culture, 217, 266; defined, 217, 265-266
Cushman, D. P., 140
Czitrom, D. J., 125

D'Annunzio, Gabriele, 186
Darwin, Charles, 89; *Origin of the Species*, 89
Das Reich, 186
David, Jacques Louis, 72, 73
Davidson, E. S., 144
Davison, W. Phillips, 16, 17, 73
Day, Benjamin, 80
Declaration of Independence, 71
DeFleur, M., x, 130, 142, 143, 144, 145, 146
Delia, J., 150
DeParles, J., 256
Department of Information (Br.), 163
Dependency theory, 147
Deutsche Welle, 106
Deutschlandfunk, 106
Devil Dogs of the Air, 95
Dewey, John, 85
Dickens, A.G., 48
"Diffusion of Innovations," theory of, 136
Direct Broadcasting Satellites (DBS), 112
Disinformation, 13-17; defined, 13; models, 15-16; Deflective Source model, 16; Legitimizing Source model, 16
Dissociation hypothesis, 131

Dobrogaev, 219
Donnerstein, E., 144
Doob, L. W., 3, 15, 35, 215, 216
Dowd, M., 8
Dovzhenko, Alexander, 74
Duffey, B., 5
Dutch Reformed Church (South Africa), 40-41

Earth, 94
Ebbeson, E., 20
Ebon, M., 13
Edwards, W., 140
Einstein, Albert, 128
Eisenstein, Sergei, 30, 94
Elaboration Likelihood Model, 137
Ellul, Jacques, 13, 221
Emery, E., 63, 87, 88
Emery, M., 63, 87, 88
Enthymeme, 28
Ethos, 28
Ewige Jude, Der, 187-188
Explicit/implicit conclusions, 132

Facilitative communication (as subpropaganda), 16, 17
Fear appeals, 132-133
Federal Communications Commission (FCC), 243-245; "Fairness Doctrine," 243
Federal Housing Authority, 230
Federal Public Housing Administration (FPHA), 235
Federal Trade Commission (FTC), 86, 243
Ferdonnet, P., 9, 10
Festinger, L., 41, 134
Fielding, Raymond, 91
Filene, Edward A., 182
Finan, J., 130
Fishbein, M., 23, 138
Fiske, J., 152
Fleming, D., 128
Fonda, Jane, 99
Ford, J., 215
Forman, Henry James, 93-94; *Our Movie-Made Children*, 93-94
Foulkes, A. P., 227
"Four-Minute Men," 166

Franklin, Benjamin, 64, 70-71; *Boston Independent*, 71; *Poor Richard Almanacs*, 71; *Sale of the Hessians, The*, 71
Fremantle, A., 44, 45
French Revolution, 56, 72-77; propaganda techniques, 72-73
Freud, Sigmund, 89
Friedrich, L. K., 144
Fritschler, A. L., 241, 245
Fulbright Awards Program, 219
Furhammer, L., 92, 93
Futuribles, 23

Galtieri, Leopoldo, President-General, 226
Garbo, Greta, 171
George, Lloyd (P. M.), 163
George, III, King, 56, 70
Gerbner, George, 143
Gideon, 156
Gillray, James, 56, 60, 69
Ginsberg, B., x
Glennon, L., 145
Godson, R., 13
Goebbels, Josef, 30, 185-187, 214, 221, 225
Gompers, Samuel, 123
Gorbachev, Mikhail, 33
Graff, H. J., 55
Grandin, T., 104
Greenberg, B. S., 144
Greenwald, A. G., 131
Griffith, D. W., 92
Griffith, William E., 20
Grosse Liebe, 143, 188
Group norms, 224; defined, 224
Gruening, Ernest, 86
Gustainis, J., 100
Gwyn, R., 256

Hale, J., 102, 107, 110
Hall, S., 151
Hanke, H., 113
Hardt, H., 125, 128
Harper's Weekly, 88
Hart-Davis, D., 208
Hartmann, S. M., 231, 239
Hayden, D., 237, 238
Hearst, William Randolph, 88; *New York Journal*, 88

Hearts of the World, 92
Heider, F., 133
Heilbroner, R. L., 119
Henry, Patrick, 264
Here Comes the Navy, 95
Herzstein, Robert, 194
Hess, S., 59, 64
High Noon, 227
Hill, Anita, 148, 264
Hill and Knowlton, 261-262
Hitler, Adolf, 9, 38, 39, 77, 89, 94, 95, 103, 148, 177, 185-194, 216, 264; *Mein Kampf*, 30, 89, 164, 185, 216, 217, 257, 259
Hogarth, William, 56
Honey, M., x, 235
Horkheimer, M., 128
House Un-American Activities Committee (HUAC), 98
Housing Authority of Portland (HAP), 236, 237
Hovland, Carl I., 31, 129, 130, 131, 133, 135
Hunt, E. L., 27
Hussein, Saddam, 5, 6, 199, 207, 250-262
Hymes, James L., 237
"Hypodermic Needle Theory," 125; "Magic Bullet Theory," 125

Ideology, 1, 2, 8, 152, 213-214, 219, 220, 227, 267; defined, 213
If You Love This Planet, 100
Informative communication, 19-20; defined, 19
"Inoculation Theory," 134
Institute for Propaganda Analysis, 182-184, 221, 257
Invasion of the Body Snatchers (1956), 227
Iran-Contra hearings, 15
Irish Republican Army (IRA), 40, 108, 209
The Iron Curtain, 6, 98
Irwin, Will, 87-88
Isaksson, F., 92, 93
Islam, 40, 44, 45, 47, 264
I Was a Communist for the FBI, 98

Jackson-Beeke, M., 143
Janis, F. L., 130, 133
Jefferson, Thomas, 69; *Declaration of Independence*, 70, 71

JFK, 97
Johnson, Hugh S. (Gen.), 180-181
Johnson, J. M., 32, 33, 218
Johnson, Lyndon B., 141
Johnson, M., 258
Joint U.S. Public Affairs Office (JUSPAO), 204
Jones, Dorothy, 97
Jones, M., 10
Jowett, Garth, 16, 91, 93, 94, 96
Jud Süss, 187-188

Kable, June, 21, 142
Kaiser, Edgar J., 235
The Kaiser, the Beast of Berlin, 92
Kaiserville, 236
Kapferer, J. N., 80
Kaplan, M., 59, 64
Karlins, M., 154, 224
Kasnechev, Alezander, 14
Katz, E., 148
Kecskemeti, P., 25, 213, 214, 219
Kelly, H. H., 133
Kelman, H. C., 131
Kennedy, John F., 13, 268
Kennedy, Robert (U.S. Sen.), 266
Kerensky, Alexander, 175
KGB, 10, 13, 14
Killing Ground, The, 100
Kincaid, D., 19
King, Martin Luther, 13
Kneitel, T., 10
Knox, John, 50
Koop, C. Everett (U.S. Surgeon-General), 246
Korean War, 1991, xi, 200-202
Kuby, R., 146

Lakoff, G., 258
Lamay, C., 252, 257
Lanham Act, 235, 238
Land, R. E., 33
Lang, K., 125, 131
Lapierre, Richard, 127
Lasswell, Harold D., 86, 123, 124, 125
Lazarsfeld, Paul F., 128, 129, 131, 150
League of Nations, 103
Learning Theory, 125

Lee, Alfred M., 183-184
Lee, C., 112
Lee, Elizabeth, 183-184
Leilen, K., 205
Leippe, M., 134, 136, 138, 141
Lenin, Vladimir, xi, 42, 94, 102, 175-176
Lerner, Daniel, 156
Liebert, R. M., 144
Likert, R., 125
"Limited Effects Theory," 125
Lincoln, Abraham, 215
Linebarger, Paul M., 155, 161, 169
Lippmann, Walter, 33, 85
Literaturnaya Gazeta, 14
Locke, John, 59, 70; *Treatises on Government*, 70
Long, Huey, xii; propaganda techniques of, 177-179; *Everyman a King*, 178; Share the Wealth Society, 178, 181
Lorimer, George H., 87; *Saturday Evening Post*, 87
Lowery, S., 130, 142, 143, 144, 145, 146
Loyola, Ignatius, 53; Society of Jesus (Jesuits), 53
Ludendorff, E. (Gen.), 92, 175
Lueger, Karl, 136
Luke, T. W., 210
Lumsdaine, A. A., 129 130
Lusitania, 171
Luther, Martin, 47-53, 265; *An Appeal to the Christian Nobility of the German Nation*, 49; *Deutsche Messe*, 48; propaganda techniques, 48-53; Ninety-five theses, 50
Lutz, W., 266

Maben, M., 235, 236, 237, 238
Maccoby, N., 148, 150
MacCunn, J., 28
Mach, E., 128
Machiavelli, Niccolo, 29; *The Prince*, 29
Maclean, M. S., 19
"Magic Bullet" theory, 125; "Hypodermic Needle" theory, 125
Maine Incident, 88
Maisel, Robert, 123
Malamuth, N., 144
Mandell, W., 31
Marchand, R., x

Martin, E. D., 125
Martin, L. J., 16
Marwell, G., 140
Marx, Karl, xi, 175
Mata Hari (Margaret Gertrude Zeller), 171
McArthur, Douglas (Gen.), 200
McArthur, J. R., 261-262
McBride Commission (UNESCO), 114
McBride, Sean, 114
McCarthy, Joseph (U.S. Sen.), 98
McCarthyism, 227, 265
McCombs, M., 146
McCrosky, J. C., 31
McGuire, W. J., 135, 136, 137, 143
McLaine, I., 198
McPhee, R. D., 140
Melanchthon, Philipp, 29
Merton, R., 129
Military Assistance Command (Vietnam) (MACV), 204
Miller, A., 227
Miller, Clyde R., 182
Miller, G. R., 22, 34, 140
Miller, Michael, 235
Mills, Peter (M.P.) 226
Ministry of Information (Br.), 198
Miss Pacific Fleet, 95
Mission to Moscow, 97-98
Missing, 97-98
Mitchell, M., 33
Modeling, 24; theory of, 138-140
Mohammed, 264
Mongeau, P., 133
Moon, Sun Myung, 141
Morgan, M., 143
Morley, D., 145
Motion Picture Research Council, 93
Motion pictures, propaganda appeal of, 90-101
Mr. Rogers, 144
"Multi-Step Flow" model of communication, 131, 220, 269
Mussolini, Benito, 39, 104
Mutual vs. Ohio (1915), 91
My Four Years in Germany, 92
Myth, 215

Naisbitt, John, 154

Nanook of the North, 93
Napoleon, 38, 39, 56, 72-78; coronation of, 74; Napoleonic Code, 74; propaganda techniques, 74; use of plebiscites, 74, 77
Nast, Thomas, 56-59, 60, 61
Nation, The, 88
National Commission on the Causes and Prevention of Violence, 141; Report on Violence on the Media, 141
National Electric Light Commission (NELA), 86
National Film Board of Canada, 100
National Housing Authority, 235
National Institute of Mental Health (NIMH), 143; Television and Behavior, 143, 144
National Liberation Front (Viet Cong), 203
National Tuberculosis Association, 244
National War Aims Committee (Br.), 163
Neall, J., 144
Negrine, R., 112
Neutral Countries Committee (Br.), 163
New English Broadcasting Station, 9
New World Information Order (NWIO), 113-114
Newspapers, 88; in the American Revolution, 71; early nineteenth century, 79-80; penny press, 88-89; yellow journalism, 89
Newsweek, 89
New York Times, The, 7
Newton, Isaac, 70
Nicholas II, Czar, 175
Nichols, J. S., 198
Nietzsche, F., 265
Night Line (ABC), 8
Nine to Five, 99
Nixon, Richard M., 268
Nordenstreng, K., 112, 114
The North Star, 97-98
Nuremburg Rallies, 193
Nye, Gerald P. (U.S. Sen.), 95, 99

Observational Learning Theory, 24, 138
O'Donnell, Victoria, 16, 21, 142, 223
Office of War Information (OWI), 97, 104-105, 199

Ohm Kruger, 187
Olympic Games; Berlin—1936, 104, 208; Los Angeles—1984, 8-9, 208; Seoul—1988, 209
O'Neill, W. L., 177
Operation Desert Shield, 5
Operation Desert Storm, 5, 6
Opinion leaders, 131, 218, 268-269
Ordering of argument (primacy-recency), 130-131
Oregonian, 236
Otis, M., 128
Osgood, C.E., 127, 133

Pacific Northwest Bell, 239
Paine, Thomas, 62, 69-70; *American Crisis*, 69
Palestine Liberation Organization (PLO), 107, 209
Papathanassopoulos, S., 112
Patai, R., 258
Pathos, 28
Patriot, The (India), 14
Payne Fund Studies, 90, 9394, 125, 127
Pearl Harbor, 157, 160, 185, 231
Pennsylvania Journal, 64
Pentagon Papers, 209-210
People's Crusade (1096), the, 46
Persian Gulf War, xi, 5, 6, 7, 8, 116-117, 199, 207, 209, 212, 215, 229, 247-262; "Nayirah incident," 261; propaganda analysis of, 247-262
Persuasion, 2, 21-26; attitudes, group norms, values, and group norms, 22-25; 224; defined, 21; ethics of, 27-31; interactive or transactive nature of, 21; McGuire's model of, 135-136; research in, 126-141; resistance to, 135; rhetorical background, 27-31
Peter the Hermit, 46
Petty, R. E., 137
Phillipe, R., 57
Plato, 27, 28; *Gorgias*, 27; *Phaedrus*, 27,28
Pletka, D., 259
Poindexter, John, 15
Pool, I. D., 25
Pope, D., 118
Pope Gregory XV, 53-54
Pope Pius VII, 74

Pope Urban II, 44-46
Pope Urban VIII, 54
Pratkanis, A. R., x, 3, 131, 224
Prelude to War, 199
Presidential election of 1940, 131
President's Research Committee on Recent Social Trends, 125
Price, Richard, 62; *On Civil Liberty*, 62
Printing press, 47, 48, 50, 78, 265; increased rates of literacy, 50; invention, 45, 49
Proctor and Gamble Company, 80
Provisional Irish Republican Army (PIRA), 40
Propaganda; agitative, 8, 214; analysis of, 212-220; black, 9, 10, 13, 215; bureaucratic, defined, 32; as communication, 31; definition of, 4; disinformation, 13-17; forms of, 8-15; gray, 13; integrative, 8, 214; purpose model, 18; purpose model discussed, 17-26, 31-35; process model, 265; process model discussed, 263-270; and rhetoric, 29-31; special techniques of, 221-226; subpropaganda, 15-16; white, 9, 20
Prosser, M., 29
Public Opinion, 125
Public opinion, defined, 33
Public Opinion Quarterly, 125
Pueblo, USS, 268
Pulitzer, Joseph, 88; *New York World*, 88

Qualter, T. H., vii, 4, 121, 124, 221
Queen, 226
Quintilian, 29; *Institutes of Oratory*, 29

R. J. Reynolds Company, 246; Camel cigarettes, 246
Radio Baghdad, 254
Radio Cairo, 107
Radio Free Europe, 10, 105, 106, 109, 110
Radio Free Hungary, 10
Radio Liberation, 105
Radio Liberty, 106, 109
Radio Luxembourg, 106
Radio Marti, 106, 111-112
Radio Monte Carlo, 106
Radio Moscow, 8, 13, 102, 106, 109

Radio Peking, 87, 90
Radio, propaganda appeal of, 101-112
Radio Tokyo, 104
Randall, R. S., 91
Rather, Dan 14
Read, J., 172
Reader's Digest, 89
Reagan, Ronald, x, 11, 115
Red Brigade (Italy), 209
The Red Menace, 98
Reeves, N., 92
Reinard, J. C., 13
Reasoned Action Model, 138
Reformation, The, 29, 47-55
Resonance, 25-26, 214
Revere, Paul, 63-64, 69
Rhetoric, background and ethics of persuasion, 27-31; and propaganda, 29-31; defined by Aristotle, 28; dramatistic pentad, 30; enthymeme, 28; ethos, pathos, and logos, 28
Rhodes Scholarship, 219
Riefenstahl, Leni, 187
Richards, Julius, B., 143
Roberts, I. F., 148, 150
Robespierre, Maximilien, 73
Robison, Robert, 29
Roetter, C., 9, 124, 126, 143
Rogers, E. M., 19, 131, 136
Roloff, M. E., 22, 34
Roman Catholic Church, 2, 29, 44, 270
Ronalds, F. S., 108
Roosevelt, Franklin D., 178, 185, 195, 199
Rosenberg, H. L., 100, 101
Rosenthal, S. P., 127
Rowlandson, Thomas, 56
Rubin, A., 148

Saar Plebiscite (1936), 187
Sachs, Hans, 50
Sacra Congregatio de Propaganda Fide, 2, 29, 54-55
Said, E., 253
Saturday Evening Post, 237
Saturday Night Live, 256
Sandinistas (El Salvador), 15
Schiller, H. I., 112, 113
Schmitt, D. R., 140
Schudson, M., 81, 120-121

Schrecker, E. W., 202
Schreiner, S. A., 89
Schultz, R. H., 13
Sears, D. O., 33
Self-attribution theory, 134, 141
Seljuk Turks, 44
Shannon, C., 18
Shaw, D., 146
Shaw., J. F., 29
She Wore a Yellow Ribbon, 215
Sheffield, F. D., 130
Sherwood, Robert, 105
Shinto, 40
Shoemaker, F. F., 131
Short, K. R. M., 110, 111
Short, Rev. William, 93
Shulman, H. C., x
Siegelman, J., 218
Signorelli, N., 143
Skelt, B. 103
Sleeper effect, 131
Smith, Albert E., 91
Smith, B. L., 37
Smith, M., 130
Smith, T., x, 16
Soley, L. C., 198
Solidarity Movement, 7, 224
Song of Russia, 98
Sorensen, T. C., 201
Source credibility, 132, 222-223
Soviet Friendship Scholarships, 219
Spanish American War, 88
Spanish Inquisition, 39
Sparks, A., 41
Speer, Albert, 193
Speier, H., 33
Spiral of Silence, 146
Sproule, J. M., x, 84-85, 125, 182, 184
Stanton, F. N., 128
St. Augustine, 29; *On Christian Doctrine*, 29
St. Hill, T. N., 59
Steele, R. W., x
Stein, A. H., 144
Stewart, R., 140
Stone, Oliver, 97
Stoneman, L., 145
Storm Over Asia, 94
Stowe, Harriet Beecher, 89; *Uncle Tom's Cabin*, 89
Subjective Expected Utility Model (SEU), 140

Sunday Express (London), 14
Surgeon-General's Advisory Committee on Television and Social Behavior, 142
Surgeon-General's Report on Smoking (1967), 242-243
Szanto, G. H., 8

Tannenbaum, P. G., 127, 133
Taylor, R., 94
Tearing Down the Spanish Flag, 91
Thatcher, Margaret, 108
Thirty Years War, 49-50
Thomas, Clarence, 128, 148
Thomas, W. I., 125
Thompson, Daley, 9
Thomson, O., 38, 42, 45, 55, 71, 74, 185
Thurstone, L. L., 126
Tiananmen Square (Beijing), 33, 126, 127, 266
Time, 89
Tobacco Institute, 242, 244-245
Triandis, H. C., 34
Triumph of the Will, The, 187
Trotsky, Leon, 175
Tunney, John (U.S. Sen.), 204
Tweed, William Marcy ("Boss"), 59, 60-01
20/20, 266
"Two-Step Flow" model of communication, 131
TV Marti, 115-116

UNESCO, 23
Unification Church (Moonies), 141
United Nations, 200
Universium Film Aktiengesellschaft (UFA), 75
U.S. Committee on Public Information, 17
U.S. Department of Agriculture, 241
U.S. Fourth Psychological Operations Group, 6
U.S. House Committee on Intelligence, 14
U.S. Information Agency (USIA), 3, 16, 17, 100, 110, 218, 223, 226, 269; USIA Fact Sheet, 17
U.S. Information Service (USIS), 204
U.S. Justice Department, 100
U.S. Maritime Commission (USMC), 235
U.S. Public Health Service, 243
U.S. State Department, 14

U.S. War Department, Information and Educational Division, 128
Uses and Dependency Theory, 149
Uses and Gratifications Theory, 149

Valins, D., 141
Vanport City, Oregon, 229-239
Vatican Radio, 107
Vaughn, S., 165
"Video Journal" (Czechoslovakia), 7
Vietnam War, xi, 199, 202-207
Voice of America (VOA), 6, 8, 13, 17, 20, 104, 105, 106, 108, 109, 110, 111, 254
Voice of America "Worldnet," 17
Voice of the Andes, 107
Voice of the Gulf, 6
Volksempfänger, 187, 189
Volkische Beobachter, 186

Walesa, Lech, 7
Wallas, Graham, 83; *Human Nature in Politics*, 83
Walsh, K. T., 5
Walter the Penniless, 45
Wanger, Walter, 96
Ward, L. N., 92
War Brides, 92
War Manpower Commission, 231
War Propaganda Bureau (Br.), 163
Washington, George, 62, 69
The Washington Inquirer, 14
Weaver, W., 18
Weisman, S. R., 160
Wells, H. G., 165
Werthlin Group, 262
Weschler, Lawrence, 222, 224
Westley, B. H., 19
Wheelis, L. R., 140
Whip Hand, 98
Whiteside, T., 242, 243
Why We Fight films, 129-130, 199
Wicker, Tom, 7
Wilkerson, M. M., 88
Williams, F., 148
Williams, R., 151
Wilson, Thomas, 29; *Arte of Rhetorique*, 29
Wilson, Woodrow, 165
Winkler, Alan, 199

Wisan, J. E., 88
Wish, H., 62
World Radio Gospel Hour, 107
Wright, J., 209

Xerography, propaganda uses of, 157

Yale Studies, 132-133

Zajonc, R., 134
Zeman, Z. A. B., 186, 188
Zimbardo, P., x, 20, 134, 136, 138, 141
Znaniecki, F., 125

About the Authors

Garth S. Jowett is currently Professor of Communication at the University of Houston. He obtained his Ph.D. in communications history from the University of Pennsylvania, and has served as Director for Social Research for the Canadian Government Department of Communication, and was a former consultant to various international communications agencies. He was appointed a Gannett Center Fellow in 1987-1988, and has published widely in the area of popular culture and the history of communications. His book, *Film: The Democratic Art* (1976), was an important benchmark in film history. This book is being completely revised and will reappear as *Moviegoing in America: A Social History*. His volume in Sage's Comm-Text Series, *Movies as Mass Communication*, 2nd ed (with James M. Linton), is a unique and widely appreciated study. His current major project is a social history of American television. He is the advisory editor of the Sage Foundations of Popular Culture Series, and (with Kenneth Short) advisory editor of the Cambridge History of Mass Communications Series. He is on the editorial boards of several communication and film journals.

Victoria O'Donnell is Professor and Director of the Basic Communication Course at Montana State University. She was the Chair of the Department of Communication and Public Address at the University of North Texas and Chair of the Department of Speech Communication at Oregon State University. In 1988 she taught for the American Institute of Foreign Studies at the University of London.

She received her Ph.D. from the Pennsylvania State University. She has published articles and chapters in a wide range of journals and books on topics concerning persuasion, the social effects of media, women in film and television, British politics, and Nazi propaganda. She is also the author (with June Kable) of *Persuasion: An Interactive-Dependency Approach*. She is currently writing a book on television criticism as well as a text for the basic course in speech communication. She made a film, *Women, War, and Work: Shaping Space for Productivity in the Shipyards During World War II*, about the case study on pages 229-239 for Public Television. Copies can be purchased through KUSM Public Television at Montana State University. She serves on editorial boards of several journals as well. The recipient of numerous research grants, honors, and teaching awards, including being named Honor Professor at North Texas State University, she has been a Danforth Foundation Associate and a Summer Scholar of the National Endowment for the Humanities. She has taught in Germany and has been a visiting lecturer at universities in Denmark, Norway, Sweden, and Wales. She has also served as a private consultant to the U.S. government, a state senator, and many American corporations.